Louis XI enthroned, surrounded by his Lords. At his feet,
Commynes, seated, dictates his *Memoirs* to a scribe

North

Sea

Holland

Gelderland

Zeeland

Brabant

Bruges

Brussels

Flanders

Neuss

Cologne

Boulogne

Artois

Arras

Liège

Amiens

Péronne

cardy

St. Quentin

Luxembourg

Compiegne

Rheims

Champagne

Senlis

le de

Paris

rance

Montlhéry

Nancy

R. Rhine

R. Seine

Lorraine

Alsace

Orléans

Duchy of

County of

Bâle

R. Loire

Dijon

Burgundy

Swiss

Burgundy

Confederation

erry

Charo-

lais

Bourbon

Geneva

Auvergne

Lyons

Rodez

R. Rhône

Grenoble

Dauphiné

Castres

Languedoc

Provence

Marseilles

Perpignan

oussillon

Mediterranean Sea

PHILIPPE DE COMMYNES

THE UNIVERSAL
SPIDER

The Life of Louis XI of France

TRANSLATED AND EDITED BY
PAUL KENDALL

The Folio Society
London 1973

PRINTED IN GREAT BRITAIN
Printed by Richard Clay (The Chaucer Press) Ltd, Bungay

Contents

Maps

All the maps have been drawn by K. C. Jordan, FRGS

Illustrations

All the miniatures are reproduced from the Dobrée Manuscript of Commynes Memoirs by kind permission of the Musées Departementaux de Loire-Atlantique, Nantes, from transparencies supplied by Studio Madec, Nantes.

Introduction

1. Preface

The *Memoirs* of Philippe de Commynes have been celebrated for more than four hundred years both as a remarkable literary work and as a priceless contribution to the history of the fifteenth century. They fall into two quite different parts. The first (comprising Books I–VI) narrates the intense, violent struggle for the dominance of Western Europe between Louis XI of France and his greatest vassal, Charles the Rash, Duke of Burgundy, which was resolved by the triumph of the king; it begins with the appearance of Commynes on the political scene in 1464 as a young squire in the service of the House of Burgundy and ends in 1483 with the death of Louis XI, at which Commynes was himself present. In the second part (Books VII–VIII) he recounts the first French invasion of Italy in 1494 under Louis XI's feeble son, Charles VIII. He took part in that ill-fated expedition, as a royal councillor and diplomat, and fought at Charles VIII's side in the desperate battle of Fornovo; but the chief adviser and confidant of Louis XI enjoyed little influence in King Charles' frivolous household. The *Memoirs* conclude in 1498, following the death of Charles VIII, with Commynes' entering the service of that monarch's successor, Louis XII. It is the earlier, and much the richer, part of the *Memoirs* that is here translated.

Commynes' work was first published, Part One only and very corrupt, in 1525; in the next five years five more editions of this Part appeared and Part Two was twice issued; the succeeding centuries have seen fresh editions in France and translations in several European tongues. It was first Englished in a forthright Elizabethan translation of 1596; unfortunately, the scattering of subsequent English versions, and a recent American one, have been distinguished neither by the scholarship of the editing nor by the vigour and flexibility of language the work demands. Commynes' style is alternately discursive and terse, pungently colloquial and yet at times entangled in generalizations, ironic and racy and grave by turns—the style of a man dictating, whose voice haunts the phrases. Any translator of Commynes is optimistic, or immodest, if he counts his labours a success or even supposes that he has adequately conveyed the tone and flavour of Commynes' utterance. The present translator hopes that he has profited from the work of his predecessors; he has ventured to undertake his task not in the expectation of finally domesticating Commynes in English but with the aim of offering unobtrusive annotation to clarify the historical context of Commynes' writing and of editing the *Memoirs* so as to elicit their essential form and purpose.

It is said that the famous Emperor Charles V, the rival of Francis I of France and Henry VIII, called the work 'a textbook for princes'. Montaigne a little later admired both the style of the *Memoirs* and the man who created them: they are 'illuminated by the obvious good faith of the author', who is 'exempt from vanity in speaking of himself and from prejudice and envy speaking of others'. They have continued to win praise, though less for their political wisdom than for their historical and literary appeal. One aspect of Commynes' work, perhaps the most significant, has not received much attention: Part One of the *Memoirs* can be regarded as the earliest exemplar of life-writing in the modern, i.e., post-medieval, world, and remains incomparably the greatest biography of that wizard of statecraft Louis XI. Indeed, the first two biographies of the Renaissance spring not from Italy (where the form was devoted to panegyrics of tyrants) but from France, in the *Memoirs* of Commynes, and from England, in Master Thomas More's unfortunately unfinished *History of Richard III*, written some twenty years (about 1513) after the *Memoirs*. If More's irony is the more exuberant and glossier, Commynes' is drier and subtler. It is this irony of Commynes, as well as his detached view of men and things, his insight into the realities of power, and his belief in man's capacity to mould the conditions of existence, that make him seem 'modern' to a twentieth-century reader. More's *Richard III*, further, imitates the classical tradition of inventing appropriate speeches for historical figures, whereas Commynes—who, ironically enough, for us, rues his lack of such an education as More exemplifies—confines himself to reporting only what he has heard people say or has had on good authority. It is as a biography of Louis XI that the present edition of the *Memoirs* has been prepared. The following brief sections offer a sketch of Commynes' life, a comment upon the reliability of the *Memoirs*, a short account of the life of Louis XI up to the time in that life when the *Memoirs* begin, and a note on the translation.

2. *The Life of Commynes*

With characteristic modesty Commynes provides no information about his early days, nor does he even furnish the date of his birth. He records merely that he began his career in the House of Burgundy 'at the end of my boyhood' when he was 'of an age to be able to manage a horse'. It is generally conjectured that he was then seventeen and hence born about 1447, probably at the castle of Renescure in the County of Flanders, of which Philip the Good, Duke of Burgundy, was count. Commynes' mother died apparently when he was in infancy and his father, in 1453, when the boy was but six. Colart de Commynes had enjoyed a brilliant career as a high officer of the Duke of Burgundy: he rose to become the 'Sovereign Bailli', chief administrator, of the County of Flanders and a member of Duke Philip's famous chivalric Order of the Golden Fleece (*Toison d'Or*). The duke had acted as godfather to Colart's son; hence, his name Philippe. But Colart had died in debt, leaving his son nothing but the opportunity created by his services to the House of Burgundy. Philippe, reared by his uncle, was given the typical education of a gentleman, that is, he was trained in arms rather than in letters. Such was the situation of the youth who in November 1464 entered the Burgundian court, having been appointed to the coveted position of a squire in the household of Duke Philip's only son and heir, Charles, Count of Charolais, then thirty-one. By the time Charles succeeded his father as Duke of Burgundy in June 1467, Commynes had become a chamberlain and an influential counsellor of his tough, ambitious, violent-natured master.

At some date unknown during his years with the Duke of Burgundy, Commynes apparently performed a mission to England, ally of Duke Charles who in 1468 married Margaret of York, sister of Edward IV. The chief trace of this journey appears in the *Memoirs* in the author's profound admiration for Parliament—a 'sacred institution', he calls it, which in its control of taxation and capacity to express the will of the English people is the great buttress of the monarch's power and moral authority. Commynes had other opportunities to inform himself about English affairs. In the early autumn of 1470, Edward IV, temporarily driven from the realm by Richard Neville, Earl of Warwick (the 'Kingmaker') and Warwick's Lancastrian allies, sought refuge, with but a handful of followers, in the domain of his brother-in-law, Duke Charles. In the months before King Edward's triumphant return to England (March–May

1471) Commynes talked with the king and made friends with Edward's favourite and Great Chamberlain, William, Lord Hastings. For British readers the *Memoirs* offer much valuable information and an interesting viewpoint on the Wars of the Roses and the chief figures in that conflict between York and Lancaster.

Meanwhile, at Charles' side, Commynes had participated in the war and intricate diplomacy—the battle of Montlhéry, the siege of Paris, the formation of princely coalitions against the monarchy, all vividly recounted in the *Memoirs*—which opened the mortal struggle between Charles the Rash and Louis XI. In October 1468 occurred their dramatic interview at Peronne; and, though Commynes keeps himself effaced, other documents fully attest that this adroit, cool-headed servant of the lion saved the day for the royal fox who had of his own volition entered the lion's den. Louis XI, a connoisseur of good service, did not forget—and Philippe de Commynes could not fail to compare the impolitic duke who thought only of grandiose conquests, with the king who was the master political intelligence of his time. During the summer of 1472, the Duke of Burgundy stormed into northern France with fire and sword, failed to capture Beauvais, and in vengeful anger left a trail of devastation across Normandy. On the night of 7–8 August, Philippe de Commynes stole from the Burgundian camp—abandoning his possessions (confiscated at six a.m. on the eighth) and a distinguished career—and made his way to royal headquarters at Ponts-de-Cé on the Loire, where Louis XI was probably not surprised by his appearance.

This king, who valued brains over battles and paid higher than anybody else for services, expressed his gratitude to Commynes by royal decree and his expectation of Commynes' worth as a counsellor by lavish endowments—the principality of Talmont in Poitou, an heiress for wife, Helène de Chambes, by which marriage he became the lord d'Argenton, as he is henceforth known, and, soon, the high office of Seneschal of Poitou and other lands and offices. From now on, except for a military tour of duty in the Burgundies, a brief relegation from court caused by a difference over policy with his master, and an important diplomatic mission to Lorenzo de' Medici ('Lorenzo the Magnificent'), Commynes was seldom out of the presence of the king, of whom he was an intimate as well as counsellor. Theirs was a remarkable collaboration in statecraft; and though Louis XI was always the master, it is clear that Commynes played a leading role in the grand strategy by which the Duke of Burgundy was brought to destruction and the feudal Kingdom of the Lilies set upon the road to becoming a national state. A Milanese ambassador, in 1476, reported that Commynes was the 'all in all' with Louis XI; while the Magnificent Lorenzo wrote to the king, 'I think there are few in Italy or France who are his equal'.

The death of King Louis, 22 August 1483, produced a harsh alteration in Commynes' fortunes. In the struggle for power that opened the reign of the boy king Charles VIII (born June 1470), Commynes supported the conspiracies of Louis, Duke of Orléans, heir to the throne, against the regency government of Anne and Pierre de Beaujeu, Louis XI's very able daughter and son-in-law. As a result, he was imprisoned for more than two years, for five months of which he 'tasted', as he himself reveals, one of the notorious iron cages in the castle of Loches. At the same time he lost to another claimant the great estates in Poitou which Louis XI had bestowed upon him without sufficient regard for their true ownership. He was, however, restored to moderate favour at court, and took part, as has been indicated, in Charles VIII's Italian expedition of 1494–95. The accession to the throne of Louis XII (the former Duke of Orléans) in 1498 promised much, but Commynes was employed only intermittently as a counsellor and diplomat. He apparently retired to his castle of Argenton about 1508 and there died on 18 October 1511.

There is general scholarly agreement that he dictated the first six books of the *Memoirs* here translated during the years 1489–91 in the interval between his release from prison and his return to court, and dictated the second part, Books VII–VIII, in the course of the four years 1495–98 following the Italian expedition. He informs us in a prologue that he undertook the work merely in order to furnish information for a Latin history of Louis XI projected by Angelo Cato, physician and astrologer and counsellor, who in 1476 left the service of Duke Charles of Burgundy for that of the king, being elevated in 1482 to the archbishopric of Vienne. Though from time to time Commynes addresses remarks to Cato, it seems clear almost from the beginning of his work that the chief counsellor of Louis XI, given leisure for reflection by imprisonment and then for composition by his sequestration from affairs, intended to set forth, in the form of *Memoirs*, an account of the rare ruler he had served, his ideas about the nature of power and the education of princes, and, indirectly, an *apologia*, a defence of the life of statecraft to which he had devoted himself.

3. *The Memoirs*

Philippe de Commynes freely admits, dictating his memoirs some ten years, on average, after the crowding events in which he figured, that he does not always recall dates exactly or the sequence of happenings. Such errors as he makes, mostly unimportant, have generally been corrected within brackets in the text. On the other hand, minor inaccuracies regarding an enterprise of which Commynes did not have firsthand knowledge—Edward IV's successful recovery of his kingdom in the spring of 1471—have been allowed to stand in order to avoid burdening the *Memoirs* with footnotes. One distorted sequence of events, however, perhaps calls for comment here. In Book Three, Commynes recounts the intrigues of the princes which stimulated Louis XI to take up arms against Duke Charles of Burgundy in the winter and early spring of 1471. He afterwards reverts to Louis XI's alliance with the refugee Earl of Warwick, which led to Warwick's ruling England, under the restored Henry VI, from October 1470 to March 1471, when Edward IV made his triumphant return. Thus in describing Louis' war and Warwick's rule one after the other, Commynes obscures the fact that it was the alliance with Warwick and the king's expectation that Warwick would attack the Duke of Burgundy from Calais which were in great measure responsible for King Louis' initiating hostilities.

In the nineteenth century Commynes and his work were subjected to harsh attack prompted by Belgian pride in the Burgundian inheritance. Baron Kervyn de Lettenhove sought to demonstrate in a three-volume study that Commynes had betrayed his country, i.e. the domain of Burgundy, and that the *Memoirs* were not to be trusted—a view that is manifestly flawed by relentless prejudice. In the present century two very lengthy works—both announced as only the opening volumes—have sought, on somewhat different grounds, to demonstrate Commynes' unreliability. Karl Bittman in *Ludwig XI und Karl der Kuhne*, 1964, diligently amasses significant source materials but deploys them to maintain, not convincingly, the rigid thesis that Commynes employed deceptive stratagems, deliberate or unconscious, to explain himself and his world. An even larger tome, in French, of 710 pages, Jean Dufournet's *La Destruction des Mythes dans les Mémoires de Ph. de Commynes*, 1966, tediously attempts to show, more by intuition than by evidences, that Commynes, a guilt-laden renegade, intricately falsified history in order to justify himself. When Commynes' work is checked, however, against such prime sources as the letters of Louis XI and the hundreds of dispatches written by Milanese ambassadors at the court of France, it is remarkable how sturdily the good faith of the author and the reliability of the *Memoirs* stand up. Threading by memory and perhaps a few notes a complexity of events which he himself had helped to shape, Commynes writes with a capacity for recall, perception and detachment which vindicate his reputation through the centuries.

4. *Louis XI*

When Philippe de Commynes placed himself on the stage of history in November 1464, Louis XI was already forty-one years old, though he had been king for but three years. His had been a strange and tempestuous life. He came into the world, 3 July 1423, the heir of miserable Charles VII and Marie of Anjou, at a moment when the fortunes of the French monarchy were desperately low. Though conquering Henry V of England had died the year before, shortly followed by Louis' grandfather, the mad King Charles VI, English armies with the aid of their ally Philip, Duke of Burgundy, occupied almost all northern France, including Paris; and before long their spearheads would be thrusting southward through Maine and Anjou towards Orléans on the Loire, the gateway to the south of France, of which they already held the great province of Guienne. Factional strife at Charles VII's threadbare court caused little Louis to be sequestered in the gloomy fortress of Loches, where he grew into boyhood, seeing almost nothing of his parents and reared in quite unprincely simplicity. Then the victories of Joan of Arc in 1429—the little Dauphin met her briefly at Loches—led to the crowning of Charles VII at Rheims; and though she was captured the following year and burned at the stake in 1431, she had lit a fire of national resistance. The fortunes of the monarchy improved. In 1435 the Duke of Burgundy made a separate peace with France, the Treaty of Arras. It cost Charles VII the northern province of Picardy and towns along the Somme river, but foretold the end of the English occupation. In 1437 the French regained Paris. The princes of the realm—who in France's misery had acted like independent potentates—began to jockey for influence at court; and men of ability, lesser lords and commoners (like Jacques Coeur, the great merchant), filled royal offices.

In 1440, at the age of sixteen, Louis Dauphin became the figure-head of a court faction, led by the Dukes of Bourbon and Alençon, aimed at assuming charge of the royal government. This revolt (dubbed the 'Praguerie' because of similar upheavals in Bohemia) was quickly crushed in the field; the rebellious Dauphin was the last to submit. Evidently he had for years been chafed by the igno-minious history and unkingly slackness of his father. Charles VII, for his part, passive and dependent on favourites but of shrewd in-telligence, showed little affection for his unusually energetic and strong-willed heir. Reduced to impotence (and in any case quite antipathetic to the airs and ways of feudal magnates), Louis diligently set about learning the trade of war, as a subordinate captain, and studying the arts of ruling. In 1443 he won a decisive victory over an English force besieging Dieppe and a few months later forced the submission of the unruly Count of Armagnac. He was rewarded by one of the most perilous and bizarre missions ever undertaken by a royal heir.

In the spring of 1444 English commissioners had arrived at Tours to treat for peace—as France recovered strength, the realm of England under pious, ineffectual Henry VI, torn by the rapacity and dissensions of the magnates, was moving towards the civil strife of the Wars of the Roses. A preliminary truce of two years was agreed upon, supported by the betrothal of Margaret of Anjou, the beautiful and high-spirited daughter of René, Duke of Anjou and titular King of Naples, Charles VII's brother-in-law, to King Henry. Welcome though the truce was to the French, it presented a serious problem: the free-booting companies who constituted much of the French military power would pillage the country to the bone in time of peace; yet, should the truce not continue, they would then be needed. Fortunately the emperor, an ally of France, and his cousin the Duke of Austria were appealing for aid against the Swiss, whom, as usual, they found it impossible to subdue. Dauphin Louis was chosen to lead these fearsome companies—*Écorcheurs*, they were called, 'Flayers'—eastward towards the city of Bâle, leagued with the Swiss, in support of the Hapsburgs. Outside the walls of that city Louis' army fought a bloody battle, at St Jacques, in which a small force of Swiss were almost annihilated. When the emperor did not provide the quarters and supplies he had promised, the dauphin forcibly occupied most of Austrian Alsace and there prepared to winter. Refused support by his father, however, he had to return to France, followed in the spring of 1445 by the surviving contingents of *Écorcheurs*. The best of these were incorporated in the standing army which Charles VII's government now created. It consisted of fifteen companies of one hundred mounted lances each—a lance being comprised of a mailed man of arms, with two attendants, and three archers, a team of six. There were also regiments of franc, i.e., free, archers, so called because they or the communities providing them were granted freedom from taxation.

Charles VII saw to it, however, that his son was deprived of occupation and political responsibility. After making sufficient trouble at court, the frustrated dauphin was permitted at the end of 1445 to go to his province of Dauphiné for a few months. He remained there ten years. His astonishing success in transforming that backward, wild region, a feudal jigsaw of jurisdictions and privileges, into what was for its time a model state, his reforms including the foundation of a university at Valence, aroused his father's jealousy; as did his marrying without parental consent, in 1452, Charlotte of Savoy, a daughter of the duke of that state which straddled the Alps from Italian Turin to Neufchâtel north of Lake Geneva. By August 1456 a French army was invading Dauphiné. But Louis had already departed—fleeing northward with his chief followers until he reached the Low Countries, domain of Philip of Burgundy, 'the Grand Duke of the West', scion and rival of the House of France. Philip gave him a splendid welcome, and provided him with an income and the charming castle of Genappe. The malcontent heir of France, become the self-exiled King of Dauphiné, was now a refugee guest of the richest ruler in Europe. Duke Philip was seeking to weld his French Duchy of Burgundy and imperial County of Burgundy (i.e., nominally a fief of the Empire), his French counties of Artois and Flanders and his imperial lordships in the Low Countries, into a genuine state. It would be the grander, and violent, dream of his son Charles, ten years Louis' junior, to revive the long ago Kingdom of Lotharingia, which, briefly, after the breakup of Charlemagne's dominion, had stretched between France and the Empire from the Mediterranean to the North Sea. Five years after the dauphin had fled to Duke Philip, the death of Charles VII, on 22 July 1461, transformed the fugitive into His Most Christian

Majesty, Louis XI. He inherited a kingdom still deeply scarred by the long wars with the English, still a feudal domain of high-flying princes who, like their ancestors, sent and received ambassadors, coined money, administered the High Justice, the Middle and the Low.

The new monarch hurled himself with enormous zest, energy, ability and imprudence, into demonstrating what, in his view, a royal government should be and do. He rode up and down the realm of France as no king before him had ever done; he sought to do everything immediately, and he saw to everything himself. A number of his father's ablest officers took refuge with Francis II, Duke of Brittany; others were disgraced or, for a time, imprisoned. Great lords were no longer welcome at court or in council. Louis' advisers and agents, many of them of bourgeois origin or undistinguished rank, he drove as hard as he drove himself. At home he instituted judicial and fiscal and administrative reforms, some of which had soon to be modified. Abroad he embarked upon an ambitious foreign policy which scored some resounding successes. As a pledge for his aid to the King of Aragon, he secured the counties of Roussillon and Cerdagne on the southern border. He allied himself with the greatest Italian *condottiere* of the age, Francesco Sforza, who in 1450 had made himself Duke of Milan. In 1463 he succeeded in persuading Duke Philip of Burgundy to honour a clause in the Treaty of Arras which allowed for the repurchase of Picardy and the Somme towns for 400,000 gold crowns—then he combed his kingdom until he had brought in the money which restored northern France to the realm. In the same year he brought the war with England to an end by a year's truce, prolonged the following year, in the course of which he won the friendship and stimulated the ambitions of Richard Neville, Earl of Warwick. Their agreement upon the marriage of Louis' sister-in-law, Bona of Savoy, to Edward IV was spoiled, however, in the summer of 1464 when that handsome and easy-going young monarch showed that he was not entirely under the domination of the Kingmaker, by marrying, 'for love', an English widow with two sons, Elizabeth Woodville, a daughter of Lord Rivers.

Louis XI had also in these three years succeeded in frightening and alienating the princes of his feudality. The House of Anjou, headed by 'King' René and his warrior son Duke John, was angered by its sovereign's alliance with Francesco Sforza, who had thwarted

Angevin attempts to regain the Kingdom of Naples. Southern lords like the turbulent Count of Armagnac were outraged by Louis' cracking down upon their flouting of royal authority. The Duke of Brittany, himself ineffectual but supported by refugee officers of Charles VII, haughtily resisted Louis' attempts to impose royal sovereignty. The House of Burgundy, most powerful and therefore most important of all, had by 1464 turned against its quondam guest. Aged Duke Philip, who had expected to be the king's benevolent mentor, was deeply hurt by Louis' inattention to his wishes. Worse yet, Philip's heir, the smouldering Count of Charolais, infuriated by the repurchase of Picardy, broke his friendship with Louis, a friendship which the king had carefully cultivated. All the great lords were appalled by Louis' efficiency, disturbed by his unprincely manners, frightened by his obvious hostility to their pretensions, and, so they claimed, justly indignant at his making peace with the English, especially since they suspected that such peace would free him to take measures against them. By the summer of 1464 the buzz and hum of princely plotting could be heard all over France.

At this critical moment (September 1464) the king learned that his friend Warwick was not coming to sign the marriage contract of Bona and Edward IV. At almost the same moment a sensational scandal broke. A rakish adventurer, the Bastard of Rubempré, leaving his warship in a small Dutch port, had come in the guise of a merchant to Gorcum in Holland, where he was apprehended by the Count of Charolais in the act of furtively spying on the count's castle there. At once the inflammatory rumour ran through the Burgundian domains that the King of France had hired the Bastard to kidnap the heir of Burgundy. A ducal officer, Olivier de la Marche, brought the news to Philip of Burgundy's castle of Hesdin, not far from English Calais, where Louis XI, quartered close by, had persuaded the duke to remain in order to help him welcome the Earl of Warwick. Without a word to the king, old Philip hastily took his departure from Hesdin, and shortly after, to Louis' chagrin, effected a reconciliation with his headstrong son, with whom he had long been bitterly quarrelling. The king let it be known that he had dispatched the Bastard of Rubempré not to abduct Charolais but the Vice-Chancellor of Brittany, who, after treasonable negotiations in London, had arranged to visit the Count of Charolais at Gorcum on his way home. (Most scholars agree that the king's statement is

B

probably true, since such an attempt against Charolais would have been foolhardy in the extreme, whereas the king was already on openly hostile terms with Brittany.) Snubbed by the English, humiliated by the House of Burgundy, aware that his princes were conspiring against him, Louis XI decided to put a bold face on the matter by dispatching to Duke Philip a formal embassy to protest against Burgundian behaviour. It is this embassy, arriving at the ducal court at Lille in early November 1464, 'only some three days after' young Philippe de Commynes had entered the Count of Charolais' household, which forms the opening subject of the *Memoirs*.

In December Louis convoked an assembly of his principal lords, before which he defended his record as king and, in effect, received from them an ardent vote of confidence. But in March 1465 the king's weak and timorous brother Charles was persuaded to steal away to Brittany; the Duke of Bourbon raised the standard of revolt; the Duke of Brittany put forward the king's brother as the figurehead of the movement; princely proclamations called for reforms of government and made other demands that rebels in all ages (including Louis himself in the Praguerie of 1440) have used; and, harshest blow for the king, the Duke of Burgundy, declined into senility, relinquished his government to the king's mortal foe, the Count of Charolais. Louis XI, leaving a strong force under his cousin, the Count of Maine, and Pierre de Brezé, Great Seneschal of Normandy, to face the Breton army, marched for the Bourbonnais in an attempt, nullified by treachery, to knock the Duke of Bourbon out of action and win a quick pacification. Thus began the 'War of the Public Weal', which Commynes narrates from the Burgundian side. To the *Memoirs* can be left the subsequent history of Louis XI's life and reign.

5. *A Note on the Translation*

Of the half dozen extant manuscripts of the *Memoirs*, all scribal copies, the two best are the Polignac, of about 1530, which Bernard de Mandrot prints in his two-volume edition, 1901–3, and the incomplete Dobrée, some ten years older, which forms the basis for the first six books of the edition in three volumes of Joseph Calmette, 1924–25. The present translation uses the Dobrée manuscript, in Calmette's edition, as principal text, though in cases of doubtful or manifestly corrupt readings, Mandrot's reproduction of the Polignac and, on a few occasions, emendations by various French editors have been followed.

The reader will notice inconsistency in the translation of titles. In deference to custom, the titles of princes are Englished, i.e., the Duke of Burgundy, the Duke of Orléans; but the generality of nobles are designated by their French titles, the lord du Bouchage, the lord d'Argenton (Commynes himself), etc. The earliest critical edition of Commynes, by Denis Sauvage, published in 1552, first uses the title *Mémoires* and divides the work into books, each with heading, and chapters, an arrangement which almost all subsequent editions, including this one, have observed. For the sake of brevity and clarity, however, the headings of books in this translation have been supplied by the editor. Dots indicate where cuts have been made; the omitted material either concerns details of Burgundian happenings not relevant to the story of Louis XI or represents repetitions of ideas and of events elsewhere set forth. No attempt has been made to give a modern value to fifteenth-century money, simply because all such attempts, it is generally agreed, are inaccurate and misleading. In most cases, context will suggest the relative importance of the sum mentioned.

THE LIFE OF
LOUIS XI

PROLOGUE

MY LORD ARCHBISHOP OF VIENNA, IN FULFILLING YOUR request that I set down what I have known of the doings of King Louis XI—may God pardon him!—our master and benefactor and a prince most worthy of being remembered, I have kept as close to the truth as I could, according to my memory.

Concerning his youth I cannot speak, except for what I have heard him say himself; but from the time I entered his service until the hour of his death, at which I was present, I was more continuously in his household than any other man of comparable station, which has always been, at the least, that of chamberlain and of a counsellor occupied in his great affairs. In him and all other princes that I have known and served, I have seen good and bad; for they are men like us—to God alone belongs perfection. But when in a prince virtue and good qualities outweigh vices, he is worthy of great praise, since princes are more inclined than other men to be completely headstrong and wilful, partly because their upbringing in youth has been undisciplined and partly because on their reaching man's estate most people try to please their every mood and flatter their greatness.

Since I am unwilling to lie, it could be that in some place or other in this writing there may be found something not to the king's credit. But I hope that those who read this will take into account what I have said about rulers. I indeed venture to give him this praise, that I do not believe I have ever known a prince in whom there were fewer vices than in him, all things considered. As for my experience in the matter, I have had as much knowledge of great princes and as many dealings with them as any man of my time in France, including those who have reigned in this realm, in Brittany, in French Flanders [the Burgundian domains in the Low Countries], in Germany, England, Spain, Portugal and Italy, lords both temporal and spiritual. Some of these I have not seen, but knew them through negotiations with their ambassadors and through their letters and instructions, by which it is possible to learn a great deal about the character and capacities of rulers.

Nevertheless I have no intention, in praising the king, to diminish the honour or renown of others. I am merely sending you what immediately comes to my mind, hoping that you have requested the material in order to use it in a work that you propose to write in Latin, in which language you are well versed—a work that will reveal the greatness of the prince of whom you are going to speak and also your own powers. Wherever I am at fault, you can call upon my lord du Bouchage and others better able to inform you and to express themselves than I. Still, because of the obligation of honour and because of the great intimacies and benefits that were to continue without interruption until one of us was no more, I have especial reason to remember him—and also because of the losses and griefs I have suffered since his death, which indeed vividly recall to my memory the favours I received from him. However, it is the usual thing, after the decease of so great and powerful a prince, that there be great changes, by which some lose and others gain; for honours are by no means distributed according to the wishes of those who seek them.

In order to inform you of the period when I knew the king, about which you ask me, I must begin before the time that I came into his service. Then, in due order, I will pursue my narrative up to the hour at which I became his servant, and from then will continue until his death.

BOOK ONE

The War of the Public Weal
1465

AT THE END OF MY BOYHOOD AND AT THE AGE OF BEING ABLE
to manage a horse, I was brought to Lille before Duke Charles of
Burgundy, then called the Count of Charolais, who took me into
his service. This was the year 1464 [about 1 November].

Some three days later, there arrived at Lille the ambassadors of the
king [Louis XI], the Count of Eu, the Chancellor of France, called
[Pierre] Morvilliers, and the Archbishop of Narbonne. The ambassadors were heard in open audience in the presence of Duke Philip of
Burgundy and of the Count of Charolais and all their council.
Morvilliers spoke very arrogantly, declaring that the Count of
Charolais, while in Holland, had ordered the seizure of a little
warship out of Dieppe, on board which had been a certain Bastard
of Rubempré whom the count had taken prisoner on the charge of
coming there to abduct him. This accusation the count had then
spread abroad, especially at Bruges—the resort of foreigners [foreign
merchants] from all nations—through the agency of a Burgundian
knight named Olivier de la Marche.

On this account the king, finding himself charged with this
offence (contrary to truth, as he maintained), demanded of Duke
Philip that this Olivier de la Marche be sent prisoner to Paris so that
the king could punish him as the case required. At this point Duke
Philip replied to the ambassadors that Olivier de la Marche, his
Master of the Household, having been born in the County of
Burgundy [Franche-Comté] was in no way subject to the crown;
nevertheless if he had said or done anything impugning the king's

honour, and the duke found it so on evidence, he would condemn
de la Marche to fitting punishment. As for the Bastard of Rubempré,
it is true that he had been imprisoned because of the attitude and
behaviour of him and his men in the vicinity of The Hague in
Holland, where the Count of Charolais was then residing. If the
count was suspicious, he had not inherited the trait from his father—
for he himself was never suspicious—but had got it from his mother
[Isabella of Portugal] the most suspicious lady the duke had ever
known. Still, notwithstanding that he, as he said, had never been of a
suspicious nature, if he had been in his son's place at the moment that
this Bastard of Rubempré was lurking in the vicinity, he would have
had him arrested, as the Bastard had been. If the Bastard was not
found guilty of having sought to abduct his son the count, as it was
said he was aiming to do, the duke would immediately have him
freed and sent back to the king, as the royal ambassadors were
demanding.

Then Morvilliers levelled harsh and dishonourable charges
against the Duke of Brittany, named François [Francis II], declaring
that, when the Count of Charolais was at Tours with the king, the
duke and he had exchanged their seals, by which they swore themselves brothers in arms. The seals had been delivered by Tanneguy
du Chastel (since, Governor of Roussillon and of high authority in
this realm). Morvilliers made this case so enormously felonious that
he neglected nothing in his harangue that could heap shame and
obloquy upon a prince.

The Count of Charolais, violently angered by these insults cast
upon his friend and ally, several times tried to make reply. Morvilliers, however, each time interrupted him, saying, 'My lord of
Charolais, I have not come to speak to you but to my lord your
father'. The count several times begged his father for permission to
reply; but the duke said to him, 'I have replied for you, as it seems to
me a father should answer for his son. Nevertheless, if you are so hot
about it, take thought today and tomorrow say what you will'.
Morvilliers then added that he could not imagine what had moved
the count to make this alliance with the Duke of Brittany, unless it
were the fact that the king had cancelled the pension which he had
given the count with the governorship of Normandy.

Next day at the audience, the Count of Charolais, kneeling on a
velvet cushion, began by speaking to his father about this Bastard of
Rubempré, the causes of whose arrest, he said, were just and reason-

able, as would be shown at his trial. (I do not believe, however, that the truth of the matter ever came to light, but there were great suspicions; and I saw the Bastard delivered from a prison where he had been for five years.) The count, then beginning his vindication of the Duke of Brittany and himself, said that it was true the duke and he had sworn alliance and friendship and become brothers in arms, but far from harbouring intentions prejudicial to the king and his realm, they had made the alliance to serve and support him at need. As for the annual pension that had been taken from him, he had received only one quarterly payment in the sum of nine thousand francs, and never had he asked for the pension nor for the governorship of Normandy. As long as he enjoyed his father's favour, he could well do without all other benefits. I believe, however, that had it not been for his fear of his father, to whom he was addressing his words, he would have spoken much more bitterly. Duke Philip's concluding remarks were very humble and prudent: he begged the king not to entertain doubts of him and his son and to hold him always in his good graces.

Then wine and spices were served, and the ambassadors took their leave of the father and the son. When the Count of Eu and the chancellor had taken leave of the Count of Charolais, who was some distance from his father, he said to the Archbishop of Narbonne, whom he saw last, 'Recommend me very humbly to the good grace of the king, and tell him that he has here had me well worked over by this chancellor but that before a year has passed he will regret it'. The Archbishop of Narbonne delivered this message to the king when he returned, as you will afterward hear.

These words engendered great hate between the Count of Charolais and the king, already on bad terms because the king had only just repurchased for 400,000 crowns the towns on the river Somme like Amiens, Abbeville, St Quentin and others, which King Charles VII by the Treaty of Arras [1435] had delivered to Duke Philip of Burgundy to be held by the duke and his heirs male. At this time the duke was growing senile and all his affairs were administered by the brothers de Croy [Antoine, Count of Porcien and Jean, Count of Chimay] and others of their family. His accepting the king's money and restoring the territory very sorely troubled the count his son, for this area was the frontier and boundary of their domains and the repurchase cost them a great many subjects, good fighting men. Charolais blamed the de Croy family for this transaction; and after

Duke Philip sank into complete senility, which was already near, his son drove the whole de Croy family from Burgundian territory, and deprived them of all their offices and holdings.

Only a few days after the departure of the royal ambassadors, there came to Lille the Duke of Bourbon, Jean (recently deceased), on the pretext of paying a visit to his uncle, who of all the noble families in the world best loved this house of Bourbon. This Duke of Bourbon was the son of Duke Philip's sister [Agnes], who had long been a widow and lived with the duke her brother, she and several of her children—three daughters and a son. The true reason for the Duke of Bourbon's coming, however, was to persuade the Duke of Burgundy to raise an army in his domains—Bourbon saying that all the other princes of France would then do likewise—in order to remonstrate to the king against the state of disorder and injustice that he maintained in his realm. They wanted to be strong enough to force him to reform his government if he refused to do so. The war that subsequently occurred was called the Public Weal, because it was undertaken on the pretext that it was for the public weal of the realm.

Duke Philip—who since his death has been called Philip the Good —agreed to the raising of troops, but the nub of the matter was never revealed to him nor did he have any expectation that things would come to the point of violence. At once soldiers began to be mustered, and the Count of St Pol, afterwards Constable of France, came to the Count of Charolais at Cambrai, where Duke Philip then was. After St Pol had arrived, and also the Marshal of Burgundy, Thibaut de Neufchâtel, the Count of Charolais convoked a great assemblage of councillors and other officers of his father in the residence of the Bishop of Cambrai. He there declared all members of the house of de Croy to be mortal enemies of his father and himself, notwithstanding that the Count of St Pol had given his daughter in marriage to [Philippe] lord de Croy [son of Antoine] many years before; but St Pol declared he had been forced to do so. In sum, all the members of the de Croy family had to flee from the domains of the Duke of Burgundy and lost a great many of their belongings.

All this deeply displeased Duke Philip, whose first chamberlain was one [Philippe de Croy, son of Jean], afterwards known as my lord of Chimay, a very accomplished young man, nephew of the lord [Antoine] de Croy, who went off without taking leave of his master for fear of his life. Otherwise he would have been killed or imprisoned, for so he had been emphatically told. Enfeebled by old age, Duke Philip endured this patiently. The cause given for these proclamations against the duke's favourites [the de Croy family] was the part they had played in the restoration of the territories on the river Somme to King Louis.

The Count of Charolais reconciled himself with his father as best he could. Then he immediately took the field with his troops, and with him the Count of St Pol, the principal governor of his affairs and chief commander of his army. St Pol had some three hundred men of arms and four thousand archers under him, as Charolais had ordered, including many fine knights and squires from Artois, Hainault and Flanders. My lord of Ravenstein, brother of the Duke of Clèves, and Antony, [the Grand] Bastard of Burgundy, had been given command of equally strong forces. There were other commanders, whose names I will omit for the sake of brevity. Among these were two knights who enjoyed great credit with the Count of Charolais. One was the lord of Hautbourdin, bastard brother [a cousin] of the Count of St Pol, who had cut his teeth in the old wars between France and England at the time that King Henry of England, fifth of that name, reigned in France and Duke Philip had joined with him as his ally. The other was the lord of Contay, of the same years as Hautbourdin. These two very wise and valiant knights had the actual command of the army.

Of young men there was a plenty: among others, one of high renown named Philippe de Lalain, from a family of whom there were few who have not been valiant, nearly all of them having been killed in serving their lords in war. The army had some fourteen hundred men of arms, badly armed and inexperienced, for the Burgundian lands had been long at peace and since the Treaty of Arras had seen little fighting of any consequence—indeed I believe that they had enjoyed repose for more than thirty-six years [since the Treaty of Arras, 1435: twenty-nine years] save for some small wars of brief duration against the people of Ghent. The men of arms were extremely well mounted and well accompanied, there being few you could have seen who did not have five or six powerful horses. There were perhaps eight or nine thousand archers; when they were being mustered, it proved more difficult to send away the unwanted ones than it had been to summon these troops; only the best were chosen.

At this time the subjects of this house of Burgundy enjoyed great prosperity because of the long peace and the benignity of the prince under whom they lived, who little taxed his subjects. It seems to me that at that time his territories could more truly be called lands of promise than any other domains on earth. They were overflowing with riches and in complete peace—as they have never been since, a period of some twenty-three years. [Commynes evidently wrote this passage about 1489.] The standard of living and the clothing of men and women were extravagant; the feastings and banquets were on a more prodigal scale than in any other place I have known of; the bathing parties and other entertainments with women were lavish and lax—a little on the seamy side. (I am speaking of the lower sort of women.) In sum, it then seemed to the subjects of this house that no prince was a match for them, at least that none was capable of oppressing them. And in this world today I know of no princely house so desolate, and I fear that the sins of their prosperity have brought this adversity upon these people—mainly because they did not realize that all these bounties came to them from God, who distributes them as he pleases.

The Burgundian forces having thus been quickly made ready, the Count of Charolais set forth with his army, all mounted save for those who served his artillery train, which by the standards of that time was very impressive, and so numerous were his wagons that they enclosed most of his host in a laager.* Taking the road for Noyon, Charolais besieged a little castle named Nesle, which was held by some soldiers. In a few days he captured it. Joachim [Rouault], Marshal of France, setting forth from Péronne, tracked the Burgundian army but did no damage because he had few troops; and finally he put himself within the walls of Paris when the count approached it.

The whole length of his march the count engaged in no hostilities nor did his troops take anything without paying for it. Hence the Somme towns and all others gave entry to small parties of his men and delivered to them what they wanted for their money—it appeared indeed that they were waiting to see who would prove the stronger, the king or the princes. Continuing to push forward, the count arrived at St Denis near Paris, where he was to meet all the

---

* This word—used by the Boers to designate a defensive circle of wagons and guns, and now domesticated in English—is the only term in our tongue for the method of encampment employed by the fifteenth-century Burgundians.

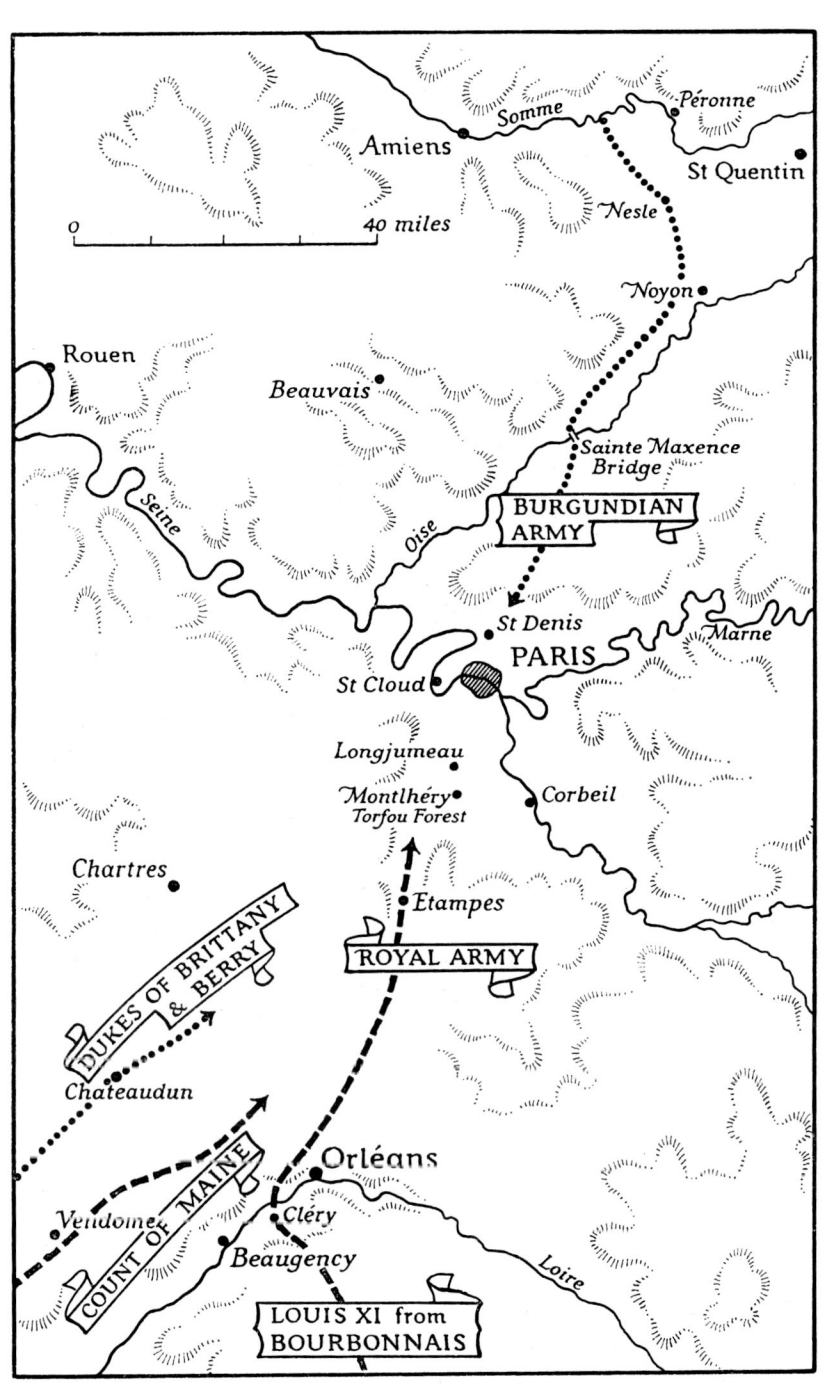

PARIS AND MONTLHÉRY

other lords of the realm, as they had promised, but none was there.

As ambassador for the Duke of Brittany there was with the Count of Charolais the Vice-Chancellor of Brittany named [Jean de] Rouville, who had blanks signed by his master and made good use of them in inventing fresh communications and messages as circumstances indicated. He was a Norman and a very clever man; and he had need of his inventions because of the grumblings of which he was the object.

The count went to show himself before the walls of Paris [early July 1465], and in a very hot fight his men thrust to the gates, to the disadvantage of those within. Of regular troops Paris had only Marshal Joachim and his force and my lord of Nantouillet [Charles de Melun], afterwards Grand Master of the Royal Household, who served the king this year as well as any subject ever served a French king in need; and in the end he was ill requited for it, more because of the persecution of his enemies than by fault of the king, though the latter was not entirely free of blame. Some of the Parisian populace, as I afterwards learned, were very much frightened that day, to the point of yelling 'They are within!'—as several people have since told me; but there was nothing to it. However, my lord of Hautbourdin, who had been reared in the city, was very much of the opinion that it could be successfully attacked—it was not then so strong as it is at present. The Burgundian troops were all for attacking, being contemptuous of the rabble they had beaten back to the gates. Nevertheless it is likely that Paris was impregnable. The Count of Charolais returned to St Denis.

The next morning council was held on the subject of whether to go meet the Dukes of Berry [Charles, the king's young brother] and of Brittany, who were near at hand, according to the Vice-Chancellor of Brittany who produced letters from them—but he had manufactured them on the signed blanks and actually had no knowledge of the princes' whereabouts. It was decided that the army should cross the Seine river, although several were in favour of returning since the other princes had failed the rendezvous and since, in their view, it was quite enough to have crossed the Somme and the Marne without crossing the Seine. On this theme some expressed great doubts and fears, since at its back the army had no strongholds into which to withdraw if there was need.

The whole host grumbled loudly about the Count of St Pol and this Vice-Chancellor. Nevertheless the Count of Charolais set forth

Omme say dit
icy dessus / quant
le conte de char
rolloys sceut le de
partement du roy qui sestoit
party du pays de bourbonoys
et quil venoit droit a luy
aumoins le cuydoit Il se
delibera aussy de marcher au
deuant de luy / et dist alors
le contenu de ses lectres sans
nommer le personnage / et
que ung chascun se deliberast
de bien faire Car il deliberoit
de tempter la fortune. Et sen
alla loger en ung villaige
pres paris appelle Longiumeau
et monss le connestable a tout
son auantgarde a Montlehery
qui est trois lieues oultre / et en
uoyrent espies et cheuaucheurs
aux champs pour scauoir la ve
nue du roy et son chemin.

The Battle of Montlhéry, showing the castle and the village

to cross the river and lodged at the bridge of St Cloud [the garrison of which surrendered]. The day after his arrival there, he received a message from a lady of this realm [Marie, Duchess of Orléans], who wrote in her own hand that the king was leaving the Bourbonnais and by forced marches was advancing to meet him.

It is now necessary to say something about the king's going to the Bourbonnais. Realizing that all the lords of the realm were declaring themselves against him, or at least against his government, he decided to put down the Duke of Bourbon first, because it seemed to him that the duke had committed himself more deeply than the other princes and because, the ducal territory being weak, it might be the sooner subdued. The king took several places and would have won the rest had it not been for the aid that the Marquis of Rothelin, the lord of Montagu and others brought from [the Duchy of] Burgundy. Soldiering with them was the present Chancellor of France, a man highly esteemed, my lord Guillaume de Rochefort.

This force, which had been raised in Burgundy by the Count [Pierre] de Beaujeu and [Charles, Archbishop of Lyons, later] the Cardinal of Bourbon, brothers of the Duke of Bourbon, had been introduced into Moulins [the Duke's chief town]. From the opposite direction there came in Bourbon's aid [Jacques d'Armagnac] the Duke of Nemours, [his cousin Jean] the Count of Armagnac, the lord [Charles] d'Albret, with a great number of men, among whom were some first-class soldiers, natives of their territories, who had deserted the royal standing army and withdrawn to these lords. Most of these troops were a sorry lot, however, for they were given no pay and had to live off the country.

Notwithstanding the size of these enemy forces, the king gave them plenty of trouble. Finally some form of peace was arranged, the leading role in it being played by the Duke of Nemours, who took an oath of allegiance to the king, promising to uphold his cause. Nevertheless he then did exactly the opposite, on which account the king conceived the hate that he long harboured against the duke, as several times he told me.

Now, the king, seeing that he could not, so soon as he had hoped, make an end in the Bourbonnais and that the Count of Charolais was approaching Paris, feared that the capital might open its gates to him and to the king's brother [the Duke of Berry] and the Duke of Brittany coming from Brittany, because they all proclaimed their devotion to the public weal of the realm; and he likewise feared that

c

what the city of Paris might do, all the other cities would do also. He therefore decided to make his way to Paris by forced marches and prevent those two great armies [Burgundian and Breton] from joining. He had no intention of giving battle, as several times he told me in speaking of these matters.

As I said above, when the Count of Charolais learned that the king had left the Bourbonnais and was advancing right at him (at least he so believed), he decided for his part to march to meet the king. He then revealed the contents of the letter [from the Duchess of Orléans] without naming its author and said that each one should make up his mind to do his best, for he had decided to put fortune to the test. He set up camp in a village near Paris called Longjumeau, while my lord the Constable [St Pol] with his whole advance guard went on to Montlhéry three leagues beyond, and dispatched spies and scouts to discover by what route the king was coming.

When St Pol was still with the Count of Charolais, a field of battle had been chosen in the vicinity of Longjumeau; and it had been agreed that if the king did come, St Pol would retire to this prepared position, among those present at this council of war being the lord of Hautbourdin and the lord of Contay. Now it must be understood that my lord [Charles, Count] of Maine with seven or eight hundred men of arms was facing the Dukes of Berry and Brittany. They had in their army a number of sagacious and distinguished knights whom King Louis had deprived of office at his succeeding to the crown, notwithstanding that they had well served his father in the recovery of the realm [from the English] and its pacification—and many times the king, recognizing his mistake, afterwards regretted his treatment of them. Among these knights were the Count [Jean] of Dunois, highly esteemed in all things; [André de Laval] Marshal Lohéac; [Antoine de Chabannes] the Count of Dammartin; the lord [Jean] de Bueil; and many others. These knights had left the royal standing army, a good five hundred men of arms with them, and had withdrawn to the Duke of Brittany —being natives of the province and his subjects—and now were the flower of the Breton host.

As I said, the Count of Maine, not believing himself strong enough to combat this force, retired before it day after day, thus drawing ever nearer to the king. The Dukes of Berry and Brittany, on the other hand, were seeking to unite with the Burgundians. Some have hinted that the Count of Maine had an understanding with them but I have never had any knowledge of it and I do not believe it.

The Burgundian army being at Longjumeau, as I have said, and its advance guard at Montlhéry, there was brought to the Count of Charolais a prisoner who informed him that the Count of Maine had joined with the king and that with them were all the companies of the standing army, some 2,200 men of arms, and the feudal levy of Dauphiné, along with forty or fifty gentlemen of Savoy, men of rank.

The king meanwhile held a council of war with the Count of Maine and the great seneschal of Normandy, named [Pierre de] Brezé, and the admiral of France [Jean], who was of the house of Montauban, and others. In conclusion, whatever opinions he received, he decided not to give battle but instead to put himself within the walls of Paris without going any nearer to where the Burgundians were encamped. It is my view that his judgement was correct.

He had suspicions of this great seneschal of Normandy and demanded to know whether or not the seneschal had given his seal of allegiance to the enemy princes. The great seneschal replied that he had done so indeed, but that though the seal remained with the princes, his body would serve the king—he said this jokingly, for so was he accustomed to speak. The king, satisfied, gave him command of the advance guard and the scouts, because he wanted to avoid battle, as has been indicated. The grand seneschal, who meant to have his own way, then said to one of his intimates, 'I will put them so close together today, these two armies, that it will be a clever man who can separate them'. And so he did. And the first who perished were he and his men. These words the king later told me, for at that time I was with the Count of Charolais.

Thus it was that on 27 July [actually, 16 July] 1465, the royal advance guard approached Montlhéry, where the Count of St Pol had encamped. St Pol in all diligence signified their coming to the Count of Charolais, three leagues to the rear of the field which had been prepared for battle, and requested Charolais to come succour him at once; for his men and arms and archers had already dismounted and enclosed themselves in a laager of wagons, and it was impossible for him to retire to Longjumeau as he had been ordered to do, because to break camp and retreat would seem to his men like flight and thus his whole force would be endangered.

The Count of Charolais hastily sent him Antoine, Bastard of Burgundy and a great number of the Bastard's troops. Charolais debated with himself whether he should go or not. In the end, he marched after the others and arrived at St Pol's position about seven o'clock in the morning. Already five or six royal banners were to be seen along a great ditch which ran between the two forces.

The Vice-Chancellor of Brittany, Rouville, was still with Charolais' army, and also an aged man of arms named Madré who had surrendered the Sainte-Maxence bridge [over the Oise]. Frightened by the threats muttered against them because, with battle imminent, the forces for whose arrival they had given assurances had not appeared, they fled before the battle began in the direction that they thought to find the Bretons.

The Count of St Pol was on foot when the Count of Charolais came up with him. All the troops as they arrived took up positions in the battle order. We found the archers with their footgear off, each with a stake planted before him, and several casks of wine had been opened so that they could drink. In my small experience, I never saw men with a better will to fight, the which seemed to me a very good sign and great source of comfort.

It was first decided that everyone would combat on foot, with no exception. Then the order was changed, and most of the men of arms mounted their horses. Several of the best knights and squires, however, were ordered to remain on foot, including [Philippe de Crevecoeur] lord d'Esquerdes and his brother [Antoine]. Philippe de Lalain was already prepared to fight dismounted, for at that time among the Burgundians those were most honoured who stationed themselves with the foot-archers; and a large number of men of high rank were always thus positioned so that the common soldiers would be thereby heartened and would fight better—it was an idea borrowed from the English, with whom Duke Philip had waged war in France in his youth. . . .

What with the Burgundians first dismounting and then remounting their horses, much time was lost and harm came of it. That young and valiant knight, Philippe de Lalain, perished in the field because he was poorly armoured. The king's troops continued to defile, man after man, from the forest of Torfou [to the south of Montlhéry]. They had not numbered four hundred men of arms when we arrived; and had we attacked immediately (it seems to many), we would have encountered no resistance, for the royal troops still coming up could only proceed in single file, as I have said. Still, their numbers continually increased. So seeing, that sagacious knight, my lord of Contay, came to tell his master, my lord of Charolais, that if he expected to win the battle, it was time for him to advance—Contay giving reasons for his statement and adding that if Charolais had moved sooner, the enemy would have already been defeated for he had found them to be, at first, inferior in numbers, which were visibly increasing all the time. And it was true enough.

Then all the plans of battle were changed about as everybody took it upon himself to put in his opinion. Meanwhile there had already erupted a hot skirmish, at the foot of the village of Montlhéry, between royal and Burgundian archers. The king's men, commanded by Poncet de Rivière, were all élite archers of the standing army, smartly outfitted with gold insignia on their uniforms. The Burgundians were a disorderly lot, under nobody's command, as is often the case when skirmishing begins. With them, on foot, were Philippe de Lalain and Jacques du Mas, a man of renown, later grand equerry to [Charolais when he had become] Duke Charles of Burgundy. Outnumbering their enemies, the Burgundians won a house, ripped two or three doors from it and used them as shields; and then they began to advance up the village street and they set fire to one of the houses. The wind favoured them, blowing the flames towards the king's men, who began to pull out and take to their horses and flee.

On perceiving this tumult, the Count of Charolais began to advance, abandoning, as I have said, all the plans previously devised. It had been agreed that the march would be accomplished in three stages, since a great distance separated the two armies. The king's forces were around the Castle of Montlhéry and had a stout hedge and a ditch in front of them; beyond were fields of wheat and beans and other crops, a very thick growth for the land was fertile there.

All the archers of the count haphazardly advanced on foot ahead of him. It is my opinion that the supreme resource for battle is archers—provided that there are thousands of them, for in small number they are worth nothing, and that they have sorry mounts, for then they will not regret losing their horses, or, better yet, have no mounts at all. And for the day of battle, those who have never seen anything are better than veteran archers. Such also is the view held by the English, who are the flower of the bowmen of the world.

It has been agreed that there would be two halts on the road, to give a breathing-spell to the foot soldiers; for the route was long and the crops tall and luxuriant, which made the going difficult. Nevertheless, the opposite was done, as if we were deliberately trying to lose the battle. Thus God shows that battles are in his hand and that he awards the victory as he pleases. I do not believe that a single man is capable of controlling so large a number of troops nor that things work out, in the field, as they are ordained in council. . . .

To return to the point, the count advanced without giving a breathing-spell to his archers and other foot-soldiers. The king's forces moved forward around both ends of the hedge, all mounted men of arms; and as they came close enough to lower their lances to position of attack, the Burgundian men of arms broke through the archers and trampled them down without giving them a chance to release a single flight of arrows—these archers who were the flower and hope of their army, for I do not believe that of our twelve hundred men of arms or thereabouts there were fifty who knew how to handle a lance. There were not four hundred of them armoured in cuirasses nor did a single attendant have any armour, because there had been such a long period of peace and because the house of Burgundy, in order to relieve their people of taxes, maintained no paid standing army. But ever since that day of Montlhéry, the Burgundian domain has known no peace to this hour, and now the situation is worse than ever.

Thus they themselves destroyed the flower of their hope. Nevertheless God, whose ways are mysterious, willed that the wing commanded by the count, which was on the right towards the castle, should triumph without even encountering any opposition. I was continually at his side that day, feeling less fear than I have ever felt in any place since, because I was young and knew nothing of peril. I was astonished, though, that no one dared put up a defence against this prince my master, and concluded that he must be greater than any other. That's the way people without experience are, whence it comes that they often maintain ill-founded and irrational views; and it is therefore good to espouse the opinion of him who says that one never repents saying little but often repents saying too much.

On our left were the lord of Ravenstein and Jacques [de Luxembourg, lord of Richebourg, brother of the Count] of St Pol and several others. They did not believe they had sufficient men of arms to sustain the attack of those they were facing, but the two forces had then come so near that it was no use thinking about changing troop dispositions. The upshot was that that Burgundian force was knocked flat and pursued all the way to the laager, and most of them fled even further, into the forest, which was half a league behind the lines. At the laager some Burgundian foot-soldiers made a stand. The main contingents engaged in this pursuit were the nobles of Dauphiné and the Savoyards and a great many men of arms also; and they thought they had won the battle. On this side a large number of Burgundians fled, including some great personages, and most of them were heading for the Sainte-Maxence bridge [over the river Oise], believing that it was still in Burgundian hands. Many remained in the forest; among others, the Count of St Pol, with a sizeable force, had withdrawn there. The laager was quite close to the forest. St Pol clearly demonstrated a little later that he did not yet consider the day lost.

The Count of Charolais, on his side of the field, pressed his pursuit for half a league beyond [i.e. south of] Montlhéry, and with a very small company. However, though there were numerous enemy troops, none turned to offer opposition, and already the count believed he had won the victory. An old gentleman of Luxembourg named Antoine le Breton came in search of him and told him that the French had rallied their forces on the field and that if he pursued further, he would be lost. The count, though he was told this two or three times, did not slacken his pace. At this moment arrived my lord of Contay, of whom I have previously spoken, who told the count just what the old gentleman of Luxembourg had said, and so emphatically that, heeding the warning, the count abruptly turned back. I believe that had he gone two bow-shots further he would have been captured, as were some others who were pursuing ahead of him. Passing by the village, he came upon a wave of fleeing foot-soldiers. He pursued them, though he did not have a hundred horse with him. One man only turned to fight, and gave him a pike-thrust in the stomach; the mark of it could be seen that evening. Most of the others escaped through the gardens, but that one was killed.

As the Count of Charolais swung around the castle, we saw before the gate the archers of the king's guard solidly holding the position. The count was very much amazed, for he had thought the royal army was beaten. He turned aside to reach the field, at which point some fifteen or sixteen men of arms charged upon us (part of the count's little force had now separated from him), and in the first shock they killed his square-carver, named Philippe d'Oignies, who was bearing a standard with the count's coat-of-arms. The count was in very great danger and took several blows, among them a sword-thrust in the neck—the scar of which stayed with him all his life—because his gorget, badly fastened that morning, had fallen off (I had seen it fall). Hands were laid on him. Someone cried, 'My lord, surrender! I know you well! Don't get yourself killed!'

He continued, however, to defend himself. In this struggle the son of a Parisian doctor named Master Jean Cadet, a big heavy hulk of a man astride a horse as massive as himself, drove between the count and his assailants. Then all the king's men drew back to the edge of the ditch where they had stationed themselves in the morning—having taken fright when they saw some soldiers approaching. The Count of Charolais for his part, bleeding freely, withdrew to these troops of his in the middle of the field. There was the banner of the Bastard of Burgundy, all shredded—it was not a foot long—and the banner of the count's archers looked no better. They did not number forty men in all and we, on joining them, did not add thirty, the whole party in great trepidation. Immediately the count changed horses, a fresh one being brought to him by his page, Simon de Quingey, who has since made a name for himself.

The count then rode about the field to rally men to him; but I experienced then quite a half hour, for those of us who remained there would have thought only of flight if we had glimpsed a hundred men on the march. There came to us ten men, twenty men, both foot and horse; the foot-soldiers weary and wounded, some as the result of the violence we had done them that morning [in riding down our archers], some as the result of enemy action. Little by little our numbers grew. The battlefield was now a flat expanse, there where half an hour before the wheat had stood so tall. The dust was terrible; the whole field was strewn with dead men and dead horses. None of the dead could be recognized because of the dust.

At this moment we saw the Count of St Pol sallying from the woods, a good forty men of arms with him and his banner. He headed directly for us, men rallying to his company as he advanced, but to us they seemed far away. Though three or four messages were sent to beg him to hasten his march, he did not change his measured pace. He had his men arm themselves with lances lying on the ground; they kept good order, which greatly comforted our people; and when, now become a large force, they reached us, we found them to number some eight hundred men of arms. Foot-soldiers he had few or none, which lack prevented St Pol from winning a complete victory, for a ditch and a great hedge separated the two armies.

On the king's side, the Count of Maine had fled, and some others, and with them a good eight hundred men of arms. It has been insinuated that the Count of Maine had an understanding with the Burgundians, but in truth I do not believe there was any such thing. A greater flight, on both sides, there never was, especially considering that the two princes remained on the field. On the king's side there fled a man of rank all the way to Lusignan without halt for food; and on the count's side, a man of similar rank fled all the way to Quesnay-le-Comte [in Hainault]. These two were not interested in biting each other.

The two armies thus being face to face, there were fired several cannon shots which killed men on each side. No one wanted any more fighting. Our force was larger than that of the king. However, his being there in person meant a very great deal, as did the hearten-ing language he used to his troops. I truly believe, from what I have since learned, that if it had not been for him alone, his whole army would have fled. A few on our side wanted to resume the battle, especially my lord of Hautbourdin, who said that he could see royal troops streaming in flight; and if a hundred archers could have been found to fire through the hedge, our whole force would have moved to attack.

As thus we were talking and thinking, there being no resumption of hostilities, night fell. The king withdrew to Corbeil [a few miles to the east on the Seine river]. We, however, believed that he and his host were encamped beyond the hedge. By chance fire broke out in a powder keg, there where the king's army had been, and it spread to some carts and then all along the hedge: we thought that these flames were the enemy campfires.

The Count of St Pol, who seemed indeed a great commander, and my lord of Hautbourdin—who seemed even more so—ordered the baggage wagons to be brought where we were, so as to enclose us in a laager, as was done. When we had first come together to reform our ranks, there returned from pursuit a great many of the king's men, who had to try to make their way through our forces. Some escaped but more were killed.

Of men of name on the king's side, there perished in the battle Geoffroy de Saint-Belin, the great seneschal [of Normandy, Pierre de Brezé], [Robert de Floques, called] Floquet, one of the chief captains. On the Burgundian side was killed Philippe de Lalain. Of foot-soldiers and lesser folk we lost more than did the king, but the king suffered greater cavalry losses. As for prisoners who could pay fat ransoms, the king's men had the better of it in the fugitives they captured. On each side there were killed at least two thousand men. The battle was well fought, and on both sides were men who showed their mettle and men who showed their heels. It was, in my opinion, a tremendous thing—each army reforming on the field and then for three or four hours the two forces remaining face to face. The two princes had reason to think highly of those who stayed at their side in this need. But they acted like men, not like angels: some, for having fled, lost offices and lands, which were given to men who had fled ten leagues further. One of ours who was deprived of power and forbidden to come into his master's presence, a month later enjoyed greater authority than before.

Enclosed as we were within the laager, each made himself comfortable for the night as best he could. We had a large number of wounded, and most of our force were disheartened and apprehensive, fearing that the Parisians and Marshal Joachim [Rouault], royal lieutenant in the capital, with two hundred men of arms, would issue from the city and that we would be attacked from two sides. When it was completely dark, fifty lances were ordered to scout the king's position. Perhaps twenty went off on the mission. It may have been three bow-shots from our camp to where we believed the king to be. Meanwhile, my lord of Charolais drank and ate a little—and thus each of us, in his fashion—and the wound in his neck was dressed.

To clear a place for him to eat, four or five dead men had to be removed, and two bundles of straw were spread. As the bodies were being carried away, one of these poor naked creatures began to beg for drink. Someone poured in his mouth a little herb tea, part of the brew which the count had drunk. The man revived; he was recognized—an archer (named Savarot) of the count's bodyguard, very famous too—and he was treated and eventually cured.

A council was held to decide what should be done. First to give his opinion was the Count of St Pol. He said that, the situation being perilous, we should at dawn take the road for the Duchy of

Burgundy, burn most of the baggage train excepting only the artillery, and forbid any officer commanding fewer than ten lances to have any wagons. To remain where we were, without supplies, between Paris and the king's forces, St Pol summed up, was impossible. Then my lord of Hautbourdin gave a like opinion, save that he counselled that we should first learn what the scouts had to report. Three or four expressed much the same view. The last to speak, my lord of Contay, said that the moment word of the retreat ran through the host each one would take to flight and every single man would be captured before he had gone twenty leagues. Offering good reasons for this conclusion, he gave as his advice that everybody should stand fast that night and in the morning, at break of day, we should attack the royal army, live or die. This he regarded as a surer way to safety than to take to flight.

Around midnight those who had been sent out scouting came back—you can believe that they had not gone far—and reported that the king's forces were encamped where the fires had been seen. Immediately other scouts were dispatched. An hour later each one was readying himself to fight—though most would have much preferred to flee. As day was breaking, the scouts met a wagon-driver, one of ours, who had been captured the previous morning as he was transporting a cask of wine from the village of Montlhéry. He told them that the whole royal army had decamped. Dispatching this news to our host, the scouting party sent men forward to investigate. Finding that the wagon-driver spoke the truth, the scouts came back with the news, which made our men very happy indeed—and there were plenty of folk who then said that we should pursue the enemy, the same folk who an hour before were pulling very long faces. I had an extremely weary mount, an old horse. He drank a pail of wine—by chance he had thrust his muzzle in it. I let him finish—I never knew him so willing and animated.

When it was broad daylight, everybody mounted horse, and the respective corps, much thinned, formed ranks. However a great many men returned who had been hiding in the woods. The lord of Charolais had arranged for a friar to appear and say that he had come from the Breton army, which would arrive that day. This performance very much heartened our company, though it was not believed by everyone. Shortly after, about ten o'clock in the morning, arrived Rouville, the Vice-Chancellor of Brittany, and

Madré with him; they brought two archers of the Duke of Brittany's guard, wearing their master's insignia, which greatly comforted the army. After being questioned, Rouville was praised for having slipped away—in view of the hostility towards him—and still more for having returned; and everybody gave him and Madré a warm welcome.

For the whole rest of the day my lord of Charolais remained on the field, very joyously treasuring the vision that the glory of victory was owing to him—a notion that afterwards cost him dear, for thenceforth he heeded no counsel but his own. Up until that day he had had no military experience and cared for nothing connected with war. But from this time forth his attitude was altered, and he was continually preoccupied with waging war until his death. And it was this that put an end to his life and destroyed his house—if it is not entirely destroyed, it is certainly desolate.

Three great and sagacious princes, his predecessors, had raised the house of Burgundy high; there are few monarchs, save the King of France, more powerful than he was; and for beautiful cities, no domains surpassed his. A man must not take too much credit to himself, especially a great prince: it is to be recognized that grace and good fortune come from God. Two things more I will say of Charles of Burgundy: I believe that never man had more stamina than he, in all situations requiring physical exertion; and, in my experience, I never knew a bolder man. Not once did I ever hear him say that he was weary, nor did I ever see him show fear—and I was seven years in a row at his side in war, summers at least and sometimes summer and winter. His visions and his projects were on a grand scale, but no man could have made them good, unless God had lent the aid of His power.

The next day, the second after the battle, we left the field and lodged in the village of Montlhéry. Its inhabitants had fled, some to the church steeple and others to the castle. The Count of Charolais ordered them to return to their homes; and they did not lose a single penny, for each Burgundian paid his reckoning as if he had been in Flanders. The castle still held for the king, and was not attacked. The following day the Count of Charolais, on the advice of the lord of Contay, took the road [southward] for Étampes, a commodious town situated in fertile country, partly in order to arrive sooner than the Bretons, who were likewise coming there, and also to provide shelter for the exhausted and wounded, the rest of the army encamping in the field. These comfortable quarters, and our sojourn at Étampes, saved the lives of many.

There arrived at Étampes the king's only brother, Charles, then Duke of Berry, the Duke of Brittany, my lord of Dunois, my lord of Dammartin, Marshal Lohéac, my lord de Bueil, and my lord de Chaumont [Pierre d'Amboise] and Charles d'Amboise his son who has since been a great man in this realm. All of these men the king had deprived of their offices and estates when he succeeded to the crown, notwithstanding that they had well served the king his father [Charles VII] and the realm in the reconquest of Normandy [1449–50] and in several other wars.

My lord of Charolais and his chief lords rode out to welcome them and escorted them to the lodgings prepared for them in Étampes, while their forces encamped in the fields. Their company numbered eight hundred men of arms, handsomely equipped, including a large contingent of Bretons who had recently deserted the royal standing army, as I have here and elsewhere said, and had greatly strengthened the Breton army. There was a very large number of archers and other soldiers armoured in good brigandines, amounting to some six thousand horsemen, smartly turned out. The sight of this army vividly suggested that the Duke of Brittany was a very great lord, for all these men were living out of his coffers.

The king, who had gone to Corbeil, as I have said, was not unmindful of what had to be done. He went into Normandy to assemble troops, and also because he feared there might be trouble in the province; and he stationed part of his forces in the environs of Paris, as need dictated.

On the evening of the arrival of the Breton army at Étampes, the two parties exchanged news. The Bretons had taken prisoner some of the fugitives of the king's army. Had they advanced a little further, they would have captured or killed a third of the royal force. They had indeed held council about sending troops forward, judging that the king's army and the Count of Charolais' were about to join battle. Some [of the Burgundians] blamed them for their inaction. However, Charles d'Amboise and some others did ride ahead of their army to see what they would encounter, and they took a number of prisoners, as I have said, and some artillery. These prisoners declared that for certain the king was dead—so they thought because they had fled at the beginning of the battle.

Charles d'Amboise and his party brought this news back to the Breton host, who were overjoyed at it, believing it true and thinking of the good things that would be theirs if my lord Charles [of France, heir of Louis XI] were king. A council was held—as was afterwards told me by a man worthy of credence who was there—to consider how these Burgundians could be got rid of; and it was the opinion of nearly all that if possible they should be picked clean in the process. This joy was of short duration, but it shows you the kind of dark dealings that go on in this realm whenever there are upheavals.

To return to the armies at Étampes, when everybody had supped and there were many walking along the streets, my lord Charles of France and my lord of Charolais were standing at a window exchanging protestations of devotion. Among the Bretons there was a humble fellow who liked to toss fuses in the air which when they fell squirted between peoples' feet and went off with a small flash. The fellow was called Master John Fire-setter or Master John the Gunner. At this moment he was throwing a few fuses among the crowd, doing it from the upper storey of a house so that nobody noticed him. One struck against the sash of the window at which the two princes aforesaid had their heads together—so close to each other were they that there was not a foot between them. Both jerked upright, started, and looked at each other; they were nursing the suspicion that the fuse had been thrown expressly to harm them. The lord of Contay came to speak to his master; as soon as he had murmured a word in the count's ear, he went below and ordered all the count's household and the archers of his bodyguard and others to arm themselves.

When the Count of Charolais then told the Duke of Berry of the measures being taken, the king's brother likewise ordered the archers of his guard to arm. In a moment two or three hundred men of arms, armed, were standing before the door of the house together with a large number of archers, and people were searching everywhere to discover where the fuse had come from. The poor fellow who had thrown it came up and, casting himself on his knees before them, said that he was the one, and he threw three or four other fuses to demonstrate. In so doing, he relieved many minds of dark suspicions, and people began to laugh. Everyone went off to disarm and retire for the night.

The next morning there was held a very great and impressive council, all the lords and their principal officers being present, the object of which was to decide what to do. Since they were of several parties—rather than being responsible to a single master, as is indeed almost requisite in such assemblies—so also did they have differing points of view. Among the speakers to whom particular attention was paid, my lord of Berry, who was very young and had never seen such exploits, seemed to imply that he was already weary of the enterprise. He instanced the great quantity of Burgundian wounded he had seen, indicating that he felt very sorry for them and using such words as suggested that he would rather these things had never been begun than already to see so many evils resulting from him and his cause.

These remarks displeased my lord of Charolais and his people, as I shall explain hereafter. In any case, it was decided at this council that they would advance to the walls of Paris in order to see if they could persuade the inhabitants to heed their case regarding the public weal of the realm, on behalf of which they all claimed to have assembled. They were quite sure that if the Parisians lent ear to them, all the other cities of this realm would do likewise.

As I have said, the words spoken by my lord Charles in this council so aroused the mistrust of my lord of Charolais and his people that they began to say, 'Have you heard what this man said? He is over-whelmed by the sight of seven or eight hundred wounded men about the town, men who are nothing to him and whom he does not know. He would very quickly lose his nerve if the matter touched him somewhat; and he would be the sort to come to terms very rapidly and leave us in the lurch.' [The Count of Charolais said:] 'Because of the wars waged in time past between King Charles [VII] his father and the Duke of Burgundy my father, the Duke of Berry might very well take sides with the king against us. We must therefore see to providing ourselves with friends.'

With this single thought in mind, the Count of Charolais dis-patched Guillaume de Cluny, [Apostolic] Prothonotary, who would die Bishop of Poitiers, to King Edward [IV] who was then reigning in England. My lord of Charolais had always considered him an enemy and was supporting the House of Lancaster against him, from which the count was descended through his mother [Isabella of Portugal, grand-daughter of John of Gaunt, Duke of Lancaster]. De Cluny was instructed to enter into negotiations for the hand of King Edward's sister Margaret, but not to conclude the match—the Count of Charolais knowing that the King of England had strongly desired it and estimating that, as a result of this semblance of an offer, King Edward, at the least, would do nothing against him and that if he encountered trouble he would thus win the king to his side. Though the count had no intention at all of contracting this marriage and the thing in the world he most hated in his heart was this House of York, yet the match continued to be so actively negotiated that several years later it was concluded; and in addition Charles of Burgundy accepted membership in the Order of the Garter and wore the Garter all the rest of his life.

Many such businesses are carried on in this world, like the one I have just recounted, especially between the great princes who are much more suspicious than other people, because of the mistrusts that are implanted in them and the warnings they are given—often mere words to curry favour that have no basis in fact.

As had been agreed, all the lords quitted Étampes, after sojourning there a few days, and went to Larchant and to Moret-sur-le-Loing in the Gatinais. My lord Charles [of Berry] and the Bretons remained in these two little towns, while the Count of Charolais went off to encamp in broad meadows on the bank of the Seine, having ordered proclamation to be made that everyone should carry stakes by which to tether his horses. He had ordered seven or eight little boats to be transported on wagons, along with some staves of casks, in the intention of constructing a bridge over the Seine—the lords having no means of crossing the river.

My lord of Dunois accompanied the count, riding in a litter with his banner borne after him, because gout prevented him from mounting horse. As soon as they reached the river they had the boats put in the water and thus a crossing was made to a little island approximately in the middle of the stream. Archers disembarked and began a skirmish with some horsemen who were holding the passage for the king. Marshal Joachim [Rouault] and [the famous captain] Jean de Salazar were there. Their position put them at a grave disadvantage, because they were on very high ground amidst vineyards. And the Burgundian army had powerful artillery commanded by a very renowned gunner named Master Girault de Samien (and others with him) who had been taken prisoner at the battle of Montlhéry. The upshot was that the royal force had to abandon the defence of the passage, and they withdrew to Paris. In the evening a bridge was thrown across to the island and

Quant toute ceste compaignie fut passee que lon estinoit a Cent mil chevaulx que bons que mauvais ce que ie croy ie delibererent lesd seigneurs de partir pour tirer devant paris et misdrent toutes les avantgardes ensemble pour les bourguygnons les coduisoit le route de San

les ducz de berry et de bretaigne Oudet deffac depuis Conte de Commynges et le mareschal de Loheac comme il me semble: Et ainsi se achemynerent. Tous les pces demouremt a la bataille. Led conte de Charrolovs et le duc de Calabre prenomt grand peine de comander et de faire temr ordre a leurs

The arrival of the Count of Charolais and his army before Paris, with
the Bastille shown in the foreground of the city

immediately the Count of Charolais had his great tent set up there and spent the night within it, and fifty men of arms of his household with him. At dawn a large number of coopers were set to work making barrels from the staves that had been brought; and, before midday, the bridge had reached the further bank of the Seine. The Count of Charolais at once crossed the river and ordered his tents, of which he had a great number, to be pitched there. He had his whole host and his artillery cross by the bridge, and his forces encamped on a slope running down to the river. The host so encamped made a very handsome sight for those still on the other side.

Only the Burgundians could pass the Seine that day. At dawn the next morning the Dukes of Berry and Brittany and their whole host began to cross, finding the bridge very handsome even though it had been built in haste. They moved a little beyond the Burgundian army and likewise encamped on the height.

As soon as night fell, we began to perceive a large number of fires; they were at a considerable distance from us and stretched as far as the eye could reach. Some believed that it was the king. Before midnight, however, we were informed that it was Duke John of Calabria, only son of René [Duke of Anjou, Count of Provence, and titular] King of Naples, who had with him a good nine hundred men of arms from the Duchy and County of Burgundy accompanied by numbers of horsemen, but of foot-soldiers only a few. Given the small size of the Duke of Calabria's force, I never saw so fine a company nor one that seemed such an exemplar of the military art.

He had some six score men of arms, horse and rider magnificently armoured, all Italians or others battle-hardened in the Italian wars, including Giacomo Galeotto, [Nicolas] Count of Campobasso, lord Jean de Baudricourt, now governor of Burgundy. The duke's men of arms were very athletic, and, to say truth, they could almost be called the flower of our army, at least man for man. Duke John also had four hundred crossbowmen lent by the Count Palatine of the Rhine [Frederick], all well mounted, who had the look of professional troops; the duke likewise had five hundred Swiss foot, the first to be seen in this realm; and they were the ones who made a reputation for the others who afterwards came, for they conducted themselves very valiantly wherever they went.

Duke John's company drew near us in the morning and that day crossed the river by our bridge—so it can be said that, save for the king's forces, the entire military power of the realm of France had

D

been on view upon our bridge. And I assure you that it was a grand
and splendid host, which included large numbers of handsomely
equipped men of rank. It is to be wished that the friends and well-
wishers of the realm had seen it and had valued it at its worth—and
likewise the enemies, for at no hour would they have felt greater
fear of the king and kingdom.

The commander of the Burgundians with Duke John was my lord
[Thibaut] of Neufchâtel, Marshal of Burgundy; with him were his
brother, the lord of Montagu, the Marquis of Rothelin and a large
number of knights and squires, some of whom had been in the
Bourbonnais, as I said at the beginning of this account. The Burgundians had joined forces, for greater security, with the Duke of
Calabria, who seemed as great a prince and military leader as any
other that I saw in our combined forces. And there was born a great
friendship between him and the Count of Charolais.

This whole company having passed the river—an army estimated
at a hundred thousand horse (good troops and poor), a figure that I
believe—the lords decided to set forth for Paris and put all their
advance guards together. For the Burgundians, the Count of St Pol
commanded; for the Dukes of Berry and Brittany, Odet d'Aydie,
who afterwards became Count of Comminges and Marshal Lohéac,
as I recall; and thus the army marched. All the princes remained with
their respective forces. The Count of Charolais and the Duke of
Calabria took great pains to exercise command and maintain military
order, riding in full armour, and it seemed indeed that they were
eager to fulfill their responsibilities.

The Dukes of Berry and Brittany ambled on little hackneys at
their ease, clad in brigandines that were very light indeed, to say the
most for them. Some said, moreover, that the 'brigandines' were
merely satin tunics spotted with gilded nails, which the dukes wore
to avoid the fatigue of bearing armour—though I can't be sure of
this. Thus rode all these contingents to the bridge of Charenton,
scarcely two leagues [eastward] from Paris, which was quickly won
from the handful of royal franc archers guarding it; and the whole
army crossed the Marne river on this bridge. The Count of Charolais
encamped his forces along the [right bank of the Seine] river from
this bridge of Charenton to a dwelling of his at Conflaus; he enclosed
a great expanse of land with his baggage train and artillery wagons
and established his host within this laager; and the Duke of Calabria
set up headquarters there too. The Dukes of Berry and Brittany with

a number of their men were lodged at St-Maur-des-Fossés, and all
the rest of the army was sent to occupy St Denis, also two leagues
[northward] from Paris. Here remained this whole company for
eleven weeks, and what happened I shall explain hereafter.

The next day began skirmishes that were fought all the way to the
gates of Paris, within which were commanding [Charles de Melun]
my lord of Nantouillet, Grand Master of the Royal Household, who
did good service there as I have elsewhere said, and Marshal Joachim
[Louis XI being absent in Normandy gathering troops and supplies].
The populace read fear in each other's faces and certain other classes
wanted the lords admitted because they judged the princes' cause to
be good and profitable for the realm. Still others there were, from
the territories of the princes and involved in their affairs, who hoped
by means of their princely patrons to secure offices or lands. Such
offices are more sought after in Paris than in any other city in the
world: their possessors gain from them what profit they can, not
what they should; and there are some offices without salary that
are sold for eight hundred crowns, while others yielding very small
wages are sold for more than the wages would amount to in fifteen
years. Very seldom is any one discharged, and the Parlement of
Paris upholds this custom, and rightly so; but then it touches almost
all members of this court of Parlement—among whose counsellors
are always to be found many good and notable persons and also
some very shady ones. Thus is it among all ranks.

As soon as the lords had arrived before Paris, they all began intriguing with people in the city, promising offices and goods and
whatever could serve their purpose. Three days later at a great
assemblage in the city hall, after a prolonged discussion during
which the public demands and petitions of the lords on behalf of the
welfare of the realm (as they put it) were aired, it was decided that a
delegation should be sent to the princes to negotiate for a pacification.

With Guillaume Chartier, then Bishop of Paris, a man of great
renown, as their speaker, a large delegation of Parisian notables
made their way to the princes at St Maur. On behalf of the latter, the
Count of Dunois spoke. The Duke of Berry, brother of the king,
presided in a chair of state with all the other lords standing about
him. On one side of him were the Dukes of Brittany and Calabria
and on the other the Count of Charolais, who was completely
armed except for helmet and arm-guards and wearing a very rich

short-cloak over his breastplate. He had to come to St Maur from Conflans, and, the castle of Bois de Vincennes being strongly garrisoned for the king, he therefore needed a sizeable escort. What the lords requested was entry into Paris in order to hold amicable consultations regarding the reformation of the realm, which they declared to be badly governed, making a number of weighty accusations against the king. The replies of the delegation were very gentle—though before answering they duly paused to take Counsel together. Ever after, the king disliked the bishop and those with him.

On the return of the delegates to Paris, intrigues were intensely pursued; for, before their departure from St Maur each of the lords took individual members of the delegation aside to speak with them. And I do believe it was agreed in secret by some that the lords, with their retinues only, would enter the city and their troops could pass through, if they so desired, in small contingents one after the other. Such an agreement would have meant not only Paris won but the whole enterprise; for the populace could easily, for several reasons, have been swayed to their side, and as a consequence all the rest of the cities of the realm would have followed the example of the capital.

God gave wise counsel to the king and he executed it well. Warnings of all these goings-on reached him before the city delegation had made their report; and he arrived in his capital the way a ruler should come to hearten people; for he entered the city in great strength, bringing with him two thousand men of arms, all the nobles of Normandy, a powerful contingent of franc archers, the gentlemen-pensioners of his household and other men of rank who are with such a king at such a time. Thus was this intrigue with the princes broken and the whole city now turned to the king—nor was there to be found a single one of the delegates who dared say another word about the negotiating, and trouble overtook some of them.

However the king used no cruelty in this matter, though some lost their offices and others he banished from Paris. I think it greatly to his credit that he took no further vengeance, for if the bargaining that had been begun had come to effect, the best he could have hoped for was to flee the realm. Indeed several times he told me that if he had not been able to enter Paris, finding its allegiance altered, he would have sought refuge with the Swiss or with the Duke of Milan, Francesco [Sforza], whom he reputed his great friend—and the duke showed himself to be so in the aid that he sent the king. The duke's eldest son, named Galeazzo-Maria, afterwards duke, led a force of five hundred men of arms and three thousand foot, which advanced as far as Forez [in the region of Lyons] and made war on the Duke of Bourbon; but upon the death of Duke Francesco [8 March 1466] they returned to Milan. The Duke of Milan also aided the king by the counsel that he offered: that the king should refuse nothing demanded of him—except for insisting upon keeping control of the standing army—in order to divide the princes, and so the king acted in eventually accepting the terms set forth in the Treaty of Conflans [October 1465].

I believe we had not been more than three days before Paris when the king entered the city. He at once began hostilities in force, especially against our foragers, who had to go long distances in foraging and be guarded by many troops. It must be pointed out that this region of Ile-de-France and the city of Paris are well situated to supply two such powerful hosts. Never did we lack food, and the Parisians hardly realized that they had an extra mouth to feed. Nothing became dearer except bread, and that by only a *denier* a loaf. For eastward from the city we did not block the rivers, which are three, the Marne, Yonne and Seine, and several of their tributaries.

All things considered, I have never seen a town surrounded with a lovelier or more fertile countryside: it is almost unbelievable—the produce that is brought to Paris. I was afterwards with King Louis for half a year there without interruption, lodged in the royal mansion, *Les Tournelles*, eating at his table and usually sleeping in his chamber, and since his death I have spent twenty months—not of my own volition—as a prisoner in the Conciergerie of the palace, where from my windows I saw arriving the laden boats from Normandy which moved upstream against the current; while from the other direction there arrived products more numerous than I had ever expected to see.

So then, there sallied from Paris every day many bands of soldiers, and hot skirmishes developed. Our outposts numbered fifty lances who were stationed in the vicinity of a manor called Grange-aux-Merciers, and they kept their outriders as near Paris as possible. The latter were very often driven back upon the outposts, and quite often they too had to turn tail and withdraw all the way to our laager, sometimes at a measured pace and sometimes fleeing at a trot. Then we sent them forth again with reinforcements, and in turn our men very often drove the royal troopers back almost to the gates of Paris. This sort of thing went on at all hours; for in the city there were more than 2,500 men of arms, crack troops and comfortably lodged, a large force of Norman nobles and franc archers. And then these fighters saw the ladies every day, which prompted them to display their prowess.

On our side we had a mass of troops, but not nearly so many horsemen—only the Burgundians, about two thousand lances, some good and some poor, who were not so well equipped as those within the city because of the long peace the Burgundian domain had enjoyed, as I have formerly explained. Then too, of this number there were two hundred men of arms stationed at Lagny under command of the Duke of Calabria. Of foot-soldiers we had a great number, and good ones.

The army of the Bretons was at St Denis, waging war as best they could; and the other lords were scattered here and there for the sake of maintaining food supplies. Finally there arrived the Count of Armagnac, the Duke of Nemours, and the lord d'Albret. Their troops remained at a distance because, unpaid as they were, they would have starved our army if they had taken supplies without paying. I know well that the Count of Charolais gave these southern lords up to five or six thousand francs, as a result of which he was informed that their troops would come no closer. They numbered fully six thousand horsemen, who were marvellously adept at pillage and destruction.

To return to the siege of Paris, you may be sure that no day passed without loss and gain, as much on one side as on the other. But no large engagements took place, for the king would not allow his troops to sally forth in strong contingents. He was unwilling to hazard a battle and hoped, by dividing the princes, to secure peace.

Nevertheless, early one morning four thousand franc archers, the nobles of Normandy and a few other troops established themselves on the bank of the Seine opposite the Count of Charolais' dwelling at Conflans. Other troops of the standing army were stationed a quarter of a league from there in a village, and between the two forces stretched a handsome plain. The river Seine was between us and them. The king's men began a trench running from opposite Charenton, where they constructed a bulwark of wood and beaten earth, to the further flank of our army; it passed in front of Conflans, the river between, as has been said. There they planted a large number of artillery pieces, which, right off, drove all the troops of the Duke of Calabria out of the village of Charenton, who having to move in great haste, came to camp with us, and some men and horses were killed in the process. And Duke John took up lodging in a small house in front of the Count of Charolais' dwelling and facing the river.

This artillery soon began training its fire throughout the army and badly frightened our men, for it immediately killed some people and put two shots through the Count of Charolais' chamber, as he was dining, and killed a trumpeter who was bringing a platter of meat up the stairs. After dinner the Count of Charolais went down to the ground floor, decided not to move from there, and had it furnished for him as best it could be.

Next morning all the lords arrived to hold council—it was never held elsewhere than at the Count of Charolais' quarters, and always, after the council meeting, the lords dined together, with the Dukes of Berry and Brittany sitting on the bench [in the place of honour] and the Count of Charolais and Duke John of Calabria opposite them. The count did honour to them all, ceremoniously seating them at table, as indeed was fitting since he was the host.

It was decided that the whole artillery of the army would be trained on the enemy trench. The lord of Charolais had a great many field pieces; the Duke of Calabria had some fine ones and so did the Duke of Brittany. Large openings were made in the walls along the river behind the count's dwelling at Conflans, and the best guns were planted there (except for the siege-bombards and other large pieces, which did not fire at all) and the remainder placed where they would be most useful. Thus the lords had many more cannon than did the king. The trench that the king's men had made was very long, extending towards Paris, and they continually lengthened it, throwing up the earth on our side in order to protect themselves from our artillery; for they were all hidden within the ditch nor would any have dared to show his head. They were in a place as flat as a man's hand, a beautiful plain.

I have never seen so much artillery fire within such a few days; for we, on our part, expected to drive them away by means of our artillery. The other side, reinforced from Paris every day, was just as diligent, and did not spare the powder. Large numbers of our troops dug holes in the earth near their quarters, even though there were already a great many holes, the place having been a quarry. Thus each one entrenched himself and so passed three or four days. On each side, there was more fear than loss, for no man of note was killed.

When these lords saw that the king's men were not at all worried, they thought it both shameful and perilous thus to hearten the inhabitants of Paris, for, on any day of truce, so many people came out [to watch] that it seemed that nobody had remained in the city. It was decided at a council meeting that a great bridge would be erected on large boats—the bows and sterns to be cut off and the wood used to make the passageway across the widest part of the boats, the pair at the end having stout anchors to fasten them to shore. Accordingly, several boats were assembled, so large that in one crossing they could have transported a great number of foot-soldiers. Thus was it arranged to pass the river. Master Girauld, artillery chief, was put in charge of this work. He thought it a great advantage for the Burgundians that the king's men had thrown up the ridge of earth on our side, because, when the former had crossed the river, the latter, in their trench, would be much below the level of their assailants, and yet they would not dare sally from the ditch for fear of the artillery.

This reasoning greatly encouraged our men to make the crossing; the bridge was built, save for the last pair of boats which were turned to the side ready to be put in place; and all the boats were aligned. As soon as the bridge was ready, there came an officer of arms of the king to say that building it was contrary to the truce— that day and the day before there had been truce, and people had come to see what was going on. The officer of arms happened to find my lord de Bueil and several others on the bridge, to whom he spoke. That evening the truce ended. The bridge could accommodate three men of arms, lances at thigh, moving abreast. About six large boats had been used, each capable of transporting a thousand men at a time, and several small ones. The artillery was trained to cover the crossing; military units were assigned positions and the lists drawn up of those who were to cross, the Count of St Pol and the lord of Hautbourdin commanding.

Just after midnight, those who were to take part began to arm themselves, and before daylight they were armed. Some heard Mass, while waiting for day, and did what good Christians do in such a case. That night I was in a large tent in the middle of the camp, headquarters of the watch, for I was on guard duty from which no one was excused. The commander of the watch was [Louis de Chalon] lord of Châteauguion, later killed at the battle of Morat [actually, Grandson, 1476]. As we were all waiting to see the fun begin, suddenly we heard those in the trenches across the river cry out, 'Adieu, neighbours, adieu!' And immediately they set fire to their quarters and withdrew their artillery. Day began to break. Those taking part in our enterprise were even then on the river, at least some of them; they saw the king's men, already at a distance, retiring to Paris. Hence each one went off to disarm, very happy with this departure.

In truth, the king had established this position only to pound our host with artillery, not with any idea of combating for he was not willing to put anything to hazard, as I have said elsewhere, notwithstanding that, despite this assemblage of princes, his power was very great. His aim, as indeed he would demonstrate, was to treat for peace and divide the princes of the league, without putting his situation—the splendid one of being king of this grand and obedient realm of France—in peril of anything so uncertain as a battle.

Each day little bargains were struck to win people over from one side to the other; there were several days of truce, during which the two parties negotiated for peace. These negotiations were held at the Grange aux Merciers, quite near our army. As representatives of the king, there came the Count of Maine and several others. The lords were represented by the Count of St Pol and several others. Many times meetings were held without accomplishing anything. Meanwhile the truce continued; and standing on either bank of a great ditch about half way between the armies—crossing the ditch being forbidden by terms of the truce—a great many men from each side saw each other.

As a result, there was not a day passed that ten or twelve men did not come over to the lords' side, and sometimes more. Another day, as many of ours went over to the king. On this account the place was afterwards called the Market since so many such bargains were struck there . . .

I have mentioned this matter because I have seen a great many deceptions in this world—and a great many servants deceiving their masters, more often those puffed up princes and lords who have small desire to listen to counsel than humble men who are happy to hearken to it. Among all the princes I have ever known the most skilful at getting himself out of a bad situation in time of adversity was King Louis XI, our master, and the humblest in words and dress. Nor have I known any who worked harder to win a man who could serve him or one who could injure him. He was not at all put off at being once refused by such a man, but pressed on his campaign, making large promises and fulfilling them with gifts of money and offices that he knew would please the man; and those whom he had dismissed and driven away in time of peace and prosperity he brought back, very dearly indeed, when he had need of them, and made good use of them and harboured no hate against them because of the past.

He was by nature the friend of those of middling rank and the enemy of all great ones, who showed that they could do without him. No man ever lent ear so readily nor inquired into so many things as he did, nor sought to know so many people. For he was truly as well acquainted with all men of authority and importance in England and in Spain, in Portugal, in Italy, in the domains of the Duke of Burgundy and in Brittany, as he was with his own subjects. These methods and ways of his, of which I have spoken above, saved his crown for him—considering the enemies he had himself created at his accession to the realm.

What served him best was his grand liberality. Wisely he managed matters in adversity, but, on the other hand, as soon as he believed himself secure, even if only by a truce, he began to annoy people by petty means which did him little good; and peace was almost unendurable to him. He let his tongue wag in talking about people— as readily in their presence as in their absence—save for those whom he feared, who were numerous, for of his own nature he was quite nervously timorous. When, as a result of his loose talk, he had received some injury, or suspected that he would, and wished to make amends, he spoke like this to the person himself: 'I am well aware that my tongue has done me a great deal of harm; at times it has also given me a great deal of pleasure. In any case, it is only right for me to make amends.' And he never uttered such a private confession without conferring some benefit on the person to whom he was speaking—and no small one either.

Moreover, God grants grace to a prince when he knows the difference between good and evil, and especially when good predominates in his nature, as was true of the king our master. Again, it is my opinion that the trials he suffered in his youth, when, a fugitive from his father, he took refuge with Duke Philip of Burgundy and spent six years thus, were worth much to him, for he was obliged to practice the arts of pleasing on those of whom he had need. And this experience taught him the meaning of adversity, which is no little thing. When he found himself in power, a king crowned, he at first thought only of vengeances, but they brought him trouble at once, and with it, repentance; and he made amends for this folly and this mistake by winning back those whom he had wronged, as you will learn hereafter.

If he had had no other upbringing than that of some lords I have seen reared in this realm, I do not believe he would ever have recovered from his reverses. For such lords are taught only to make fools of themselves in dress and speech; of letters they have no knowledge; not a single man of sense is placed in their entourage; they have governors to whom one speaks of their affairs—to them, nothing—and these governors manage their business. Such lords there are who do not have a yearly income of thirteen pounds in silver, who glorify themselves in saying, 'Speak to my people'— thinking by such language to imitate the manner of the great. Also, I have often seen their servants make a good thing out of this, at the same time openly treating their masters like brute beasts. If by chance such a lord does wake up and wants to find out where he stands, it is so late that the effort is of little use; for it must be noted that all men who have ever been great and done great things have begun very young; and the capacity to do so lies in nurture or in the grace of God.

Now I have a long time held to this subject, but it is not one that I find it easy to dismiss. To return to the war—you have heard how the royal troops in the trench along the Seine withdrew at the moment they were going to be attacked. Periods of truce never lasted more than a day or two. On other days war was waged very bitterly and skirmishing went on from morning till night. No large companies sallied from Paris. Nevertheless, our watch was often driven back to the encampment, only to be reinforced and attack in turn. I never saw a single day that there was not a skirmish, however small it might be; and indeed I believe that if the king had so willed the fighting would have been much hotter; but he was deeply suspicious of a great many people, not without cause. Later he told me that one night he found unlocked the gate of the Bastille St Antoine that opens on the fields outside the walls, which discovery caused him to entertain great suspicion of Charles de Melun because Melun's father [Philippe] was the captain of the Bastille. I will say no more about Messire Charles than I have already said, but a better servant the king did not have that year.

One day plans were laid in Paris to attack us—I believe that the king had no hand in the matter; it was the captains. The design was to assail us on three sides: one band to push directly forward outside the walls, which was to be the main force; a second band to attack by way of the Charenton bridge (they could hardly have hurt us); and a third, composed of two hundred men of arms, to come through the Bois de Vincennes [a large walled park with a royal castle]. Around midnight our host was informed of these arrangements by a page who shouted from the other bank of the river that some good friends of the lords were herewith warning them of this enterprise and he named some of the friends and immediately went off.

As dawn broke, there came Poncet de Rivières [captain of a hundred lances of the standing army] before the Charenton bridge and [Antoine] lord du Lau [captain of a hundred lances, and a favourite of the king] and others through the Bois de Vincennes and penetrated to our artillery and killed a gunner. Our men were greatly alarmed, believing that this was the attack of which the page had warned in the night. Almost at once the Count of Charolais was armed; but even sooner, Duke John of Calabria, for at every disturbance he was the first man armed, and armed completely, and his horse always barded. He wore a suit of armour such as the *condottieri* of Italy wear, and he indeed appeared a prince and a great captain. In an alarm he always headed right for the outer defences of our host, to prevent men from sallying forth haphazardly. He was obeyed as readily as was the Count of Charolais, and the whole host was happy to obey him, for in truth he was worthy of such honour.

In an instant, the whole host was in arms and stationed on foot behind the wagon-walls of the laager, save for two hundred horse who were outside on watch. Except for this day, there was none which offered any hope of a battle, but this time everybody expected one. Responding to the alarm, the Dukes of Berry and of Brittany arrived. I never saw them armed except this day. The Duke of Berry was in complete mail. They had few men with them. Passing through the encampment, they went a little way outside to find my lords of Charolais and of Calabria and the four had a conference. The scouts,

reinforced, rode closer to Paris and spied a number of royal outriders, who were coming to investigate the noise made by our army.

Our artillery had opened a heavy fire when my lord du Lau's
troops approached so near. The king had powerful artillery mounted
on the walls of Paris, which fired several shots that carried all the
way to our host—a tremendous feat for the distance is two leagues,
but I believe that the cannon muzzles had been greatly elevated. The
sound of the artillery fire made both sides believe that some great
enterprise was on foot; the weather was bad and visibility very poor;
our scouts, who had ridden very close to Paris, saw numerous horsemen; and they discerned, further off, a great quantity of erect
lance-shafts—so it seemed to them. They concluded that they were
looking at all the forces of the king deployed in the fields and the
whole militia of Paris. It was the poor visibility that made them
imagine this.

Hastily turning back, they rode straight to these lords of ours conferring outside the laager and reported the news, assuring them that
the king's main forces had taken the field. The outriders from Paris
continued to draw nearer the Burgundian encampment because they
saw our scouts withdrawing; the approach of these outriders made
our lords believe more readily the report of the scouts. The Duke of
Calabria then came up to the battle flag of the Count of Charolais,
who had most of his household gentry with him—his banner and the
standard bearing his arms ready to be unfurled, as was the custom of
the House of Burgundy. The Duke said to all of us: 'Well then, we
are about to have what we have all desired. Look there on the king
and all these people who have sallied from the city! And they are
advancing, as our scouts tell us. Therefore, let each one be of good
heart. Even as they issue from Paris, we will measure them with the
standard measure of this city, which is the great measure!' Thus did
he talk in order to encourage the company.

Our scouts had recovered a little of their morale, seeing that
the royal horsemen were few in number; they went back towards
the city and again spied the enemy battalions in the place they had
last seen them, which once more gave them something to think
about. They approached as close as they could, and by this time the
weather had cleared a little and it was lighter. What they had taken
as lances they found to be tall thistles, and though they were close by
the gates of Paris, they saw nobody outside the walls. They sent word
to the lords, who then went off to hear Mass and dine. The scouts

felt ashamed of themselves, but the weather excused them, that and what the page had shouted during the night.

Peace negotiations continued to be carried on more intensely between the king and the Count of Charolais than with the other princes because the power lay with those two. The demands of the lords were very large, especially because the Duke of Berry wanted Normandy as his share of the realm, which the king was not willing to accord. The Count of Charolais wanted the Somme towns, such as Amiens, Abbeville, St Quentin, Péronne and others that the king had repurchased for 400,000 crowns not three months before from Duke Philip, who had secured them by the Peace of Arras from Charles VII. The Count of Charolais claimed that the king had no right to repurchase them during Duke Philip's lifetime, and reminded him under what obligation he was to the House of Burgundy, since as a fugitive from his father King Charles, he was received into that House and there maintained for six years, supplied with money for his needs, and then escorted to Rheims for his coronation and to Paris. Hence the Count of Charolais had taken great umbrage at the repurchase of these territories.

As a result of arrangements made at the peace negotiations, the king came one morning by water to a place where our army, mostly the cavalry, were drawn up on the bank of the river. In his boat there were but four or five persons, except for those who were rowing. There were my lord du Lau, my lord [Jean] de Montauban, then Admiral, my lord of Nantouillet [Charles de Melun] and others. The Counts of Charolais and St Pol were at the river bank awaiting him. The king asked this question of my lord of Charolais: 'My brother [the count's first wife having been the king's sister Catherine], do you guarantee my safety?'

The Count replied, 'My Lord, yes'. I heard him; so did many others.

The king disembarked with his entourage. The counts did him great honour, as was proper. He, not sparing of charm, opened the conversation.

'My brother, I know that you are a gentleman and of the House of France.'

The count asked, 'Why, my lord?'

'Because', said he, 'when I dispatched my ambassadors to Lille to my uncle, your father, and to you, some time ago, and that fool

Morvilliers spoke so well of you, you sent me a message by the Archbishop of Narbonne (who is a gentleman, as he indeed showed, for everybody was pleased with him) that before the end of the year I would repent those words Morvilliers had spoken.' Then the king added, 'Well, you have kept your promise to me—and much before the end of a year!' He said these words with a smiling countenance, knowing that the character of him to whom he was speaking was such that he would take pleasure in this remark; and it certainly did please him. The king then disavowed Morvilliers' embassy, saying that he had not at all instructed the chancellor to say the words he had spoken.

In effect, the king walked up and down between the two counts for a long time, with the forces of the Count of Charolais looking on from close by. In the course of the conference the Duchy of Normandy was demanded, as were the Somme towns: further requests were made on behalf of each of the other princes; and some of the items concerning the welfare of the realm were again put forward—but this was the least of the matter, for the public weal had been converted into private gains. Under no circumstances would the king hear of yielding Normandy, but he accorded the Count of Charolais his demands and offered to the Count of St Pol the office of Constable, as a favour to the Count of Charolais; and the farewells of the two counts were very gracious. The king re-embarked in his boat and returned to Paris, while the others went back to Conflans.

So the days passed, some in truce and others in war. However, negotiations at the Grange aux Merciers, where the delegates of both sides had been accustomed to meet, were broken off. Instead, negotiations were pursued between the king and the Count of Charolais. They sent envoys back and forth, even when hostilities were going on. One of these envoys was named Guillaume Bische and another, Guyot d'Usie, both of whom were the count's men. However, they had formerly received favours from the king; for Duke Philip had banished them, and King Louis, at the request of the Count of Charolais, had taken them in.

These goings back and forth did not please everybody. Already the princes were beginning to mistrust each other and to grow weary of the cause. Had it not been for what happened a few days later they would all have shamefully abandoned the siege of Paris. I saw them hold three consultations among themselves in a chamber where they were all assembled; and I saw one day that this behaviour very much displeased the Count of Charolais, for they had already acted in such a way twice in his presence and it certainly seemed to him that, since the main strength of the army was his, their consulting together in his chamber without calling on him was grossly improper.

In speaking of this conduct, the lord de Contay, a very shrewd man (as I've formerly told you), said to the count that he should bear it patiently, for if he angered them, they would be able to get better terms from the king than he; that, as he was the strongest, so must he also be the wisest; and that he should therefore keep them from separating into factions and with all his power maintain their unity. All these considerations, however, should be concealed from them. In truth, de Contay added, there was much amazement, even in the count's own household, that such insignificant persons as the two above named should be involved in so important a matter—it was a dangerous proceeding, especially since they were dealing with so generous a king as Louis XI. The lord de Contay hated Guillaume Bische; however, he was only saying what several others were likewise saying; and I believe that he was not moved by personal feeling but rather by the urgency of the affair. This advice pleased the lord of Charolais, and he saw to it that he was more convivial with these lords than he had been, and offered them better cheer, and kept in closer touch with them and their people than he had been wont to do.

In my opinion, it was very needful that he did so, for there was great danger of their becoming disaffected. . . .

While these negotiations were being carried on through the meetings of envoys the people on both sides were able to communicate with each other, instead of treating for peace there were some who were intriguing to have the Duchy of Normandy put into the hands of the Duke of Berry, sole brother of the king, which he would take as his share of the realm, leaving Berry to the king. These dealings so turned out that the widow of the Great Seneschal of Normandy, and a number of her adherents, servants and relatives, introduced Duke John of Bourbon into the Castle of Rouen and thus gave him entry to the city.

The people of Rouen immediately accepted this change, being only too eager to have a prince as their ruler who would dwell in the province of Normandy. With few exceptions, the rest of the Norman towns and places did likewise. It has always seemed to the Normans,

Inablement, toutes choses furnt accordees et le lendemain fist le conte de charrolois vne grand monstre pour scauoir qz gens il auoit et ce quil pouoit auoir perdu. Et sans dire gare / y keuint le Roy auecques trente ou quarante cheuaulx / et alla voir toutes les compagnies lune apres lautre / sauf celle de ce mareschal de bourgongne / lequel naymoit pas le Roy A cause que despieca en lorrayne que ledict seigneur luy auoit donne espinal / et puis oste pour la donner au duc Jehan de Calabre dont grant dommage en auoit eu led mareschal

The Treaty of Conflans, with Louis XI on the left and the Count of Charolais on the right and does so still, that so great a duchy as theirs should have its own duke; and, to tell the truth, it is a rich province and raises very large revenues—I have seen it raise 950,000 francs in taxes yearly, and some say it raises more.

When Rouen changed allegiance, all the inhabitants took an oath to the Duke of Bourbon, as proxy for the Duke of Berry, save for a man named Guillaume Picard, afterwards General of Finances of Normandy, and for the royal Bailli of the city, Houaste [de Montespédon], who had been with King Louis from his youthful days, the king's *valet de chambre* when the king had been a refugee Dauphin in Flanders, and one of the Dauphin's closest intimates. Also the present Great Seneschal of Normandy [Jacques, son of Pierre de Brezé] refused to take the oath but instead went to the king against the will of his mother, who was responsible for the yielding of Rouen as has been recounted.

When the king learned of this change in Normandy, he decided to have peace, seeing that there was no way of remedying what had happened. He immediately made known to the Count of Charolais, at that moment with his army, that he wished to speak with him and named the time that he would appear in the fields neighbouring the Burgundian encampment near Conflans. At the appointed hour the king came forth with perhaps a hundred horse, most of them Scots of his guard, and with but few others. The Count of Charolais, bringing hardly any escort, went to the meeting without ceremony. Nevertheless, a great many Burgundians followed, so many that they far outnumbered the men with the king. The count ordered them to remain some little distance away; he and the king then talked, the two of them, for a while. The king told him that peace [on Charolais' terms] was accorded, recounting what had happened at Rouen, of which the count as yet knew nothing. He would never have yielded such a share of the realm to his brother of his own free will, the king continued, but since the Normans themselves had produced this new development, he was content with it and would approve the treaty of peace as it had been drawn up several days before. There remained but few matters yet to be agreed.

The lord of Charolais was very joyous at this news, for his army was in dire need of supplies, especially of money; and if this event had not occurred, all the lords before Paris would have ignominiously abandoned the siege. However, this day or a few days later the count received from his father Duke Philip of Burgundy reinforcements,

E

brought by my lord [Philippe] de Saveuses, which included six score men of arms, fully 1,500 archers, 120,000 crowns in bags of coin on ten pack-horses, and a large quantity of bows and arrows. Thus the Burgundians were very well provided for, at the very time they were suspecting that the rest of the princes might come to terms with the king without them.

This conversation regarding a treaty of peace was very pleasing both to the king and to the Count of Charolais. Indeed, I afterwards heard the count relate that so amicably were they talking about concluding what terms remained that they had no idea where they were walking; and, moving steadily in the direction of Paris, they covered so much ground that they entered a large bulwark of beaten earth and wood that the king had had constructed, quite some distance from Paris, at the head of a trench leading to a gate of the city. The count had but four or five persons with him. On finding themselves within the bulwark, they were stunned; however, the count kept his composure as best he could. It is to be believed that, since no harm came to either of these lords, they never afterwards had so much joy as at this moment.

The news that the Count of Charolais had gone within the bulwark caused a great sensation in the Burgundian army. The Count of St Pol, the Marshal of Burgundy, the lord of Contay, the lord of Hautbourdin and several others, having met together, bitterly blamed the lord of Charolais and the others of his retinue for this folly, referring to the fate which had befallen Charolais' grandfather [on the bridge] at Montereau in the presence of King Charles VII [where Duke John the Fearless of Burgundy was killed, in 1419, by members of the king's entourage]. Immediately these lords ordered all those walking in the fields to withdraw inside the laager; and the Marshal of Burgundy spoke as follows: 'If this young prince out of folly or lunacy has gone to his destruction, let us not permit his House to be ruined or his father's rule or our own lives. Therefore let each one withdraw to his quarters and there remain on the alert, without being upset by whatever chances to occur, for we are strong enough, if we hold together, to withdraw to the marches of Hainault or of Picardy or into [the Duchy of] Burgundy.'

The marshal then mounted horse, as did the Count of St Pol, and they rode forth to see if there would be any developments from the direction of Paris. After a long time, they spied forty or fifty horse, and with them were the Count of Charolais and some king's men acting as escort, archers and others. The count, on seeing the approach of the marshal and St Pol, had his royal escort turn back. He then spoke to the marshal, whom he feared, for the marshal used very harsh language and was a good and loyal knight for his side, and he had dared to say to the count, 'As long as your father is alive, I am yours only on loan'. The Count of Charolais said to him, 'Don't scold me, for I am well aware of my great folly; but I did not realize until too late that I was near the bulwark'. The marshal used stronger language to his face than he had in the count's absence. The count lowered his head without making reply and went back to the camp, where all were joyous to see him again and each one praised the good faith of the king. Nevertheless, the count never afterwards put himself again in the king's power.

Finally all the treaty terms were concluded, and the next day the Count of Charolais held a great review of his army in order to establish how many troops he had and how many he had lost. Without sending word, the king came there with thirty or forty horse, and inspected all the companies, one after the other, save for that of this Marshal of Burgundy, who had no love for the king because some time before the king had given him the town of Épinal in Lorraine and afterwards taken it from him to give to Duke John of Calabria, a loss which cost the marshal dear.

   Little by little the king was reconciling himself with the good and notable knights who had served the king his father, and who, the king having discharged them from office at his accession to the crown, had therefore taken part with the princes. And the king thus acknowledged his error. It was announced that the next day he would be at the castle of Bois de Vincennes, and likewise all the lords, who were obligated [by the treaty] to do homage to him; and for the security of all the king would deliver the castle to the Count of Charolais.

   The next day the king was there, and all the princes without exception; and the portal was strongly guarded by armed soldiers of the count. It was in this castle that the treaty of peace was signed. My lord Charles did homage to the king for the Duchy of Normandy, the Count of Charolais for the Picard territories which have been mentioned, and other princes accordingly; and the Count of St Pol took the oath of office as Constable. There is never so bounteous feasting at weddings that some guests aren't left with scraps.

Some of the princes had what they wanted; the others secured nothing. The king won over some valuable men of middling rank. Nevertheless the majority of such men remained with the new Duke of Normandy and with the Duke of Brittany, who were going to Rouen for the ceremony of Duke Charles' taking possession of the province.

On quitting the castle of Bois de Vincennes, they all took leave, one of the other, and each returned to his quarters, the letters of remission and pardons and other instruments required by the treaty having been executed. The day that the Duke of Normandy and the Duke of Brittany set out together, the Count of Charolais likewise departed for Flanders. As the count took to the road, the king joined him and accompanied him as far as Villiers-le-Bel, a village four leagues from Paris, thus demonstrating his great desire for the count's friendship; and both lodged that night in the village. The king had few people with him but he had summoned two hundred men of arms to escort him back to Paris. The Count of Charolais, informed of their arrival as he was going to bed, became very suspicious and ordered large numbers of men to arm. Thus you can see that it is almost impossible for two great lords to be true friends, because of the rumours and reports that every hour engender suspicions. Two great princes who genuinely desire to live in amity should never see each other; instead they should make use of sagacious and honest ambassadors, who would maintain their amity or repair the rifts in it.

The next morning the king and the count bade each other farewell with warm and prudent expressions of esteem. The king returned to Paris with his escort of men of arms, and thus removed any suspicion that their coming could have produced. The Count of Charolais took the road for Compiègne and Noyon—the gates of all towns being opened to him by the king's command—and then went to Amiens. There he received the homage of its citizens as well as that of the other Somme towns and Picard territories that had been restored to him by this treaty—for which the king, not nine months before, had paid 400,000 gold crowns, as I have previously said.

The count, at once continuing his march, headed for the territory of Liége, because in his absence the people of Liége had been making war on his father, in the regions of Namur and Brabant, for five or six months, and had had some success. Nevertheless, because of winter weather, the count accomplished little. A large number of villages were burned and a few minor defeats were inflicted in the Liégeois; and they made peace. They bound themselves to observe the treaty, under penalty of a great sum of money; and the Count withdrew into Brabant.

Coming back to the Dukes of Normandy and of Brittany who had gone to take possession of the Duchy of Normandy—as soon as they had made their state entry into Rouen, they began to fall out over the issue of sharing the booty; for still with them were those knights I have mentioned who had been accustomed to receiving great estates and honours from Charles VII and who now, believing that they had attained their ends and that they could put no trust in the king, wanted, each of them, to secure the best office he could. On the other hand, the Duke of Brittany wanted some of the Norman offices at his disposal, since it was he who had staked the most and borne the brunt of the expenses. This quarrel [between the two dukes] grew so fierce that the Duke of Brittany, for fear of his person, found it necessary to withdraw to [the monastery of] Mont-Sainte-Catherine near Rouen. Matters so much worsened that the Duke of Normandy's people and the men of Rouen were preparing to attack the Duke of Brittany at the monastery, on which account the latter was forced to take the quickest road back towards Brittany.

On learning of this quarrel, the king moved upon Normandy. And you may be sure that he understood the dissension very well, and indeed had helped to fan the fire, for he was a master of this science. Some of those who held the best Norman places began to deliver them to him and come to terms with him. I know about these matters only what he afterwards told me, for I was not present there. He had a conference with the Duke of Brittany, who was holding some places in lower Normandy, in the hope of bringing the duke entirely to abandon his brother. The two of them spent a few days together at Caen, and they signed a treaty by the terms of which Caen and other towns remained in the hands of [Odet d'Aydie] the lord de Lescun [chief adviser to the Dukes of Brittany and Normandy], the garrisons being paid by the king. But this treaty was so confused that in my belief neither of them ever really understood it. The Duke of Brittany then went off, and the king took the road towards his brother [at Rouen].

When the Duke of Normandy perceived that he could offer no resistance, the king having captured Pont-de-l'Arche and other places, he decided to take to flight and go to Flanders [i.e., Burgundian territory]. The Count of Charolais who was still at St-Trond, a small town in the territory of Liége, was in no condition to take action, his army dispersed and enfeebled, it being the winter season, and he still involved in his campaign against the Liégeois. It grieved him deeply to learn of this falling out of the dukes, for the thing in the world he most desired was to see a duke in Normandy since by this means he considered the king to be one third diminished in his power. He ordered an assemblage of troops in Picardy in order to put them within Dieppe. Before they were ready, the town of Dieppe came to terms with the king. Thus was restored to Louis XI the whole Duchy of Normandy, save for the places that remained in the hands of my lord de Lescun by the treaty made at Caen.

The Duke of Normandy, as I said, had decided all of a sudden to flee into Flanders; but at that moment the Duke of Brittany and he were reconciled, both of them having realized that they had erred and that through quarrelling all the good things of the world are lost . . .

So the Duke of Normandy withdrew into Brittany, poor, downcast and abandoned by all those knights who had been high in Charles VII's favour and had now come to terms with Louis XI and received better offices from him than ever they had enjoyed under his father.

The two dukes were wise after the event (as it is said of the Bretons), and they remained in Brittany. The lord de Lescun, the chief of their servants, kept many embassies going and coming between the pair of them and the king, between them and the Count of Charolais, and between the king and the count (afterwards Duke of Burgundy)—some to learn news, others to win people over and to drive all sorts of nasty bargains under the pretence of good faith. Some took part with the best of intentions, believing that they could keep the peace. But it is great folly those commit who think themselves so upright and so prudent as to suppose that their presence can maintain peace among princes so powerful and so cunning as were these and so well aware of what they were after, especially considering that neither one side nor the other gave these envoys any reason to entertain such hopes. But then there are honest folk vainglorious enough to think that they can manage matters about which they in fact know nothing, for sometimes their masters do not reveal to them their secret thoughts . . .

BOOK TWO

The Interview at Péronne
1466–69

THUS PASSED SEVERAL YEARS DURING WHICH THE DUKE OF
Burgundy [i.e. Charles of Charolais] waged yearly war against the
Liégeois. When the king saw him thus occupied, he attempted some
new move against the Bretons while giving a little aid to the
Liégeois. Either the Duke of Burgundy then turned against the king
in order to succour his allies or they themselves made some sort of
treaty or truce with Louis XI.

In 1466 the Count of Charolais captured Dinant, a town in the
territory of Liége that was very strong for its size and very rich
because of its trade in copperware, called *dinanderie* [i.e. Dinantware]
—pots and pans and the like. This event occurred before the demise
of his father, Duke Philip, who died in June 1467. Philip of Burgundy, though in extreme old age, had had himself carried in a litter
in order to accompany the expedition, such hate did he harbour
against the inhabitants of Dinant because of the great cruelties they
had perpetrated against his subjects in the County of Namur,
especially against the citizens of Bouvignes, a small town situated
but a quarter of a league from Dinant, with only the river Meuse
between them. The people of Dinant, only a little before, had
besieged Bouvignes, from across the river. They had committed
several cruelties in the neighbouring region. During the siege, with
two bombards and other large artillery pieces they continually
pounded the houses of Bouvignes, forcing the unfortunate inhabitants to hide in their cellars and remain there.

It is unbelievable, the hate these two towns had for each other.

Yet the young people of the two places rarely married except with each other, for Bouvignes and Dinant were far off from all other sizeable towns. The year preceding the destruction of Dinant—the season when the Count of Charolais had returned from the siege of Paris—its inhabitants had come to an accommodation with that lord and given him a sum of money. Thus they had parted company with the city of Liége and made a separate peace. This is a sure sign of the coming destruction of a country—when those who should stick together go their separate ways and abandon each other . . . Now, it is to be noted that King Louis our master better understood this art of dividing people than any other prince I have ever known, in the process of which he did not spare money or possessions or trouble— not only in regard to rulers but as well in regard to their men . . .

The eighth day after the Burgundians had besieged Dinant, they took the town by assault, burned and razed it to the ground, and drowned some eight hundred prisoners in the river. The next day there appeared an army of the Liégeois, but, upon their asking for terms, the treaty made the previous year was reconfirmed, Liége paying an indemnity and delivering up three hundred hostages as security.

The Count of Charolais returned to Flanders. At this time died his father [15 June 1467] for whom he celebrated high and solemn obsequies at Bruges [on 16 August 1467] and he sent word of Duke Philip's demise to the king.

Secret intrigues, each different from the last, were continually being hatched among the princes. The king nursed an implacable anger against the Dukes of Burgundy and Brittany. [By the conquest of Normandy] he had interposed himself between the territories of the Duke of Burgundy and those of the Duke of Brittany. Consequently the two dukes had great difficulty in maintaining communications, for often their messengers were intercepted, and, in time of war [between them and the king] their messengers had to go by sea—at the best, those from Brittany had to cross the Channel to England, then go by land to Dover and recross to Calais. If they took the direct road through France, they put themselves in great peril.

   These times, and later ones, of strife lasted about twenty years or more, some of them in war, others in truces and dissimulations— during which each of the princes included his allies in any truce that he made. In this period God bestowed upon the realm of France a great blessing—that the wars and civil strife in England, begun some fifteen years before, with their great, cruel battles and the killing of many men of note, were still going on. The warring parties called each other traitors, for there were two royal houses that claimed the crown of England, namely the House of Lancaster and the House of York. And it need not be doubted that if the English had been in the state they once enjoyed, this realm would have been gravely menaced.

The king continually sought to make an end with Brittany his prime objective, for he thought it easier to conquer since it was weaker than the House of Burgundy; and, in addition, the Bretons were the ones who harboured his enemies, like his brother and others, and who had secret affiliations within the realm. Therefore the king worked on Duke Charles of Burgundy, by all kinds of offers and bargainings, to bring him to consent to abandon the Bretons, and he, the king, would in turn abandon the Liégeois and other enemies of Burgundy. But a settlement could not be managed. Instead, the Duke of Burgundy again went against the Liégeois, who had broken the peace. They had taken a place called Huy [September 1467], driven out the inhabitants and pillaged the town, notwithstanding the hostages they had delivered the previous year on penalty of loss of life, and the additional penalty of a great sum of money if they failed to observe the treaty. The duke assembled his army around Louvain, in Brabant, and on the borders of the territory of Liége.

There arrived at his quarters the Count of St Pol, Constable of France, who at that time had been entirely won over to the king and was a fixture at the king's court. He, along with Cardinal [Jean] Balue and other royal envoys, signified to the Duke of Burgundy that the Liégeois were allies of the king and included in the Franco-Burgundian truce, warning the duke that their master would aid the Liégeois if he attacked them. However, the envoys offered the proposition that if the duke consented to the king's waging war in Brittany, the king would give him a free hand with the Liégeois. Their audience was short, and in public, and they remained but one day.

The Duke of Burgundy said by way of excuse that it was the Liégeois who had attacked him and they who had broken the truce, not he, and in such circumstances he had no reason to abandon his allies. The ambassadors were then given leave to depart. As they

were about to mount horse—this being the day after their arrival—
he said to them in a loud voice that he begged the king to undertake
nothing against Brittany. The Constable pressed him on the issue,
declaring, 'My lord, you do not make a fair choice, for you take all
and insist on waging war as you please upon our friends, and at the
same time you expect to keep us quiet without our daring to attack
our enemies, as you do yours. This cannot be, nor will the king
permit it.'

The duke bade them farewell in these words: 'The Liégeois are
mobilized and I expect a battle within three days. If I lose it, I quite
believe that you will do as you please; but if I win it, you will leave
the Bretons in peace.' He then mounted horse, and the ambassadors
went to their lodgings to prepare their departure. As for the duke,
quitting Louvain, armour-clad, with a very large army, he marched
to lay siege to a town called St Trond. . . .

*Three days later the army of the Liégeois occupied the village of Brusthem,
half a league from the besiegers. On 28 October battle was joined. 'I was
never with the Duke of Burgundy', writes Commynes, 'when I saw him of
himself effectively command an army, except this day.' After routing the
Liégeois, the duke received the surrender of St Trond, shortly followed by
that of Tongres. The Burgundian army then moved upon Liége. The
Liégeois, however, brought the duke the keys of the city and yielded without
conditions, save that Liége was to be spared fire and pillage. After Charles
of Burgundy had made a triumphant entry into the town, 17 November
1467, he had the walls, towers and gates razed, imposed a heavy indemnity
and carried off all the municipal artillery.*

Thus had the Liégeois continued in their foolish and malevolent
ways, without really knowing what moved them to behave so,
except too much prosperity and overweening pride. King Louis
had a favourite saying, in my opinion a very wise one, that when
pride rides before, shame and ruin follow close behind. And of this
sin the king had no taint at all.

These matters accomplished, the duke withdrew to Ghent . . .
Several royal ambassadors came there, and Burgundian ones went
to the king. Likewise the duke received envoys from, and sent
envoys to, Brittany. Thus passed this winter. Always the king
pressed the duke to give him a free hand with Brittany, in return for
certain concessions by way of recompense. No settlement could be

reached, on which account the king was displeased, considering what had happened to his allies, the Liégeois.

Finally, when the summer [of 1468] came, the king lost patience and invaded Brittany, or rather his troops for him; and they captured two little castles, one called Chantocé and the other Ancenis. This news soon reached the Duke of Burgundy, along with urgent requests for help from the Duke of Normandy and Brittany. Charles of Burgundy quickly assembled his army and dispatched to the king a request that the latter desist from this enterprise since the Dukes of Normandy and Brittany were included in the Franco-Burgundian truce as allies. Receiving no satisfactory response, the Duke of Burgundy took the field near the town of Péronne, with a very large force. The king was at Compiègne, and his army still in Brittany.

Three or four days later there arrived at the duke's headquarters an ambassador from the king, Cardinal Balue, who remained but a short time. He made some proposals, telling the duke that those in Brittany could well come to agreement without him—always was it the aim of the king to separate Burgundy from Brittany. The cardinal was soon given leave to depart, having been duly honoured and treated to good cheer. He returned to his master with the message that the duke had not taken the field to injure the king or wage war upon him but only to succour his allies. On each side there was nothing but soothing words.

Immediately after the departure of the cardinal, there came to the duke a herald named *Brittany*. He brought letters from the Dukes of Normandy and Brittany saying that they had made peace with the king and renounced all their alliances, specifically their alliance with him, and that, as his share of the realm, the king's brother Charles was to receive an annual income of sixty thousand livres and renounce the Duchy of Normandy which formerly had been delivered to him. Charles of France was not very happy about this settlement, but it was necessary for him to dissimulate.

The Duke of Burgundy was astounded at the news, since he had taken the field only to succour these dukes; and the herald found himself in very great danger—Duke Charles believed that the herald, since he had come by way of the king, had forged the letters. However, he received like letters from other sources.

It then seemed to the king that he had indeed achieved his object and that he would easily persuade the Duke of Burgundy to abandon, in turn, the Dukes of Normandy and Brittany. There began an exchange of secret messages between them. Finally the king gave the Duke of Burgundy 120,000 gold crowns, half paid in coin before the duke broke camp, as compensation for the duke's expenses in assembling his army.

The duke sent to the king a *valet de chambre* of his named Jean de Boschuse, a man very intimate with him. The king, putting great faith in this development, desired to talk with the duke, hoping to win him entirely to his will because of the bad turn that the aforesaid dukes had done Duke Charles and because of the great sum of money he had given him. The king therefore sent some word or other to the duke by way of de Boschuse and dispatched with him Cardinal Balue and Tanneguy du Chastel, Governor of Roussillon, with instructions to make clear that their master had the strongest desire for this projected interview between him and the duke to take place. They found the Duke of Burgundy at Péronne. He did not much want the interview, because the Liégeois were again showing signs of rebelling, incited by two ambassadors that the king had sent to them before the treaty of Ancenis was signed. The Liégeois, however, told the royal envoys that they would not dare revolt since the Duke of Burgundy had undone them the year before and razed their walls; and if they should see a settlement between the king and duke, they would lose all desire to revolt, if indeed they had had such a desire. In any case, it was finally concluded that the king would come to Péronne, for such was his wish. The duke wrote him a letter in his own hand giving him ample security for coming to Péronne and returning. The royal envoys then took their departure and went back to the king, who was at Noyon. The Duke of Burgundy, thinking to avoid trouble with Liége, had the Bishop of Liége [Louis of Bourbon] withdraw from the city—it was on the bishop's account that all the strife there occurred—and with him withdrew the lord of Humbercourt, ducal lieutenant in that territory, and several others.

You have heard in what manner it was settled that the king would come to Péronne. And so he did, bringing no guard with him for he insisted upon putting himself entirely in the safekeeping of the duke. He desired my lord des Cordes [Philippe de Crèvecoeur] then in the duke's service, to meet him with an escort of ducal archers. So was it done. Few people accompanied the king, but among them were men of high rank like the Duke of Bourbon, the duke's brother [Charles, Archbishop of Lyons and afterwards] the Cardinal of Bourbon, and the Count of St Pol, Constable. The latter had taken no part in the arranging of this interview and was indeed displeased by it, for at this time he had grown very proud and did not humble himself before the Duke of Burgundy as formerly, and for this reason there was no love lost between the two of them. There also came Cardinal Balue, the Governor of Roussillon, and others.

As the king neared the town of Péronne, the duke, splendidly escorted, came to meet him, and brought him into the town, and lodged him at the dwelling of the collector of taxes, a handsome mansion near the castle—accommodations in the castle being very limited and shabby . . .

The Duke of Burgundy had sent for his forces in the Duchy and County of Burgundy, where at that time there were large numbers of noblemen. With them came my lord [Philip] of Bresse, the Bishop of Geneva, the Count [Jacques] de Romont, all brothers, offspring of the House of Savoy (for Savoyards and Burgundians are at all times very closely affiliated), and also some Swiss from regions bordering Savoy and the County of Burgundy. Now you must understand that the king had at one time consigned the lord of Bresse to prison, because of his being responsible for the murder of two knights in Savoy, on which account there was little love between them. In this company was also my lord [Antoine] du Lau (whom the king had likewise kept in confinement a long time, du Lau having earlier been a royal favourite, and who had then escaped from prison and withdrawn into Burgundy), along with Poncet de Rivière and the lord d'Urfé, afterwards Grand Equerry of France.

The whole company arrived before Péronne as the king was entering. The lord of Bresse and the other three of whom I have spoken likewise entered the town, wearing the Cross of St Andrew [emblem of Burgundy]. They had expected to arrive in time to accompany the Duke of Burgundy when he went out to meet the king, but they were a little late. They went immediately to the duke's chamber, made their bows to him; and then the lord of Bresse, acting as their spokesman, begged the duke to guarantee the safety of du Lau, de Rivière and d'Urfé, notwithstanding the coming of the king, as that protection had been promised and accorded the very moment they arrived in Burgundy; and the three said that they were ready to serve him 'for and against all'. The duke granted this request by word of mouth and thanked them. The remainder of this force, commanded by the Marshal of Burgundy, was quartered in the fields, as had been arranged. The marshal bore no less ill will towards the king than the others of whom I have spoken, because of the town of Épinal in Lorraine which the king had formerly given to the marshal and afterwards deprived him of it in order to give it to Duke John of Calabria, as has been frequently mentioned in these memoirs.

The king was soon informed of the arrival of all these people and of the warlike array in which they had come. He was very much frightened and sent a request to the duke that he be lodged in the castle, declaring that these new arrivals were enemies of his. The duke, delighted by the request, arranged for him to be quartered in the castle, and heartily assured him that he need have no fear . . .

Great folly is it in a prince to submit himself to the power of another, especially when they are at war. [In this regard] it is very advantageous to princes to have read, in their youth, works of history in which they may view many such princely meetings and the great frauds and deceits and perjuries that some of the ancients practised against each other, seizing and putting to death those who had trusted to such safe conducts. This is not to say that all of them used these methods, but the example of one is sufficient to make several wise and teach them to look to their safety. Indeed (from my own experience in this world, where, having spent eighteen years or more in the company of princes, I have had full knowledge of the greatest and most secret affairs which have been transacted in this realm of France and neighbouring lordships), it seems to me that one of the best ways of achieving wisdom is for a man to read the histories of the ancients and to govern and guard himself and manage his affairs sagaciously, according to the examples provided by the history of our predecessors. For our life is too short for us to achieve so wide an experience ourselves. In addition, we are diminished in our life span since a man's life is not as long as it used to be nor his body so strong and we are likewise enfeebled in our capacity for trust and loyalty . . .

[It is especially difficult for princes to establish trustworthy relations, for they are headstrong, and, what is worse, are usually surrounded by time-servers. Though most of the princes I have known have made use of such people, I have seen some wise ones who in time of need knew how to seek out good counsellors.]

Among all the princes I have known, the king our master best exemplified this capacity and, more than any of the others, honoured and esteemed men of worth. He was well educated. He loved to ask and learn about everything under the sun, and he possessed an excellent natural intelligence, which is superior to any kind of knowledge that can be achieved in this world . . .

Now you have heard about how this army from Burgundy arrived at Péronne almost at the same moment as did the king. The duke had not been able to countermand his order, for the force had already reached Champagne when the king's coming was being negotiated. It troubled the feast because of the suspicions its presence engendered. Nevertheless the two princes commissioned representatives to treat of their affairs as amicably as possible. When they were well along in their work, having already negotiated for two or three days, there arrived from Liége news of tremendous import, as I will explain.

The king, in coming to Péronne, had not taken into account that he had dispatched two ambassadors to the Liégeois to stir them up against the duke, which ambassadors had played their parts so diligently that the Liégeois, massing in great force, had immediately gone to seize the town of Tongres, in which were the Bishop of Liége and the lord de Humbercourt with a stout force of some two thousand men or more. They captured the bishop and de Humbercourt, killed few people, and took only those two and some servants of the bishop. The rest fled, abandoning everything like men completely beaten. The Liégeois set out to return to their city which was quite close to Tongres. On the road the lord de Humbercourt came to an agreement with a knight called [Jean] de Wilde, which in translation means 'the Wild Man'. This knight saved de Humbercourt from being murdered by this mindless mob. He kept his word, though not for long since he was soon afterwards killed.

The people were overjoyed by the capture of their bishop, the lord of Liége. They hated a number of canons whom they had also captured this day. For a first course they killed five or six, among them one called Master Robert, a great intimate of the bishop, whom several times I had seen clad in complete armour like his master, for such is the custom of the prelates of Germany. They killed Master Robert in the bishop's presence and divided him into several pieces that they threw at each other's heads in derisive sport. Before they had covered the seven or eight leagues that they had to go, they killed some sixteen people, canons or others of rank, almost all of them servants of the bishop. They had heard that peace negotiations [between the king and Duke of Burgundy] were under way, and they would have been quite glad to assert they had acted only against their bishop, whom they brought prisoner to their city.

Those fleeing from the Liégeois, whom I have mentioned, spread fright and alarm wherever they passed; and the news soon reached the Duke of Burgundy. Some said that everybody had been killed; others said the contrary. Concerning such happening there is rarely just a single report. In this case, there arrived some who had seen the canons torn to pieces and thought that the bishop and the lord de Humbercourt had likewise been murdered; and they affirmed that they had seen the ambassadors of the king among the Liégeois, and named them. All this was recounted to the Duke of Burgundy, who immediately believed it and, flying into a rage, declared that the king had come to Péronne to deceive him. He suddenly ordered the gates of the town and of the castle closed, and caused to be spread abroad a very feeble explanation for so doing— namely that a casket containing precious jewels and money had been lost.

The king, finding himself shut up in this little castle with a strong guard of Burgundian archers at its gate, was not without fear; he was aware that he was quartered close by a great tower in which a Count of Vermandois had put to death one of his predecessors [Charles the Simple, who, imprisoned there, probably died a natural death in 929].

At that time I was still serving the Duke of Burgundy, as a chamberlain, and I slept in his chamber whenever I wished, for such was the custom of this house. When the duke knew that the gates were shut, he dismissed most of the people from his chamber and said to the few of us who remained that the king had come there to betray him, that he himself had sought by all means to avoid the interview, and that it had come about against his will. He kept going over this news from Liége and how the king had had the attack on Tongres instigated and directed by his ambassadors and how all the duke's people had been killed. In his violent anger against the king, the duke began uttering dark threats. I truly believe that, if those to whom he was then addressing himself had readily echoed his thoughts or advised him to use harsh measures against the king, some kind of action would have been taken; and, at the least, the king would have been put in the great tower. The only ones present besides myself were two *valets de chambre*, one of whom was named Charles de Visen, a native of Dijon, a good man and one trusted by his master. We in no way aggravated the duke's temper but calmed it as best we could.

Soon after, the duke spoke in much the same way to a number of people, and the report of what he was saying spread throughout the town and reached the chamber of the king, who was very much frightened. And in general so was everybody; for matters looked bad—considering how many things must be taken into account in order to pacify a quarrel between such great princes, and the error both committed in not giving warning to their officers who, at a distance, were involved in their affairs, and considering too the likelihood that something would happen suddenly . . .

Commynes declares that it is very foolish of great princes to have interviews with each other—better for them to sustain friendly relations by means of sagacious envoys. He then gives examples of several princely interviews that turned out badly: Louis XI and Henry IV of Castile in 1463; the Duke of Burgundy and Emperor Frederick III in 1473; the Duke of Burgundy and Edward IV of England in 1471, when the latter had taken refuge in the Burgundian domains; the Duke of Burgundy and Frederick, Count Palatine of the Rhine, in 1467; the Duke of Burgundy and Duke Sigismund of Austria in 1469; the Duke of Burgundy and Richard, Earl of Warwick (the Kingmaker) in 1469; and Louis XI and Edward IV in 1475.

The closing of the gates of Péronne and the stationing of a guard at the castle lasted two or three days. Meanwhile the Duke of Burgundy did not once see the king, and only a few of the king's people entered the castle, and then by the wicket-gate. None of his men was removed from him, but few or none of the duke's people went to speak to him or even entered his chamber, at least of those who had any authority with the duke.

The first day, all was alarm and rumour throughout the town. The second, the duke cooled down a little. He held council most of the day and part of the night. The king had approaches made to all those who, he thought, could help him, and he did not fail to hold out promises. He ordered fifteen thousand gold crowns distributed;

F

but the one charged with this mission kept back some of the money, acquitting himself badly as the king later learned. The king had great fear of those who formerly had served him, the ones who had come with this army of Burgundy of which I have spoken and who already were proclaiming their adherence to the Duke of Normandy, the king's brother.

At this council of which I have spoken, a number of opinions were expressed. The majority said that the safe conduct given the king should be honoured, in view of the fact that he was assenting to the peace treaty in the form that it had been drawn up in writing. Others opted for the king's being forthwith put under restraint without ceremony. Still others thought that the Duke of Normandy should be immediately sent for so that a peace of great advantage to all the princes of France might follow. In the view of those who offered this opinion, if such a peace were agreed upon, the king would be kept under guard, since once so great a lord has been put in captivity and thus been so egregiously offended he is never or hardly ever given his freedom. The matter was so nearly concluded that I saw a man, booted and spurred, ready to set forth; he had already been given several letters addressed to the Duke of Normandy, then in Brittany, and was waiting only for letters from the Duke of Burgundy. Nevertheless this plan was cancelled.

The king had overtures made. He offered to deliver as hostages the Duke of Bourbon, Bourbon's brother the cardinal, the Constable, and several others, on condition that, after peace had been concluded, he could return to French territory, as far as Compiègne, where he immediately would see that the Liégeois made good all the damage they had done or would declare himself against them. Those that the king named as hostages had stoutly volunteered, at least in public. I do not know whether they sang the same tune in private. I doubt it. And, in truth, I believe that he would have left them there rather than have come back.

That night, the third, the duke never undressed. All he did was lie down two or three times on his bed, and then he walked up and down again, for such was his habit when he was troubled. I bedded down that night in his chamber and walked up and down with him several times. In the morning the duke was more enraged than ever, uttering menaces and ready to do some violent deed. Nevertheless, he finally brought himself to agreeing that if the king accepted on oath the peace treaty and was willing to go with him to Liége to help him avenge the bishop, who was a close relative, he would be satisfied. And suddenly he left his quarters to go to the king's chamber and bring him this word.

The king had a certain friend [Commynes himself] who informed him of it, assuring him that he would suffer no harm if he accepted the two points, but that if he refused he would put himself in peril so great that none greater could befall him. As the duke appeared before the king, his voice was trembling, so moved was he and ready to burst out in a rage. He preserved a humble stance but his word and gesture were harsh as he asked if the king were willing to uphold the peace treaty which had been inscribed and agreed upon and take his oath upon it. The king said yes. In truth the treaty made few or no changes in the articles concerning the Duke of Burgundy in the Treaty of Conflans that had been concluded at the siege of Paris [in October 1465]. The settlement concerning the Duke of Normandy had been greatly changed, however, for it was now established that he would renounce the Duchy of Normandy and receive Champagne and Brie and other neighbouring lands as his share of the realm.

Then the Duke of Burgundy asked the king if he were entirely willing to come with him to Liége to help him get revenge for the treacherous behaviour of the Liégeois, which was the king's doing. The duke also reminded the king of how closely related the latter was to the Bishop of Liége, who was of the House of Bourbon. To these questions the king answered yes: let the peace be sworn, which he desired, and he was content to go to Liége with the duke, bringing such number of troops, few or many, as the duke thought best. These words gave great pleasure to the duke. Immediately the treaty of peace was fetched, and the True Cross worn by Charlemagne, called the Cross of Victory, was removed from the king's coffer, and duke and king swore to uphold the treaty. All the church bells in the town were then rung, and everybody was overjoyed.

On one occasion the king did me the honour of saying that I had served him well in this pacification.

Immediately the duke dispatched the news to Brittany, along with a copy of the treaty in which he had not dissociated himself from the king's brother and the Duke of Brittany. Thus did my lord Charles [of France] secure an attractive grant for his share of the realm, considering that he and the Duke of Brittany had just a little before concluded a treaty [of Ancenis], by the terms of which the king's brother was to have only a pension, as you have heard.

The day after this treaty [of Péronne] was concluded, the king and the Duke of Burgundy set out for Cambrai, and from there proceeded towards the territory of Liége. It was the beginning of winter and the weather was very bad. The king had with him only the Scots of his guard and a few troops, but he summoned to him about three hundred men of arms.

The army of the Duke of Burgundy was in two divisions. In one, commanded by the Marshal de Burgundy, were all those from the County and Duchy of Burgundy and these Savoyard lords, as you have heard mentioned above; and with them, a large number of troops from Hainault, Luxembourg, Namur and Limbourg. The other division was commanded by the duke. As this force approached Liége, there was held a council, the duke being present, in which some proposed sending back a part of the army since the gates and walls of the city had been razed the previous year, and its inhabitants could look for no help from any quarter. Furthermore, the king was there in person against them and was suggesting certain terms on their behalf which were almost identical with those that the duke was demanding.

This opinion did not please the duke, and it was well for him that it did not, for never was man so near to losing everything. It was the suspicions he nursed of the king that caused him to make this wise choice; and those who raised the issue of the army's being excessively large were very badly advised. Such an opinion represented the worst kind of pride or folly. Often have I heard such opinions. Captains sometimes advance them in order to gain a reputation for boldness or because they have failed to grasp the situation; but when princes are wise, they do not accept such advice. The king our master— whom God pardon—well understood this truth; for he was hesitant and timorous in taking action, but what he undertook he made such ample provision for that he rarely failed to be the strongest and gain the upper hand.

Thus it was decreed that the Marshal of Burgundy and all those in his force would take up quarters in Liége and, if entry was refused them, they would enter by force if they could; for already there were representatives of the city going back and forth in the course of negotiating terms. The marshal's force went to Namur, quitting that city the next day as the king and the duke arrived there. When the marshal and his troops were approaching Liége, the foolish inhabitants issued from the city to attack them but were easily destroyed, at least a goodly number of them. The rest withdrew. Their bishop, making his escape at this time, came to us.

There was a papal legate who had been sent to pacify and arbitrate the quarrel between the bishop and the Liégeois; for the city was still under sentence of excommunication for the offences and causes above said. This legate, exceeding his powers in the hope of making himself bishop of the city, had favoured the people and ordered them to take arms and defend themselves and committed numerous other follies. Now, seeing the peril in which the city was placed, the legate attempted to flee. He was captured along with all his retinue, some twenty-five well mounted attendants. As soon as the duke received this news, he sent orders to those who held the legate that they should take him somewhere without officially reporting his capture and hold him to ransom just as if he were a merchant; for if the legate's seizure was publicly made known to the duke, he would not be able to keep him under arrest but would have to order his release for the honour of the apostolic see. The legate's captors did not have enough sense to carry out the duke's command; after an argument over the matter, those who claimed to have taken part in the capture came publicly before the duke at the dinner hour to speak with him about it. Immediately he sent for the legate, dismissing those who had taken him, and had all the legate's possessions returned, and treated him honourably.

The large number of troops in this advance guard commanded by the Marshal of Burgundy and the lord de Humbercourt went directly to Liége, thinking to enter the city; and, out of avarice, they preferred to pillage it than to accept terms which were offered them. They thought it unnecessary to await the king and the Duke of Burgundy, who were seven or eight leagues behind them. They made such good time that they reached a suburb de Liége as night was beginning to fall and appeared before the city gate, which the Liégeois had partly repaired. There was some parleying, but it came to nothing. A murky darkness took the Burgundians by surprise. They had established no lodgings, for which, indeed, there was no available place, and they were in great disorder. Some walked about, others shouted for their master or their company or called out the names of their captains. Jean de Wilde and other leaders of the Liégeois beheld this folly and took heart. Their disadvantage served them well, that is, the ruin of their walls, for they could sally forth wherever they wished; and, sallying through the breaches of their walls, they came upon our troops nearest the city. Then, moving through vineyards and sheltered by hills, they attacked the pages and *valets* who were on the outskirts of the suburbs walking large numbers of horses, and killed many of them. A great number of Burgundians took to flight, for night has no shame. So successful were the Liégeois that they killed nearly eight hundred men, including a hundred men of arms.

The men of worth and valour in this advance guard kept themselves together (and they were nearly all men of arms and scions of good houses) and marched with their banners right to the gate, out of fear that the Liégeois might sally from there. Because of the continual rains there was mud everywhere and the men of arms, all on foot, were over their ankles in it. At one moment, the remainder of the Liégeois attempted to make a sally through the gate with large lanterns that lit up the scene. Our men, who were very near the gate, had four good pieces of artillery and fired two or three effective rounds down the main street and killed a great many people. That forced them to withdraw and close the gates. Meanwhile fighting continued throughout the suburb; the Liégeois who had first sallied out laid hands upon some Burgundian wagons that were near the town and used them as barricades to protect themselves; and they remained outside Liége from two hours past midnight to six o'clock in the morning. None the less, when it was daylight and friend and foe were clearly visible, the Liégeois were repulsed. In this combat Jean de Wilde was wounded and died two days later in the town, and one or two of their other chiefs likewise perished.

. . . When the alarming news of this attack reached the Duke of Burgundy, who was quartered five or six leagues from Liége, he was first told that his advance guard had been crushed. However, he mounted horse and set the army in motion, ordering that nothing of this be said to the king. As he approached the city by a different route, he was informed that all went well—many fewer having been killed than had been thought and no man of note save a knight from Flanders named my lord de Sengmeur. . . .

It was almost night when the duke received this news. After dispatching supplies to the advance guard, he returned to his standard and recounted all to the king, who was very happy to learn it, for a victory by the Liégeois could have been unfortunate for him. They were now approaching a suburb of Liége, and numbers of the gentry and men of arms dismounted to join the archers in winning the suburb and securing quarters for the army. [Antoine] the Grand Bastard of Burgundy held a high command under the duke, as did the lord of Ravenstein, the Count of Roussy, who was a son of the Constable, and several other men of rank. There was no difficulty in occupying lodgings in this suburb, all the way to the city gate, which, like the gate confronting the advance guard, had been repaired. The duke established his quarters in the middle of the suburb; and the king remained that night in a huge solidly built farmhouse a quarter of a league from the town, with many troops, his and ours, camping in the vicinity.

Liége is situated amidst mountains and valleys, very fertile country, with the river Meuse flowing through the city—a place about the size of Rouen [the second largest city in France]. At that time it had an amazing density of population. From the gate before which we were quartered to that where our advanced guard was stationed was but a short distance if one walked it within the town, but from one gate to the other outside the walls was a good three leagues, because of the rough terrain and bad roads, which were made worse by the winter weather. Since the walls of the town were demolished, the Liégeois could sally forth wherever they wished. There was but a small ditch at the foot of the walls, and there never had been a proper moat because of the hard rock just beneath the surface of the ground.

Our occupying a suburb that evening very much cheered our advance guard, for the military power of the Liégeois was now necessarily split in two. Around midnight a fierce alarm was raised in our quarter. At once the Duke of Burgundy ran into the street, and a little after, there arrived the king and the Constable, who had used great diligence to come so far in such a short time. Some were shouting, 'They are sallying by such and such a gate!' Others were giving vent to similar frightened cries. The bad weather and thick darkness served to increase people's fears. The Duke of Burgundy had no lack of boldness but was indeed at times deficient in leadership. In truth, at this moment he did not display the coolness that many of his people would have wished because the king was present. The latter assumed command, telling the Constable, 'Go with what men you have to such a spot, for if the Liégeois are coming, that's the way they'll come'. To hear his orders and see his air of authority, he seemed indeed a king with a commanding personality and great good sense who had a long experience in dealing with such situations. In any case, the alarm came to nothing and the king returned to his quarters and the Duke of Burgundy to his.

The next morning the king took up lodgings within the suburbs in a small house near the one in which the Duke of Burgundy had his quarters, and he had with him his guard of one hundred Scots, his troops being stationed in some village or other close by.

The Duke of Burgundy was prey to suspicions either that the king might enter Liége or take to flight before the duke had captured the city or even commit some outrage upon him, the king being quartered so close by. However, between their two houses there was a large barn, in which the duke placed three hundred men of arms, the flower of his household; and these men broke down the walls of the barn so that they could easily sally forth through the openings. They kept watch on the king's dwelling nearby. This garden party lasted eight days, including [the arrival of the advance guard and] the capture of the city, during which time no one disarmed, the duke or anybody else.

On the evening before the taking of the city it was decided to attack the next morning, a Sunday, 30 October 1468; and signals between us and our advance guard were agreed upon, whereby, when the latter heard the firing of a bombard and two cannon, they would immediately attack with all their power, for the duke would simultaneously be attacking from his side. The assault hour was fixed for eight o'clock in the morning. The evening before, after this plan had been settled upon, the Duke of Burgundy removed his armour, which he had not up to that time done, and ordered all his men to disarm in order to give them some relaxation, especially those within the large barn. Very soon after, the men of Liége, as if they had been informed of this order, decided to make a sally on our side, in just the way they had sallied against the advance guard.

Now observe how a great and powerful prince can suddenly find himself in a precarious situation, and one created by very few enemies, on which account all enterprises should be well weighed and discussed before being put into effect.

In this whole city, except for its surrounding territories, there was not a single man of war. Among the inhabitants there remained neither knight nor gentleman—the few that there had been, had been killed or wounded two or three days before. They had no gates or walls or defensive ditch and not a single piece of artillery that was worth anything. For a military force there were only the townsfolk themselves and seven or eight hundred foot-soldiers from a small mountain behind Liége called the territory of Franchimont, whose people have always been renowned in Liége for their valour.

Realizing that they were without hope of succour and faced by the fact that the king was there in person against them, the Liégeois decided to mount a mass attack and put everything to hazard, for they considered that all was lost. It was their plan that, through the breaches in the walls that faced the quarters of the Duke of Burgundy, six hundred men of Franchimont would sally, their best soldiers. They would have for guides the owners of the houses in which the king and the Duke of Burgundy were lodged; and they could make their way through a rocky defile quite near the two houses without being perceived, provided that they made no noise. Though they knew there would be some Burgundian outposts along this route, they believed that they could kill them or reach the houses as soon as these sentinels. They counted on the two owners leading them directly to their houses and on their men not turning aside for other diversions. The king and duke would thus be so suddenly surprised that the raiders would be able to kill or capture them before their people could assemble, and the raiding party had but a short distance to cover in withdrawing. Furthermore, if bringing off such an enterprise lost them their lives, they would be content to die such a death, for they knew they were doomed, as has been said.

In addition they ordered all the townspeople to sally forth with great shouts by the gate which opened on the main street of our suburb, with the aim of destroying all who were quartered there. They were not without hope of winning a great victory or, at worst, a glorious end. Had they been able to muster a thousand well equipped men of arms, they would have mounted a grand exploit. Even so, they failed by only a little of accomplishing their objective.

Just as they had planned, these six hundred men of Franchimont sallied through the breaches in the city walls—I believe it was not yet ten o'clock in the evening—and caught and killed most of the Burgundian outposts, including three gentlemen of the household of the Duke of Burgundy. Had the men of Franchimont then made their way directly and noiselessly to the two houses, they would without difficulty have killed the king and the duke sleeping in their beds. Behind the duke's dwelling was a pavilion in which were lodged the present Duke of Alençon [René du Perche] and [Georges de la Trémoille] lord de Craon. The raiders paused there for a moment to thrust pikes through the sides of the pavilion, and killed a *valet*. This action made some noise, on hearing which a few soldiers armed themselves, or at least got to their feet. The raiders moved on from the pavilion and headed straight for the dwellings of the king and the Duke of Burgundy. Reaching the barn near these houses, in which the duke had put three hundred men of arms, they amused themselves by thrusting their pikes through the holes that had been made in the walls. All the gentlemen within had disarmed not two hours before, as I have said, to refresh themselves for the assault in the morning. Thus the men of Franchimont found them all, or almost all, unarmed. Some, however, had thrown on their cuirasses because of the noise they had heard in my lord of Alençon's pavilion; and they fought with the raiders through the holes in the walls and at the barn door. This action proved to be the entire salvation of these two great princes, for the delay gave time for several of their men to arm and sally forth into the street.

I was sleeping in the duke's bedroom, which was very small, along with two of his other chamberlains; and on the floor below there were but a dozen archers in combat dress keeping watch, who were playing dice. The duke's main guard was stationed far off towards the town gate. This was the situation as the owner of this house where the duke was lodged led a band of the Liégeois to assault the dwelling. It happened so suddenly that we could hardly put the duke's cuirass on him and get a helmet on his head. We immediately went down the stairs with the intent of emerging into the street. We found our archers having all they could do to defend the door and windows against the Liégeois, and there was an astounding tumult in the street. Some were yelling, 'Burgundy!' Others, 'Long live the King!' and 'Kill!' It took longer than the time to say two paternosters [i.e. at least five minutes] before the archers could issue from the house, and we with them.

We did not know how it was with the king, nor on whose side he was, and this uncertainty preyed on our minds. As soon as we had emerged from the house with two or three torches, we found some other torches and so could see people fighting around us; but the combat was soon over, for our men were coming from all sides towards the duke's house.

The first of the raiders to be killed was the owner of that house, who did not, however, die immediately, and I heard him speak. His band were all killed, or almost all. The Liégeois had also attacked the king's dwelling, the owner of which had made his way inside and was there killed by the Scots, who showed themselves bonny warriors for they did not budge a foot from their master as they kept up a hot fire of arrows—with which they wounded more Burgundians than Liégeois. The inhabitants of the city who had been ordered to make a sally through the gate did so, but they encountered a stout force keeping watch and already in battle array; and they were soon repulsed, not having proved to be so tough as the men of Franchimont.

As soon as these people had thus been beaten back, the king and the duke conferred. Since many bodies were lying about, they feared that the dead might be theirs. However, only a few were, though many of their men were wounded. There is no doubt that if the raiders had not given themselves such sport in the two places I have mentioned, especially at the barn, where they encountered resistance, and had followed the two owners who were their guides, they would have killed the king and the Duke of Burgundy and I believe, would have overcome the remainder of the army. Each of these two lords withdrew to his lodgings, astounded by this daring enterprise, and took counsel to decide what should be done on the morrow regarding the attack that had been arranged. The king began to entertain great doubts and fears that, if the duke failed to take Liége by assault, he would be the one to suffer for it and would be put under restraint or made captive outright, for the duke would fear that if he were allowed to depart, he would wage war upon the duke from the other side.

Here you see the miserable situation of these two princes, who could find no way of guaranteeing their mutual security. These two had signed a final peace not two weeks earlier and solemnly sworn to uphold it loyally. Nevertheless there was no basis of trust that could be found.

In order to allay his fears, the king, an hour after he had withdrawn to his quarters following the raid of which I have spoken, sent for some of the intimate servants of the duke who had been at the duke's council and asked them what had been decided. They told him that it had been decided to attack the town in the morning in the way that had been arranged. The king expressed great doubts, and very wise ones, which were most agreeable to the duke's people, for each of them deeply feared this attack on account of the large number of people in the town and also because of the tremendous boldness they had displayed not two hours before, and these servants of the duke would have been very happy to postpone the attack for some days or to accept terms from the Liégeois. I was present when they came before the duke to make their report; they recounted all the doubts the king had expressed, and added theirs—but these they ascribed to the king, fearing that the duke would take it ill if they owned to them.

The duke replied that the king was trying to save the Liégeois, and thus took the king's fears in a bad sense. He declared that there was no doubt about the outcome, considering that the Liégeois had no artillery and no walls and that the repairs they had made to the two gates facing the Burgundian forces were already destroyed. There was no need to wait longer; he would not delay the attack planned for the morning. However, if the king wished to go to Namur and wait there until the city was captured, the duke would be quite happy for him to do so, but he was not to leave Namur until the issue had been decided.

This response pleased none of those present, for the raid had instilled fear in each of them. The response was conveyed to the king, not in the harsh terms used by the duke but as politely as possible. He fully grasped how matters stood and declared that he had no desire at all to go to Namur: the next morning would find him in the attack with the others. It is my opinion that had he wished to go off this night, he could have done so, for he had a hundred archers of his guard and some gentlemen of his household and, close by, three hundred men of arms. But doubtless he had no desire to exchange a situation which did him honour for one that would cause him to be blamed for cowardice.

Everybody took a little repose, fully armed, while awaiting the morning. Some saw to their consciences [i.e. were shriven], for the enterprise was very doubtful. As, with the arrival of full daylight, the hour fixed for the assault approached—eight o'clock in the morning, as I have said—the duke ordered the firing of the bombard and two cannon shots to signal to the advance guard at the other gate, which, as I have said, was at quite some distance from us because of the terrain outside the walls. They heard the signal. Immediately the duke's troops took up their attack positions. The duke's trumpets began to sound and the Burgundian banners led the way towards the walls.

The king was in the middle of the street, well accompanied, for all his three hundred men of arms were there and his guard and some lords and gentlemen of his household. As the soldiers thought they were about to come to grips with the enemy, they encountered no opposition. There were but two or three townsmen on watch; for all the rest had gone to dinner, supposing that because it was Sunday there would be no attack—in each house we found the cloth laid for the meal. People in the mass are worth little in combat unless they are led by a chief whom they respect and fear, except that there are occasions and times when, roused to fury, they are indeed to be feared.

These Liégeois were already beaten down before the assault, partly because of the people they had lost in the two sallies in which all their chiefs were killed, and partly because of the hardships they had endured for eight days during which they had all had to keep constant watch, since the city was open on every side, as you have heard. I believe they thought they would have this day for repose since it was Sunday; but the opposite turned out to be true. Thus there were no defenders in our quarter nor anywhere our advance guard, which entered the city before we did, attacked. They killed few people, for all had fled across the Meuse bridge to the Ardennes, and from there to places where they thought to find safety. In our quarter I saw only three men dead and one woman; and I believe that not two hundred people were killed in all, the remainder taking to flight or hiding in churches or houses.

The king advanced at his ease, for he saw plainly that there was no resistance and that both the Burgundian forces were well within the city—some forty thousand men, I believe. The duke, who had penetrated further, quickly returned to the king, whom he escorted to the palace. He then returned immediately to the great church of St Lambert, where his troops were attempting to force an entrance in order to take prisoners and booty. Though the duke had ordered some of his household to guard the church, they were powerless to prevent the soldiers from attacking both its doors. I know that on his arrival the duke killed a man with his own hand—I saw it. The attackers were forced to leave and the church was not pillaged; but in the end the Liégeois within were taken prisoner and all the precious objects seized.

Of the other churches, of which there was a great number (for I have heard my lord de Humbercourt say, who knew the city well, that there were as many masses celebrated there daily as at Rome) the greater part were pillaged under the pretext of taking prisoners. I entered no church except the great one; but so I was told and I saw the signs of this pillage. Long after, the pope pronounced severe censures against all those who had anything belonging to the churches of the city, if they did not yield up what they had taken; and the duke appointed commissioners to go throughout his territories in order to enforce the pope's mandate. Thus, with Liége captured and pillaged by about noon, the duke returned to the palace. Meanwhile, the king, who had already dined, had displayed great joy at the taking of the city and praised to the skies the courage and boldness of the duke—knowing well that what he said would be reported. He had no other desire in his heart except to return to his realm. In the afternoon he and the duke made great cheer together, and if the king had praised the duke's accomplishments behind his back, he praised them still more ardently to his face, and his words much pleased the duke . . .

Four or five days after the taking of the city, the king began to work on those about the duke whom he considered his friends in order to win the duke's consent to his departure. He spoke also to the duke, very discreetly, saying that if the duke had further need of him, he would do anything to be of service, but if there remained nothing for him to do, he desired to go to Paris in order to have their treaty published in the Parlement of Paris, because it is the French custom thus to publish all such treaties or else they're held to be invalid—however, kings can always exert great influence to secure this publication.

In addition, he proposed to the duke that the following summer they have an interview in [the Duchy or County of] Burgundy and spend a month together making good cheer. In the end, the duke gave his assent, always however grumbling a little. He insisted that the Treaty of Péronne be read to the king, in order to learn if there was any article that the king regretted, offering him the choice of approving or changing as he wished; and he made a gesture of apologizing for having brought the king to Liége. In addition, he asked the king to consent to the insertion of an article in favour of my lords du Lau and d'Urfé and Poncet de Rivière, which would restore to them the lands and estates they had possessed before the war [of the Public Weal].

This request displeased the king, for there was no reason for them to be included in the treaty as adherents of his—it was my lord Charles his brother that they served and not him. The king replied that he was agreeable provided that the duke accorded him like terms for [Jean] Count of Nevers and my lord de Croy. The duke fell silent. It was a shrewd response by the king, for the duke so much hated these two and had seized so many of their possessions that he would never have consented to such a provision. To all the other points the king replied that he did not wish to change anything but wanted only to confirm what had been sworn at Péronne. His departure thus being accorded, the king took leave of the duke, who escorted him for about half a league. As they parted company the king put to him this question: 'If by chance my brother in Brittany should not consent to the share of the realm that I am delivering to him out of love for you, what do you want me to do?' The duke answered off hand without thinking: 'If he won't take it and you can satisfy him otherwise, I leave it to you two'. From this question and response there came great things, as you will afterwards hear. So the king was free to go off; he was escorted out of the duke's territories by my lord des Cordes and my lord d'Aimeries, Grand Bailli of Hainault . . .

The king returned with great joy to his realm. He showed no signs of anger against the duke because of the way he had been treated at Péronne and Liége; and it seemed that he bore it patiently, notwithstanding that afterwards a great war broke out between them. This, however, did not occur immediately, and its cause was not the events I have just described—although they might have helped— for the treaty of Péronne was almost identical with the treaty [of Conflans] that the king had signed at Paris [in October 1465]. The main cause of the war was that the Duke of Burgundy, by the counsel of his officers, wished to enlarge his boundaries; and then some cunning intrigues were developed to stir up discord between the king and the duke, of which I will speak at the proper time.

My lord Charles of France, having been informed of the treaty signed at Péronne and of the share that he was to have, sent immediately to the king to beg him to fulfill the treaty and grant what he had promised. The king in turn sent to him regarding the matter, and there were numerous comings and goings. The Duke of Burgundy also dispatched ambassadors to my lord Charles to request him to accept no other appanage than that of Champagne and Brie, which had been accorded him by the duke's means; he pointed out the affection that he had thus shown even though Charles had abandoned him—he having refused to do the same, as Charles could see, and having also named the Duke of Brittany in this treaty as his ally. In addition, the duke instructed his envoys to say to the king's brother that the situation of Champagne and Brie was advantageous to them both: if peradventure the king sought to trample upon him, he could within twenty-four hours receive Burgundian aid, for their territories adjoined. The appanage was likewise financially attractive, for Charles would receive the royal taxes and subsidies, the king retaining only sovereignty and the jurisdiction of appeal. My lord Charles was a man who did little or nothing of himself, but was entirely managed and led by others, although he was then twenty-five or older [actually, twenty-two on 28 December 1468].

Thus passed the winter—already begun by the time the king had left us—in incessant goings and comings of embassies concerned with the appanage, for under no circumstance would the king deliver what he had promised, since he had no desire for his brother and the duke to be such close neighbours. He was therefore treating with his brother to persuade him to accept as his share Guienne and the town of La Rochelle—well nigh all of Aquitaine—which was a much more valuable appanage than that of Brie and Champagne. My lord Charles feared to displease the Duke of Burgundy; and he was also afraid that if he came to terms with the king and the latter did not keep his word, he himself would have lost his friend and his appanage and would be in a sorry plight.

The king, who was shrewder at managing such negotiations than any other prince of the age, perceived that he was wasting his time unless he won over those who had his brother's ear. Therefore, addressing himself to Odet d'Aydie, lord de Lescun, afterwards Count of Comminges, who had been born and married in the province of Guienne, he asked him to see to it that his master accepted the proposed appanage, which was very much grander than the one Charles was asking for, and that he and his brother be made good friends, living in fraternal harmony, which service would prove to the advantage of the lord de Lescun and his servants,

especially Lescun. The king would guarantee that under no circumstance would he fail to deliver possession of the province. In this
fashion was my lord Charles won over, and he took the appanage of
Guienne, to the great displeasure of the Duke of Burgundy and the
duke's ambassadors who were at his side.

The reason that Cardinal [Jean] Balue, Bishop of Angers, and
[his co-conspirator, Guillaume de Haraucourt] the Bishop of
Verdun, were imprisoned was that the cardinal had been writing to
the king's brother, exhorting him to accept no appanage but the
one which the Duke of Burgundy had procured for him by the
treaty of Péronne, which had been sworn to under the cardinal's
auspices. The cardinal set forth the arguments that he thought it
necessary to use. This proceeding was contrary to the will and aim
of the king. So it was that my lord Charles became Duke of Guienne
in the year 1469, and enjoyed full possession of the province and of
the town of La Rochelle; and he and the king had an interview and
then spent much time together.

G

BOOK THREE

Strife and Jeopardy: The Duke,
The Kingmaker, The King's Brother,
The Constable

1469–74

IN THE YEAR 1470 A DESIRE TO REVENGE HIMSELF UPON THE
Duke of Burgundy took hold of the king. Believing that the time
was ripe, he secretly intrigued and allowed others to carry on
intrigues with the aim of persuading the towns on the river Somme
like Amiens, St Quentin and Abbeville to turn against the duke and
open their gates to his troops—for great lords, at least the sagacious
ones, are always searching for a good pretext, one that is not obvious.
In order to demonstrate the kind of clever intrigues that are used in
France, I want to recount how this whole matter was managed; for
the fact is that the king and the duke were both of them hoodwinked,
and it was under these circumstances that the war again broke out,
which lasted thirteen or fourteen years and became a fierce and bitter
conflict.

It is true that the king ardently desired these towns to rebel; and
as a pretext for war he declared that the Duke of Burgundy was
extending his territorial claims further than the Treaty of Péronne
allowed. On this account ambassadors went back and forth from one
to the other, and they continually intrigued as they passed and re-
passed by the Somme towns, which had no garrisons since there was
peace throughout the realm, on the side of Brittany as well as that
of Burgundy. And the Duke of Guienne was on very friendly
terms with the king, as it seemed. However, the king had not wanted
to reopen the war merely to take one or two of these towns, but he
was seeking to stir up a great rebellion throughout the territories of

the Duke of Burgundy and he hoped by this means to triumph over
the duke.

In order to please him many folk meddled in these intrigues and
made reports to him that were much rosier than the situation
warranted. Some boasted of being able to win over a town; others
said that they would undermine the loyalties of some of the greatest
officers of the ducal household, who would turn against their master.
All this had only elements of truth in it. If the king had foreseen
what came about, he would not have broken the peace nor reopened
the war, even though he had cause to complain of the way he had
been treated at Péronne—though he had had the treaty published at
Paris three months after his return to the realm. He went to war
somewhat fearfully, but his hopes drove him to push ahead.

And now behold the wiles that were used. The Count of St Pol,
Constable of France, a very shrewd man, and certain officers of the
Duke of Guienne and some others preferred war between the two
princes rather than peace, for two reasons. First, they feared lest their
magnificent positions be diminished if peace continued; for the
Constable had four hundred men of arms [of the standing army]
who were paid according to his muster rolls which were not subject
to audit, and he received more than thirty thousand francs yearly
thereby, in addition to the wages of his office and the revenues of
several handsome places that he had charge of. Second, they wanted
to clip the wings of the king, for they said among themselves that his
nature was such that if he were not in conflict with enemies outside
the realm or the princes of his feudality, he would make trouble for
his servants, household people and officers, since his temperament
could not endure repose.

For these reasons they tried very hard to make the king take up arms
again. The Constable offered to seize St Quentin any time he was so
desired, for his lands were in the vicinity of that town. He also said
he had very important connections in Flanders and in Brabant and
could bring about a rebellion against the duke in several cities. The
Duke of Guienne, who was at court, and all his principal officers
ardently offered to serve the king in this conflict and to bring four or
five hundred men of arms that the Duke of Guienne maintained in
his pay. The aims, however, were not such as the king understood
them but entirely opposite, as you will hear.

The king wanted always to proceed with great formality, on
which account he held a meeting of the Three Estates at Tours in

March and April 1470, which he had not done before and never did again. [Commynes is confusing the Three Estates of the spring of 1468 and an Assembly of Notables convoked towards the end of 1470 to condemn the Duke of Burgundy.] He summoned only people he himself named, who, he thought, would not oppose his will. At his orders, several enterprises the Duke of Burgundy had undertaken against the crown were set forth; and the Count of Eu, appearing as plaintiff, declared that the duke had deprived him of St Valéry and other lands which he held in feudal tenure from the duke as lord of Abbeville and the County of Ponthieu, and that the duke would give him no satisfaction. The duke had so acted because a small warship of the town of Eu captured a merchant vessel of Flanders, for which seizure the Count of Eu had offered to make reparation. In addition, the duke sought to force the count to swear allegiance to him for and against everybody, which the count under no circumstances would do since such an oath would be contrary to the king's sovereign authority. At this assembly there were several judicial officers, some from the Parlement of Paris, and it was decided, in accord with the king's intention, that the duke would be summoned to appear in person before that Parlement. The king well knew that he would make an arrogant reply or in some other way defy that court's authority, on which account the king's grounds for making war on him would be still stronger.

It was in the town of Ghent, as he was going to Mass, that the duke was issued the summons by an usher of the Parlement. He was astounded and angered. He at once had the usher seized and kept him under guard for several days. In the end he was allowed to take to his heels.

Now you can see the preparations that were made to attack the Duke of Burgundy, who, however, was warned of them and assembled a large number of men retained on household wages, as they were called. This was a small sum the men received while at home for holding themselves ready for service; they were mustered every month at designated places and there were paid. After three or four months the Duke of Burgundy grew weary of this situation; he disbanded his army and dismissed all fears—for the king kept sending envoys to him—and went off to Holland. He had no standing army always ready nor any garrisons in these frontier towns, and it cost him dear.

While he was in Holland he was informed by the late Duke John of Bourbon that he would shortly be attacked both in [the Duchy of] Burgundy and in Picardy, and that the king had many secret connections in both places and also in his own household. The Duke of Burgundy, having no troops arrayed, was very much disturbed by this news; setting off by sea, he made his way to the County of Artois and then directly to Hesdin. There he began to entertain suspicion of his servants as well as suspicions about the intrigues that were being carried on in the Somme towns, of which I have spoken. He was, however, a little long in taking measures, not putting faith in all that was related to him. He sent for two of the principal dignitaries of Amiens, whom he suspected of these intrigues. They exonerated themselves so convincingly that he let them go.

Immediately some of his servants quitted his household and took service with the king, like [the duke's half brother] the Bastard Baldwin, and others, which desertions put the duke in fear that still more might do likewise. He had it proclaimed that everyone should take arms, but few were ready for it was the beginning of winter and he had arrived from Holland only a little while before.

Two days after the flight of the duke's servants, in the month of December 1470, the Constable entered St Quentin [actually, about 6 January 1471] and had the inhabitants swear an oath of allegiance to the king.

Then the Duke of Burgundy realized that his affairs were going badly, for he had no army with him, though he had dispatched officers to array the forces of his domains. Nevertheless, with the few troops he was able to assemble he advanced to Doullens, with four or five hundred horse only, intending to prevent Amiens from shifting its allegiance. Its inhabitants had already been engaged in such bargaining for five or six days, for the king's army, which had been nearby, presented itself before the city. They at first refused it entrance, for a part of the townsfolk were loyal to the duke who sent there his harbinger-marshal; and if he had had enough troops to dare entering the city in person he would never have lost it; but he did not dare enter with so small a force, though several in the city urged him to do so. When those of Amiens who were against him perceived that he was dissembling and that his position was weak, they carried out their enterprise and introduced the king's army into Amiens. The people of Abbeville were about to do the same thing,

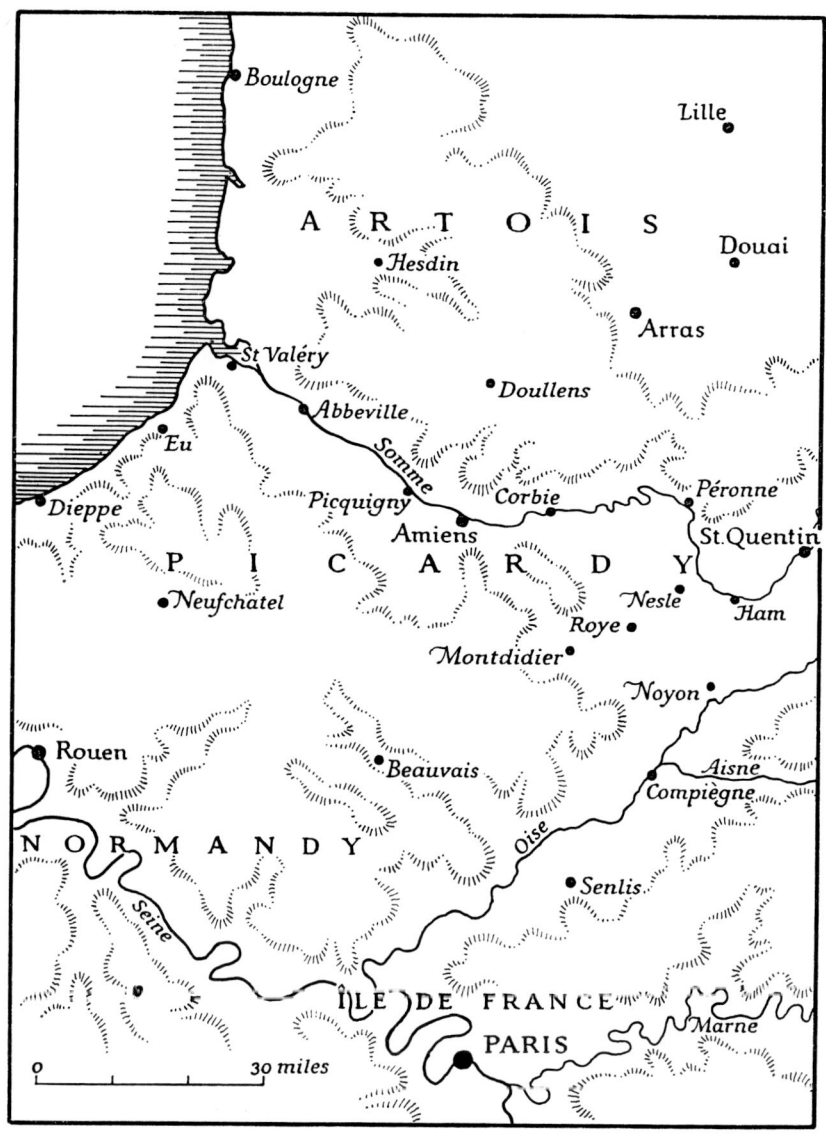

PICARDY AND THE SOMME TOWNS

but my lord des Cordes entered there on the duke's behalf and thus forestalled them.

It is hardly five leagues [some eighteen miles] from Amiens to Doullens, and the duke was therefore forced to beat a retreat as soon as he was informed that the king's troops had entered Amiens. He went to Arras in great haste and great alarm, fearing that many similar shifts in allegiance might come about, for he saw himself surrounded by relatives and friends of the Constable. Furthermore, because Bastard Baldwin had gone off, he was now suspicious of [Antoine] the Grand Bastard of Burgundy. However, troops began arriving, little by little. The king now believed that he was master of the situation, trusting as he did in what the Constable and others were telling him about these connections that they had. Had it not been for the hopes he built on these reports, he would have wished that the war was still to be begun.

It is now time for me to finish explaining what moved the Constable, the Duke of Guienne and that duke's principal officers to act as they did (considering the good turns, the aid, and the loyal support the Duke of Guienne had received from the Duke of Burgundy), and what they hoped to gain in setting these two great princes at war at a time when they and their domains were at peace. I have already said something on the subject—that their motive was to be the surer of their lands and offices and forestall the king's making trouble for them as was likely if he were free to do so—but we have not yet come to their principal motive. This was that the Duke of Guienne and they ardently desired the marriage of the duke to [Mary] the sole daughter and heiress of the Duke of Burgundy (for he had no sons). Many times the latter had been approached about this marriage, and each time he had agreed to it, but never was he willing to bring it to a conclusion; and indeed he held out such promises to others.

Now behold what device these people adopted in seeking to achieve their aim and constrain the duke to yield his daughter. The moment St Quentin and Amiens were won and the Duke of Burgundy returned to Arras, where he was assembling as many men as he could, the Duke of Guienne sent him a secret messenger who bore a note with three lines in the duke's hand, folded very small and enclosed in a ball of wax, which contained these words: 'See that you satisfy your subjects and then don't worry, for you will find friends'.

An Mil.iiii.
lxx. print vou
loir au Roy de
se venger du
Duc de bourgongne et luy
sembla quil en estoit heure.
Et secrettement traictoit et
souffroit traicter que les vil
les estans sur la kiuere de
somme comme Amyens
sainct quentin et Abauille
se tournassent contre le duc.

et quilz appellassent ses gens
darmes et les missent dedis.
Car tousiours les grans sei
gneurs Aumoins les saiges
vuillent serther quelq bonne
coulleur et vng peu appaiste.
Et affin que on congnoisse
les habilitez dequoy lon vse
en france veulx compter co
me cecy fut guide, car le kov
et le Duc y surent deceuz to9
deux / Et en kecommanca la

The Assembly at Tours

The Duke of Burgundy, who was greatly alarmed by his situation at the beginning of this war, dispatched a man to the Constable to ask him not to do his worst and not to press hostilities which had been begun against him without any formal declaration or statement of cause. The Constable was delighted with the message, for this appeal, obviously prompted by fear, signified to him that he held the duke in his hands. The only reply he made was that he realized the duke's situation was perilous and he knew only one way for him to escape from it—that was, to give his daughter in marriage to the Duke of Guienne. When he had done so, he would be succoured by a great number of people, the Duke of Guienne and many other lords would declare for him, and then the Constable would render St Quentin to him and join with the foregoing lords. However, without this marriage and the Duke of Guienne's declaration, he would not dare espouse the duke's cause; for the king was too powerful: he had marshalled his resources for this campaign and possessed widespread connections in the duke's territories—the Constable adding similar intimidating statements.

I have never known any good come to a man who sought to frighten his master and hold him in subjection or to treat thus a great prince with whom he had dealings, as you will hear concerning the Constable. Although the king was then his master, the greater part of his holdings and his children were under the duke. He constantly sought to keep both duke and king in a state of fear, using one against the other, and it was this that caused his downfall. Although everyone seeks to avoid such subjection and hates those who hold him in it, there is no one who comes near princes in this respect, for I have never known one who did not mortally hate those who applied such tactics.

After the Duke of Burgundy had heard the reply of the Constable, he realized that he would find no friendship in him and that he was in fact the principal director of this war. The duke conceived a marvellous hatred for him, which never afterwards left his heart, a hatred that sprang mainly from the Constable's attempt to constrain him by fear to give his daughter in marriage. By this time he had begun to regain his courage and had been joined by many troops. You now understand, from the messages sent by the Duke of Guienne and then by the Constable, that the stratagem had been planned between them, for a similar message, or an even more alarming one, was afterwards dispatched by the Duke of Brittany,

H

who allowed my lord de Lescun to bring a hundred Breton men of arms to serve the king. Thus it may be concluded that this war was begun to force the Duke of Burgundy to consent to the marriage and that the king was deceived by those who counselled him to undertake it, as he was deceived in the connections that they claimed to have in the duke's territories, which claim was nothing but a lie, or almost so.

Nevertheless throughout this whole campaign the king was very well served by the Constable, who had conceived a great hate against the duke, recognizing that the duke had the same feeling towards him. Likewise the Duke of Guienne, with a strong contingent, served the king in this war, and the Duke of Burgundy was in great peril. However, had that duke at the beginning of hostilities been willing to guarantee the marriage of his daughter to the Duke of Guienne, the latter and the Constable and many other lords and their followers would have decisively turned against the king and worked to deprive him of much of his power if they could. But in such matters man proposes and God disposes.

You have heard at length how this war came about and how both princes were at the beginning deceived and how they made war without understanding, either of them, its true causes— which was a marvellously clever exploit by those who managed the business. There could well be applied to this situation the saying that one half of the world does not know how the other half thinks.

Now all these things of which I have spoken came to pass in a very few days. For less than two weeks after the winning of Amiens, the Duke of Burgundy took the field near Arras—he had withdrawn no further—and then marched directly for Picquigny on the river Somme. On the road he was met by a messenger from the Duke of Brittany, just a man on foot, who informed him that the king had made known many things to the Duke of Brittany, among others that he had connections in several great Burgundian towns like Antwerp, Bruges and Brussels. The Duke of Burgundy was also thus informed that the king was determined to besiege him in whatever town he found him, were it even Ghent. It is my belief that the Duke of Brittany sent all this on the Duke of Guienne's behalf in order to increase the pressure on the Duke of Burgundy to accede to the match.

The Duke of Burgundy, however, hotly resented this warning and answered the messenger right on the spot that his master was ill-informed; that he was badly served by those who instilled such fears in him in order to make him fail in his duty of succouring Burgundy as he was obligated to do by their alliance; and that he was misled regarding Ghent and the other cities in which he said the king would besiege him, the Duke of Burgundy, since they were too large to be besieged. The duke then ordered the messenger to report to his master the size of the Burgundian army and to tell him that the situation was quite different from what he supposed it to be; for he, the Duke of Burgundy, was determined to cross the river Somme and to do battle with the king if the latter attempted to bar his way. Therefore, he told the messenger that he requested the Duke of Brittany to declare himself for Burgundy against the king and to do unto the Duke of Burgundy as the Duke of Burgundy had done unto him in making the Treaty of Péronne.

The next day the Duke of Burgundy approached Picquigny on the Somme, a very strong position. He decided to build a bridge nearby in order to cross the river. However, it chanced that there were stationed in Picquigny four or five hundred franc archers and a few nobles. This garrison, when they saw the Duke of Burgundy passing, sallied forth to skirmish along a causeway. They advanced so far from their walls that troops of the duke set out to give chase and pursued them so hotly that they killed a number of these skirmishers before the latter could reach the town, and the duke's men won the approaches to this causeway. Then four or five artillery pieces were brought up, even though on this north side the town was impregnable because it was on the other bank of the river. Nevertheless, because of the bridge that was being built, the franc archers feared lest they be besieged on the other side also. They therefore abandoned the town and took to flight. The castle held out two or three days, and then its defenders [by composition] yielded the castle and departed in their shirts [i.e. leaving baggage and weapons behind].

This little exploit heartened the Duke of Burgundy, and [having crossed the Somme at Picquigny] he quartered his army in the vicinity of Amiens. He shifted his encampment two or three times, saying that he was keeping the field to see if the king wanted to come and fight. In the end, he came very near the town, so near that his artillery, firing at random, sent cannon balls within the town. He maintained his position for six weeks. In Amiens there were a good fourteen hundred men of arms and four thousand franc archers of the king's. With them were the Constable and all the other great officers of this realm—the Grand Master [of the Household, Antoine de Chabannes, Count of Dammartin], Admiral [Louis, Bastard of Bourbon, the king's son-in-law], marshals, seneschals and a great number of men of rank.

The king meanwhile was at Beauvais, where he had assembled a very large army. With him were the Duke of Guienne his brother and Duke Nicolas of Calabria (the son of Duke John of Calabria and Lorraine [recently deceased] and sole heir of the House of Anjou) and the nobles constituting the feudal levy [arrière-ban] of the realm. There is no doubt, from what I have since learned, that this army was spoiling for a fight. The king, however, was already beginning to sense the double dealing behind this campaign, and realized that he had by no means brought it to a successful issue but was more involved in war than ever.

His forces in Amiens drew up a plan to attack the Duke of Burgundy in his laager, provided that the king was willing to reinforce them with the army he had at Beauvais. When informed of this plan, the king sent word to forbid it, ordering them to give it up entirely. Though such an attack seemed to promise success, it was risky; for the forces in Amiens would have to sally forth by two gates only, one of which was very near the Duke of Burgundy's army, and if they failed to overthrow the enemy immediately, they would be in danger, being on foot, of being cut off and overwhelmed and of thus losing the city.

In the meanwhile, the Duke of Burgundy sent to the king a page named Simon de Quingey, afterwards Bailli of Troyes, who bore a note containing six lines written in the duke's hand, in which the duke humbled himself to the king, complaining that the king had attacked him at the prompting of interested third-parties and saying he believed that if the king had really known what was going on, he would not have done it.

By this time, the army that the king had sent into [the Duchy of] Burgundy had overthrown the whole power of Burgundy which had taken the field, capturing many prisoners. The number of dead was not great, but the defeat was; and the king's army had then proceeded to besiege and capture various places, which news stunned the duke a little. However, he ordered an entirely opposite report—that the Burgundians had had the best of it—to be disseminated through his army.

When the king had seen the note written by the Duke of Burgundy, he was overjoyed, for the reason you have already heard and also because he had no liking for long-drawn-out affairs. Sending the duke an answer, he empowered some of those at Amiens to negotiate a truce, and two or three truces were taken, each lasting four or five days. Finally a truce lasting a year, as I recall, was signed, with which the Constable, the Count of St Pol, showed himself much displeased; for, without any doubt, whatever people believed and wanted to believe to the contrary, the Count of St Pol was then the capital enemy of the Duke of Burgundy, nor ever afterwards was there friendship between them, as you know from the outcome. Envoys from all sides continued to go back and forth in order to intrigue, everybody seeking to get the better of his fellow.

Whatever the Duke of Burgundy did, his constant object was to get St Quentin back. In turn, whenever the Constable was in fear of the king, he promised to yield the town to the duke . . . always believing that he could hold the king and duke in fear by encouraging the discord between them; but this was a very dangerous stratagem, for they were, the pair of them, too great, too powerful and too shrewd.

After the cessation of hostilities, the king went off to Touraine, the Duke of Guienne to his lands and the Duke of Burgundy to his. For a while things remained in this state . . . The hate between the king and the Duke of Burgundy in no way diminished, but continued in full force. After returning to his territory, the Duke of Guienne sent often to the Duke of Burgundy, persistently seeking the hand of his daughter. The latter gave him encouragement—as he did to everybody who asked to marry her. I believe he never wanted a son-in-law nor would ever have married off his daughter as long as he lived, his object being instead to encourage suitors in order to make use of them and their aid; for he pursued so many grand designs that his lifetime would not have sufficed to accomplish them; they were well nigh impossible of achievement, for half Europe would not have satisfied him. He was bold enough to undertake anything; he had a constitution that could endure any labours; he was very powerful in men and money. He had neither sufficient intelligence nor finesse, however, to manage his enterprises; and, if first-rate intelligence is lacking, all the rest is nothing—and such intelligence, you may be sure, is the gift of God. Whoever could have united in himself the capacities of the king our master and those of the duke would have made a perfect prince. For, without doubt, the king far surpassed the duke in intelligence, as in the end was made clear by his works.

I have forgotten, in dealing with these preceding matters, to speak of King Edward of England, for these three great lords lived at the same time—our king and the Duke of Burgundy and King Edward. I am not at all keeping to chronological order as historians do, nor do I indicate the years or the precise times at which events have happened, nor do I make references to past history by way of illustration, for you know all about it, and to do so would be to *parler latin devant les Cordeliers* [speak Latin to impress the Franciscans]. I merely put down roughly what I have seen and known or heard tell of the princes I name to you. You are of the times in which all these events took place, and therefore there is no need of my being exact about hours and seasons.

As it seems to me, I have formerly spoken of the reason that moved the Duke of Burgundy to espouse the sister [Margaret] of King Edward, it being mainly in order to strengthen himself against the king; for otherwise he would never have made the marriage, because of his devotion to the House of Lancaster, to which he was closely related through his mother [Isabella], a princess of Portugal whose mother was the daughter of the Duke of Lancaster [John of Gaunt, 1340–99, progenitor of the Lancastrian dynasty, Henry IV, Henry V and Henry VI]. The Duke of Burgundy's ardent devotion to this house was matched by his hatred for the House of York. Now at the time of his marriage, the House of Lancaster was entirely destroyed, and the House of York was no longer spoken of since Edward of England was both king and Duke of York and his realm was completely at peace. During the Wars ['of the Roses'] between these two houses there had been fought in England seven or eight major battles and three or four score princes or lords of these royal houses had been cruelly killed. The Lancastrian lords still alive had taken refuge in the household of the Duke of Burgundy, all young lords for their fathers had been killed in England, whom the duke, before his marriage, had hospitably welcomed as his Lancastrian kin. I saw some of them reduced to such poverty, before the duke was aware of their presence in his domains, that those who ask alms are not as poor; for I have seen a Duke of Exeter following barefoot the duke's train and begging from house to house to stay alive without disclosing his identity. He was the closest in the succession of the line of Lancaster* and had married a sister [Anne] of King Edward. After he was recognized, he was given a small pension for his support. Members of the House of Somerset were there [Edmund Beaufort, calling himself Duke of Somerset since the execution of his elder brother Henry in 1464; and his younger brother, John] as well as other lords. All have since been killed in these English battles. Their forefathers had pillaged and ruined the realm of France and held the greater part of it for many years. They all killed each other. Those who were then still alive in England, and their children, are now dead, as you know.

Yet it is said, 'God no longer punishes folk as he used to do in the time of the children of Israel and He tolerates evil princes and evil people'. I do believe indeed that He no longer speaks to people as He used to, for He has left enough evidences in this world for people to believe in Him; but you can see in reading these things, with what more you yourself know of, that of these evil princes and others ruling this world who use their power cruelly and tyrannically, none or few remain unpunished. But punishment does not come at any given time nor at the hour when those who suffer under evil long for it.

Returning to King Edward IV, the mainstay of the House of York was the Earl of Warwick [Richard Neville, 'the Kingmaker'], while that of Lancaster was the Duke of Somerset [first, Edmund Beaufort, killed at the first battle of St Albans, 1455, and then his son Henry, executed in 1464]. The Earl of Warwick could almost be called father of King Edward in respect to rearing and services. In the process he had also achieved great power, for he was himself a peer of England, he held extensive lordships by gift of the king, some of them crown lands, and others estates that had been confiscated; he was also Captain of Calais and held other high offices, and I have heard it estimated that these resources, not counting his patrimony, yielded him an annual revenue of eighty-thousand crowns a year [about £16,000 in English money of the time, a somewhat exaggerated figure].

* He was only a powerful seignorial adherent; Commynes may be confusing him with Jasper Tudor, calling himself Earl of Pembroke, half brother to Henry VI, by their mother Katherine of France, who had taken refuge in France.

The Earl of Warwick quarrelled with his master a year before the Duke of Burgundy encamped before Amiens; and the duke contributed to the quarrel. He was displeased by the tremendous power that the Earl of Warwick exercised in England; and Warwick and the duke were bitterly at odds because the earl maintained an intimate connection with the king our master. Indeed I saw at this time, or a little before, [summer 1469] the Earl of Warwick so strong that he had the king his master in his hands and put to death [Richard, Earl Rivers], father of Edward IV's queen, and two of Rivers' sons [actually one, John] with a third son being in great danger, which persons were very dear to King Edward. The earl also put to death some other English knights, kept the king his master under honourable restraint for a while, surrounded him with Neville servants to make him forget his own, and acted as if he thought his master somewhat retarded.

The Duke of Burgundy, greatly alarmed by this adventure, engaged in secret practices aiming at King Edward's escape and found the means of communicating with him. Matters so turned out that Edward indeed made his escape, and then assembled troops and defeated Warwick's forces. Edward IV has been a king highly favoured by fortune in war, for he has won nine major battles at least, all of them while fighting on foot.

The Earl of Warwick [thus defeated by the king in March–April 1470] could no longer sustain his cause. Having warned his secret friends of what they were to do, he took to the sea in his own good time [actually, in full flight] with [George] the Duke of Clarence, who had espoused his [elder] daughter [Isabel] and adhered to his party, though Clarence was the [elder] brother of King Edward. Bringing with them wives and children and a large number of their partisans, they sailed for Calais. Within the town was Warwick's lieutenant, my lord Wenlock, and a number of his household men, but instead of receiving their master, they greeted his ships with a heavy cannonade. As the fugitives were lying at anchor before the harbour, the Duchess of Clarence, Warwick's daughter, gave birth to a son. Only after repeated requests did Wenlock and his men consent to send out two flasks of wine [to ease her labour]. This was very rigorous behaviour of a servant to his master, for we may well believe that Warwick thought he had handsomely treated Wenlock in making him Lieutenant of Calais, England's greatest treasure, and in my opinion, the best and most profitable outpost of its kind in the world, or at least in Christendom. I was there several times during these hostilities, and I was assured by the mayor that (at the time of which I have spoken), from the Wool Staple, the Captain of Calais pays a yearly fee to the king of fifteen-thousand crowns, for the captain collects all the tariffs of the Staple on this side of the sea and the fees from safe-conducts [i.e. permits for ships to pass through the Channel], and he also controls the selection and payment of most of the garrison.

The King of England was highly pleased with Lord Wenlock for refusing entry to his master and appointed him Captain of Calais, for Wenlock was an old, wise knight and was a member of the Order of the Garter. My lord of Burgundy, then at St Omer, was likewise much pleased with him and sent me to him and granted him a pension of one-thousand crowns, requesting him to continue in the devotion he had shown to the King of England.

I found Wenlock entirely resolved to do so. At the headquarters of the Wool Staple at Calais he swore an oath before me to serve the King of England for and against all, as did all the garrison and the inhabitants of the town. I spent two months going and coming between the duke and him in order to keep him in that frame of mind. I passed most of this time with him while the Duke of Burgundy, at Boulogne, assembled a great fleet against the Earl of Warwick, who, on leaving his anchorage before Calais, captured a number of ships belonging to subjects of the duke. These captures did much to reopen the war between King Louis and the duke, for Warwick's men sold their booty in Normandy. In retaliation, the Duke of Burgundy seized all the French merchants who had come to Antwerp fair.

One must be aware of the deceits and evildoing in this world as well as of its goodness—not in order to be able to practice chicanery but to guard against it. I therefore want to point out an example of a deceit—or a clever stratagem, which ever one wishes to call it—which was adroitly managed, and also to reveal the deceits of our neighbours, as well as ours, and thus to show that there is good and evil everywhere.

When the Earl of Warwick came before Calais, hoping to find there his principal refuge, my lord Wenlock, who was very shrewd, sent word to him that if he entered the port he was lost, for he had all England against him and also the Duke of Burgundy and the people of Calais and many of the garrison, like my lord Duras, the royal marshal there, and several others, all of whom had men in the town. Therefore, Wenlock concluded, it would be best for the earl to withdraw to France; as for Calais, he need not worry about it, for he, Wenlock, would give good account of it for him when the time came. Lord Wenlock, in giving this counsel, very well served his captain but very badly served his king. Never was man more loyal than Lord Wenlock to the Earl of Warwick, considering that Wenlock had been made Captain of Calais and was receiving a pension from the Duke of Burgundy.

The Earl of Warwick followed Wenlock's counsel and landed in Normandy [on 1 May 1470], where he was warmly welcomed on the orders of the king, who furnished him with large sums of money to defray the expenses of his people and commanded the Bastard of Bourbon, Admiral of France, with strong forces, to help defend these English against the Duke of Burgundy's fleet. That fleet was so powerful that nobody dared challenge it at sea, and it warred on the king's subjects by sea and threatened to make landings on the coast. All this happened the year before the king took St Quentin and Amiens, as I have related.

The Burgundian fleet was stronger than the fleets of the king and the Earl of Warwick together, for in the port of Sluys the duke had commandeered many large Spanish and Portuguese vessels, two Genoese ships and several German flatbottomed freighters. King Edward was by no means a man of superior capacity, but a most handsome prince, handsomer than any I ever saw in those years, and very valiant. He did not worry nearly so much about the Earl of Warwick's making a landing in England as did the Duke of Burgundy, who was aware of movements throughout England in favour of Warwick and often gave King Edward warning of them. But the latter had no fear, which seems to me the worst kind of folly—having no fear of one's enemy and refusing to believe any warnings, despite knowledge of the enemy's preparation.

King Louis came into Normandy, assembling all the ships he had and could come by and filling them with troops. He had brought about the marriage of [Edward] the Prince of Wales with [Anne Neville] the younger daughter of the Earl of Warwick. This prince was the only son of King Henry [VI] of England, who was still alive, a prisoner [since 1465] in the Tower of London. All these people were preparing to descend upon England. This was a strange marriage for Warwick—after ruining the father of Prince Edward, to have that prince marry his daughter; not to mention that Warwick also had secured as [son-in-law and] adherent the Duke of Clarence, brother of King Edward his enemy, who had much to fear should the line of Lancaster return to power. Thus high affairs such as these are prime examples of dissembling.

Now I was at Calais in order to keep my lord Wenlock in line at the time the Earl of Warwick's expedition was being readied. Up to then I was not aware of his double dealing, which had already lasted three months. I had requested him, in view of the news he was receiving from France, to eject from Calais twenty or thirty of the household men of the Earl of Warwick, since I was certain that the combined fleets of the king and the earl were preparing to sail from Normandy; if the earl suddenly landed in England there could be a change at Calais because of these adherents of Warwick, and in that case Wenlock would no longer be master of the town. I had therefore strongly urged him to send these men away immediately. He had always given me assurances that he would do so, until this time of which I was speaking, when he drew me aside and said that he would indeed remain the master of Calais but there was something else he wanted to tell me so that I could inform the Duke of Burgundy of it. It was this: he advised the duke, if he wished to be the friend of England, to work for peace and not for war—Wenlock was thus alluding to the duke's fleet which was operating against the Earl of Warwick. Wenlock went on to say that peace would be easy to arrange, for that very day a young lady had passed through Calais, on her way into France to the Duchess of Clarence, who bore peace overtures from King Edward.

He spoke truly, but just as he was deceiving others, he in turn was deceived by this lady, for she was making the journey in order to drive a great bargain. She achieved her end, and it was the worse for the Earl of Warwick and all his following. Of the secret intrigues— brilliant stratagems or machinations—that have been carried on here on the Continent, at least those of the last twenty years, you will find no better example than the mission of this lady. The secret that she bore was to exhort the Duke of Clarence that he should not let himself be the cause of the destruction of his line by aiding in the restoration of the House of Lancaster, and that he should remember the long history of their hatreds and injuries. Furthermore, he could well suppose that, since the earl had brought about the marriage of his [younger] daughter to the [Lancastrian] Prince of Wales, he would work to make him King of England, and had already done homage to him as king. So well did this lady accomplish her mission that she won over the Duke of Clarence, who promised to come over to the side of the king his brother, but not until he had returned to England.

This lady proved herself neither lightheaded nor frivolous. She was free to go to her mistress the duchess, and therefore was better able to undertake this journey than a man. And however clever my lord Wenlock was, this lady deceived him and accomplished her mission, which resulted in the overthrow and death of Warwick and all his following . . .

I have told you previously that the combined fleets of the king and the Earl of Warwick were ready to sail and that the Duke of Burgundy's fleet, riding at anchor off the coast, intended to give them battle. God's will so disposed of matters that one night a great storm arose, so fierce that the Burgundian fleet was forced into flight and some of the ships were driven to Scotland, others to Holland. Then, a few hours later, there came a favourable wind for the Earl of Warwick, and he crossed to England without peril.

The Duke of Burgundy had informed King Edward of the port at which the earl was planning to land, and kept people at the king's side expressly to urge him to do what was good for him; but King Edward, quite unmoved, spent his time hunting and his bosom friends were [George] Archbishop of York and [John] Marquess Montagu, brothers of the Earl of Warwick, who had sworn the king a solemn oath to serve him against their brother and all others, and he trusted them.

Once the Earl of Warwick had landed, large numbers of people joined him and he found himself in a position of strength. As soon as King Edward learned the news, he began—very late—to look to his needs. He sent to the Duke of Burgundy to ask him to keep his fleet at sea, so that the earl could not return to France, assuring the duke that he himself would do very well by land. This message hardly pleased the recipient, who thought King Edward would have done better to prevent Warwick's landing in England than to be forced to give the earl battle.

Within five or six days of his landing the Earl of Warwick, now in great strength, was encamped three leagues from King Edward. The latter had the more powerful army—if its loyalty had been assured—

and he was awaiting battle. He was quartered in a fortified village, or at least in a place to which the only entry was by a bridge, as he himself told me, and it was well for him that he was so lodged. His troops were quartered in other villages round about. As he was having dinner, he was suddenly informed that Marquess Montagu, the earl's brother, and some others had taken horse and were proclaiming to all their troops, 'Long live King Henry!' At first King Edward did not believe it; but he immediately dispatched people to investigate, armed himself and had the outer defences of his quarters manned. With him was a wise knight named [William] Lord Hastings, Great Chamberlain of England, his most trusted intimate, who was married to a sister of the Earl of Warwick. Nevertheless he was loyal to his master and had brought to the army a force of three thousand mounted men, as he himself recounted to me. At the king's side were also [Antony Woodville] Earl Rivers, a brother of Edward's Queen [Elizabeth], and a number of loyal knights and squires, all of whom realized that things were going badly, for those dispatched by King Edward reported that what had been told him was true and that troops were being assembled to attack him.

By God's grace, the king was quartered near the sea, and a few ships, including two merchant vessels of Holland, had been following him, laden with supplies for the army. He had barely time to get aboard one of them. Lord Hastings, his chamberlain, stayed behind briefly in order to tell the captain of Hastings' force and a number of individuals in the army that they should go over to the enemy, asking them, however, to preserve their good will and loyalty to the king and him; and then the chamberlain joined the others in the ship, which was ready to sail.

It is the custom of the English that after they have won a battle, they kill nobody; they are especially careful to spare the commoners, for each side seeks to have their favour since they hold the balance of power and so no one is put to ransom. Hence it was that the soldiers of the royal army were left unharmed after the king left. On the other hand, King Edward also told me that, in all the battles he had won, once victory was in sight he mounted horse and proclaimed that the commoners should be spared and the lords killed, for of the latter none or very few escaped death.

Thus fled King Edward in [September of] the year 1470, with these two Dutch merchantmen and a small ship of his own, accompanied by some seven or eight hundred persons who had no other clothes than their battle dress; and they had not a penny nor did they have much idea where they were going.

How strange it was to this poor king (for thus he could well be called) to find himself thus in flight and assailed by his own servants. For twelve or thirteen years [actually, about nine] he had been accustomed to a life of pleasure, to which he was more devoted than any other prince of his time, for he had nothing on his mind but the ladies—they were an obsession—and going hunting and adorning his person. When he went off hunting in the good weather, he brought with him several pavilions for the ladies, and indeed there was royal good cheer. True it is that he had just the physique for that kind of life—as much so as anyone I have ever laid eyes on—for he was young and handsomer than any other man of his time— I mean, at the hour of this adversity, for he afterwards became very fat.

Behold now how this king begins to experience the calamities of this world. He fled directly for Holland. At this time the Easterlings [Hanseatic League] were enemies of the English and also of the French and had many warships at sea. They were very much feared by the English, and not without cause, for they are good fighters and had done the English great damage that year, capturing a number of ships. A flotilla of the Easterlings, seven or eight vessels, caught sight from afar of the ships in which the king and his party were fleeing, and began to give chase. Being far ahead, the king's vessels reached the coast of Holland, or rather Friesland, off a little town named Alkmaar. They cast anchor because the tide was low and they were unable to enter the harbour, though they came as close to the town as they could. The Easterlings cast anchor very near them, intending to board them at the next tide.

Mischances and perils never come singly. The luck of this king had changed indeed, and his thoughts with it. Only two weeks before, he would have been amazed had someone said to him, 'The Earl of Warwick will drive you from England and gain control of it in eleven days'—for it took the Earl no longer than that to master the country. In addition he had made a mock of the Duke of Burgundy, who was spending his money trying to defend him by sea, in having said that he wished Warwick were already in England. What excuse could King Edward find for having suffered this enormous loss through no other fault than his own, except to say, 'I did not think that such a thing could happen'. Any prince of mature years should certainly blush to use such an excuse, for it is totally irrelevant . . .

By chance [Louis de Bruges] lord de la Gruthuse, Governor of Holland for the Duke of Burgundy, was then at Alkmaar. Immediately informed (for the king sent men ashore) of the king's perilous situation because of the Easterlings, he at once sent word to the latter forbidding them to touch King Edward, and took boat to the king's ship and welcomed him. The king disembarked, along with a good fifteen hundred men, including his brother [Richard] the Duke of Gloucester, who afterwards took the throne as Richard III.

The king, penniless, gave a gown furred with handsome martens to the master of his ship, promising to do better by him in time to come. So destitute a company there never was. But the lord de la Gruthuse did the honourable thing, for he provided many gowns and defrayed all expenses on the journey to The Hague in Holland, to which he escorted the king, and then he informed the Duke of Burgundy of this happening.

The duke was marvellously alarmed by this news. He would very much rather have learned of the king's death, for he was in great anxiety about the Earl of Warwick, who was his enemy and was now master of England—Warwick having found, after his landing, an infinity of people embracing his cause. The army King Edward had left behind went over to him entirely, partly out of political sympathies and partly out of fear; and every day people flocked to his banners. Thus did Warwick proceed to London. A large number of knights and squires who were in the capital and loyal to King Edward took sanctuary, and afterwards well served their king. The queen likewise took sanctuary [in Westminster Abbey] and there, in great destitution, gave birth to a son [Edward, afterwards, Edward V].

On the earl's arriving in London, he went to the Tower and released King Henry VI, whom he had incarcerated there many years previously [in 1465], causing proclamation to be made before his captive as he escorted him to prison that he was a traitor and guilty of *lèse-majesté*; and now at this hour the earl hailed him as king, led him to the palace at Westminster and restored him to his royal state —this in the presence of the Duke of Clarence, who was not pleased by this proceeding. Immediately the earl dispatched three or four hundred men to Calais, who were given a good welcome by Lord

Wenlock and who made raids throughout the region around Boulogne. It could then be seen how loyal Wenlock had continued to be to his master, the Earl of Warwick.

The day the Duke of Burgundy received the news that King Edward had arrived in Holland, I had just come back to him from Calais, finding him at Boulogne. At that hour he had not yet learned of King Edward's flight—he had first heard that the king was dead. This troubled him little for he much preferred the House of Lancaster to that of York. Then too, he was maintaining in his household the Dukes of Exeter and Somerset and a number of other Lancastrian partisans; and it therefore seemed likely to him that he would easily be able to come to terms with the House of Lancaster. However, he greatly feared the Earl of Warwick. Under these circumstances, he did not know how he could satisfy the one who had taken refuge in his dominions, namely King Edward, whose sister he had espoused and whose brother he was in their chivalric orders, for King Edward wore the emblem of the Order of the Golden Fleece and he wore the insignia of the Order of the Garter . . .

Commynes was sent back to Calais by the Duke of Burgundy, with instructions to negotiate a peaceful accommodation with Lord Wenlock. Upon Commynes' dispatching a report, from the frontier, that he was heading into danger, the duke sent him a ring and ordered him to press on with his mission, promising to pay his ransom if he were seized—on which Commynes comments that his master 'had no fear of putting in peril a servant of his in order to make use of him at his need'. However, Commynes was given a good welcome by Wenlock, and it was agreed between them that the Anglo-Burgundian alliance would continue in force, Henry being now named as the King of England instead of Edward. Merchants of the Wool Staple, opposed to the interruption of their profitable trade with the Low Countries, aided in the making of this agreement and in putting an end to the raids of Warwick's men.

This appointment highly pleased the Duke of Burgundy, for the Earl of Warwick was planning to send four thousand English to Calais to make war on him . . . and it was at this very moment that King [Louis XI] took Amiens and St Quentin. And if the duke had had war with both kingdoms at once, he would have been destroyed. He did what he could to soften the Earl of Warwick, declaring that

dieu. Qui euſt peu pren
die partie des condicions du
Roy nr̄e maiſtre et partie des
ſiennes / on en euſt bien fait
vng prince parfaict / Car
ſans mille doubte le Roy en
ſens le paſſoit de trop / et la
fin la monſtre par ſes œuures.

Jcy parle par Incident
des guerres qui furent en
Angleterre ou meſme temps.

E me ſuys oublie
en parlant de ces
matieres precedẽtes
de parler du Roy
Edouard dangleterre / Car ces
trois ſeigneurs ont veſcu dug
temps grandz / Ceſt aſſauoir
nr̄e Roy et led Duc de bour
gongne et led Roy Edouard.
Je ne vous quide point lordre
deſcrire qui ſont les hyſtours
ny nomme les annees ny
proprement le temps que

The defeat of the Earl of Warwick by Edward IV at the Battle of
Barnet, April 1471

he had no wish to do anything against King Henry, that he was himself of the line of Lancaster, and making other statements serving the purpose.

To return to King Edward, he came to the Duke of Burgundy at St Pol and strongly pressed him for aid in returning to England, assuring him of his having great connections in that realm, and begging the duke not to abandon him, considering that he had married Edward's sister and that they were brothers of the Golden Fleece and the Garter. The Dukes of Exeter and Somerset were urging the Duke of Burgundy to do exactly the opposite and to support King Henry's party. The duke did not know which side to please, was afraid of offending either, and at the same time was being confronted by a bitter war. Finally he put his stock, for that moment, in the Duke of Somerset and Somerset's friends, exacting from them certain promises to oppose the Earl of Warwick, who had long been their enemy. On seeing this, King Edward, who was at the duke's court, was much disturbed. However, everything possible was done to soothe him; it was explained that the duke was thus dissembling in order not to be at war with two kingdoms at once—and if the duke were destroyed, he could not very easily then aid him.

Nevertheless, when the Duke of Burgundy perceived that he could no longer keep King Edward from going back to England (and for a number of reasons he did not dare to displease him entirely), he made a public pretence of refusing to give him aid and issued a proclamation that no one was to help him; but behind the scenes he provided King Edward with fifty thousand St Andrew florins and three or four large ships that he had equipped in the port of Vere in Holland, a free port open to all nationalities, and he secretly hired fourteen ships, well armed, belonging to the Easterlings, who promised to serve the king until he had landed in England and for two weeks thereafter. Under the circumstances this was a great amount of aid.

King Edward set sail [on 11 March 1471], just as the Duke of Burgundy was moving towards Amiens against King Louis. It appeared to the duke that matters in England could not go badly for him since he had friends in both camps. As soon as King Edward landed [at Ravenspur in Yorkshire about mid-March], he headed straight for London, for he had more than two thousand partisans in the church sanctuaries there, including three or four hundred knights

I

and squires, who would be of great aid to him since he did not land with a large force.

As soon as the Earl of Warwick, who was in the North with a great power, heard this news, he hastened to turn back towards London, hoping to be the first to arrive there, though he believed that the city would hold out for him. However, matters turned out otherwise, for King Edward was received into the capital, on Maundy Thursday [11 April], with great rejoicing by the whole population, contrary to what most people had believed would happen for everybody thought him completely done for. Indeed, had the Londoners shut their gates against him, his situation would have been hopeless since the Earl of Warwick was only a day's march behind him.

According to what I have been told, London willingly came over to him for three reasons: first, his partisans in the sanctuaries and the fact that his queen had given birth to a son; second, the great debts he owed to merchants of the city, who therefore espoused his cause; third, the influence of many ladies of rank and rich citizens' wives of London, formerly very good friends indeed of his, who won over their husbands and relatives.

He sojourned but two days in the city, quitting it on Easter eve with all the forces he had been able to assemble, and marched to meet the Earl of Warwick, whom he encountered [at Barnet, ten miles north] the next morning, Easter Sunday. As the two armies confronted each other, the Duke of Clarence, with a force of twelve thousand men or more, went over to the side of his brother, King Edward, a desertion which gave great consternation to the Earl of Warwick and great comfort to the king, who had but few troops.

You have already heard how this bargain concerning the Duke of Clarence was brought about. Yet, notwithstanding this defection, the battle that followed was very fierce and bloody. Everybody on both sides fought on foot. The king's right wing was sorely oppressed by the enemy centre commanded by the Earl of Warwick; the engagement became so hot that the King of England himself fought in the midst of the combat, and fought as well as or better than anyone else on either side.

The Earl of Warwick had never been accustomed to fight on foot but rather, after establishing his battle line, mounted horse. If things were going well for him, he thrust himself into the heart of the conflict, but if they were going badly, he soon left the field. This time he was forced by his brother [John] Marquess Montagu, a very valiant knight, to fight on foot and send the horses to the rear. The battle so turned out that the earl was killed, along with Marquess Montagu and a great number of men of rank. It was a disastrous defeat; for King Edward had resolved, on leaving Flanders, that he would no longer observe his custom of commanding the commoners to be spared and the nobles killed, having conceived a deep hatred against the English people because of the great favour which, he perceived, they bore to the Earl of Warwick, and for other reasons. Therefore the commoners on this occasion were not spared. On King Edward's side fifteen hundred men were killed. It was a bitterly fought battle.

On the day it was waged, the Duke of Burgundy was before Amiens. He [shortly] received from his duchess letters that King Edward had written to report his success. The duke did not know whether to be glad or sorry, for he felt that King Edward was dissatisfied with him, on the grounds that the duke's aid had been little enough and grudgingly granted and that the duke had come close to abandoning him altogether. Truth to tell, there was little love lost between them from that time forth. However, the duke put this news to good use, having it proclaimed far and wide.

I have forgotten to say how King Henry fared as a result of this battle. King Edward had found him in London [in the episcopal palace and had him imprisoned again in the Tower]. King Henry was a man of small sense, and well nigh out of his wits. If what I heard is true, immediately after this battle, [Richard] the Duke of Gloucester, brother to Edward and afterwards Richard III, murdered with his own hand or had killed in his presence, in some secret chamber [of the Tower], this harmless and kindly King Henry. [Actually, Henry VI was put to death three weeks after Barnet, on the night of 21 May, by hands unknown but undoubtedly upon order of King Edward's council.]

[Edward, the Lancastrian] Prince of Wales, of whom I have spoken, had landed in England [with his mother, Queen Margaret of Anjou, at Weymouth] on the very day of the battle of Barnet. The prince [and his mother] were joined by the Dukes of Exeter and Somerset and by old Lancastrian partisans, to the number of more than forty thousand persons, as I was told by people who were there. Had the Earl of Warwick been willing to await the prince's arrival, there is good reason to believe that he and the Lancastrians would have remained lords and masters. But the fear he had of the Duke of Somerset—whose father and brother he had had killed—and also of Queen Margaret, caused him to fight entirely on his own instead of waiting for the prince's landing. Behold then how long these old enmities last and how much they are to be feared and what great destruction they lead to.

As soon as King Edward had won this battle, he marched to confront the Prince of Wales. A great battle ensued [on 4 May at Tewkesbury], to which the prince had brought a larger army than King Edward's. Nevertheless the king won the victory; the Prince of Wales was killed on the field along with a number of other great lords and very many ordinary folk, and the Duke of Somerset, taken captive, had his head cut off the next day.

In eleven days the Earl of Warwick had won the whole realm of England, or at least secured nominal control of it. King Edward conquered it in twenty-one days, but only after two great and bitter battles. Thus you may behold the violent upheavals of England. King Edward put to death a great number of people in various places, especially those who had taken part in the risings against him. Of all the peoples of the world, the English are the most disposed to fight battles like these. Following this campaign, King Edward remained the ruler of a peaceful realm until his death, but not without experiencing great travail of spirit and exertions of mind.

I will say no more about English affairs until it is appropriate to do so. When I left off recounting events in France, the Duke of Burgundy [in consequence of the truce] had withdrawn from the region of Amiens, while the king had retired to Touraine and the Duke of Guienne to his province. The last named continued to seek the hand of the Duke of Burgundy's daughter; the Duke of Burgundy continued to appear to be interested in the suit, but never would he have consented to the marriage, as I have said. The Count of St Pol, Constable of France, continued his efforts to be the broker of this deal; on the other hand, the Duke of Brittany coveted this role for himself. The king, for his part, did everything he could to break the project . . . quite unnecessarily, for reasons I have explained, and thus he had his labour for nothing; but he had no way of knowing another person's thoughts. It was no marvel that the king feared the marriage; for it would have greatly enhanced the Duke of Guienne's power and prestige, and with the alliance of Burgundy, Brittany and Guienne, the king's sovereignty and that of his children after him would have been imperilled. In the meanwhile, numerous ambassadors continued to go back and forth among these princes, on missions sometimes secret and sometimes public. . . .

In the course of these marriage negotiations there was constant talk of new enterprises against the king. With the Duke of Burgundy were the lord d'Urfé, Poncet de Rivière and several other minor personages, envoys of the Duke of Guienne, while the Abbot of Begar, later Bishop of St-Pol-de-Léon, represented the Duke of Brittany. They declared that the king was working upon the servants of the Duke of Guienne, seeking to remove them from the duke by offering inducements to some and making threats to others. He had already had demolished a place belonging to my lord d'Estissac, a servant of the Duke of Guienne, and several other acts of violence had been initiated. As a result, the king had won over some of the duke's household men, on which account these envoys concluded that the king was aiming at the recovery of Guienne, as he had formerly recovered Normandy after delivering it to the duke as his appanage.

The Duke of Burgundy sent frequent representations to the king concerning these matters. The king replied that it was the Duke of Guienne, aiming at the enlargement of his territory, who began all these intrigues and that, for himself, he had no wish at all to touch his brother's appanage . . .

At this time the Duke of Guienne, or his representatives and those of the Duke of Brittany, were begging the Duke of Burgundy not to give the slightest assistance to the English, the enemies of the realm, for everything that they themselves were doing was for the welfare and relieving of that realm; when the time came to act, they would have sufficient strength of themselves, having very widespread and useful connections with a number of royal captains and others.

On one occasion I was present when the lord d'Urfé used such language to the duke, urging him to be diligent in assembling his army. The duke then called me aside to a window and said to me: 'There's the lord d'Urfé who is pressing me to make my army as powerful as I can and tells me that we will do the greatest good for the realm. Does it seem to you that if I invade France with the company I'll bring with me, I will do much good there?' I answered, laughing, that I didn't think so. He then said these words to me: 'I cherish the welfare of the realm of France more than my lord d'Urfé supposes; for, in place of the one king there reigning, I would like to see six'.

At this season King Edward of England, who firmly believed that this marriage previously spoken of was being seriously negotiated (and was thus deceived), was working as hard as was the king our master to prevent it, pointing out that King Louis had no son [the future Charles VIII had, however, been born 30 June 1470] and that if the king died, the Duke of Guienne would therefore be in line to succeed him. Hence, if this marriage were accomplished, all England would be in great peril of being destroyed because of the extensive lordships that the marriage would unite to the crown. Indeed King Edward took this matter amazingly to heart—without any need— as did the whole royal council of England; and no matter what denials the Duke of Burgundy made, they clung to their belief.

It was the Duke of Burgundy's aim—notwithstanding the requests of the Dukes of Guienne and Brittany that he call in no foreigners—to have the King of England invade the realm some- where or other, in which case he would have pretended to know nothing about it and to have taken no part in bringing it about. Never would the English have fallen in with this plan. Rather, at that time, they would have aided the king, so much did they fear lest the House of Burgundy be united to the crown of France by this marriage . . .

At this time the Duke of Guienne was somewhat ill; there were those who said he was in great danger of death, while others said his illness was nothing. His people urged the Duke of Burgundy to take the field, for it was the right season for campaigning. They said that the king's army was in the field and that his troops were stationed before St Jean d'Angély or Saintes or in that neighbourhood. As a result of their representations, the Duke of Burgundy assembled his army at Arras and then advanced towards Péronne, Roye and Montdidier. The duke had a very powerful army, the finest he had ever mustered, for there were twelve hundred lances of his [recently formed] standing army, every lance having three archers for each man of arms, all well equipped and well mounted, and each company of lances included an additional ten men of arms, not counting the lieutenant and those who bore the standards. The duke's nobles were likewise very well equipped and well paid and commanded by notable knights and squires, for the Burgundian territories were very rich at this time.

As the Duke of Burgundy was ready to leave Arras, two events occurred. One was that Duke Nicolas of Calabria and Lorraine, son of Duke John and heir of the House of Anjou, arrived there to press his suit for the hand of the duke's daughter, and the Duke of Burgundy gave him a warm welcome and reason to hope that his visit would be successful. The next day—15 May 1472, as it seems to me —there came letters from Simon de Quingey, the duke's ambassador with the king, containing the news that the Duke of Guienne had died [on the night of 24 May] and that already the king had taken a large number of his places. Immediately, however, there arrived messages from divers directions which gave varying versions of the Duke of Guienne's condition.

The Duke of Burgundy, his hopes shattered by this news and his anger fanned by some who cast suspicion upon the circumstances of the Duke of Guienne's demise, wrote letters to a number of cities in which he made accusations against the king, but nothing came of them. I believe, however, that if the Duke of Guienne had not died, the king would have had a great deal on his hands, for the Bretons were ready and had within the realm more secret understandings than they had ever had, all of which came to nothing as a result of this death.

Thus angered and embittered, the Duke of Burgundy took the field and advanced to Nesle in the Vermandois and here began to wage a foul and cruel war, which he had never done before. The countrysides through which he passed he laid waste by fire. His advance guard besieged Nesle, a place of almost no military value, in which were garrisoned some franc archers. The duke was quartered three leagues from there. Those within Nesle killed a herald who had gone to demand their surrender. Their captain then came forth, under a safe conduct, in an effort to arrange a composition. Not being able to secure terms, he returned to Nesle. At this moment there was truce because of his mission, and those within had exposed themselves on the wall without being fired upon. Nevertheless the garrison killed two more of the besiegers. On this account the truce was broken. Word was sent to the Countess of Nesle that she should quit the place with her domestic servants and her goods. She did so, and immediately Nesle was attacked and taken and most of those within were killed. Those captured alive were hanged, except for some whom the Burgundian troops, out of pity, allowed to escape; quite a large number had their hands cut off.

It displeases me to report the cruelty, but I was there and so must make mention of it. I have to add that either the Duke of Burgundy was carried away by rage in committing so cruel an act or that some great cause moved him to commit it. Two such causes were alleged: one, he had some sinister things to say, according to what I heard, about the death of the Duke of Guienne; and two, he bitterly resented the loss of Amiens and St Quentin.

At the time the duke had been assembling his army, there came to him on two or three occasions [Georges de la Trémoille] the lord de Craon and Pierre Doriole, Chancellor of France—this happening before the death of the Duke of Guienne. These royal envoys secretly negotiated with the duke a final peace, which had been hitherto impossible to achieve because the duke insisted on the restitution of the two towns aforementioned and the king was unwilling to give them back. Now, however, he agreed to restore them, in view of the duke's preparations for war and his own hopes of accomplishing certain ends, as you will learn.

The conditions of this peace were that the king would render to the duke Amiens and St Quentin and would abandon to him the Count of Nevers and the Count St Pol, Constable of France, and all their lands for him to do with as he pleased, taking their estates into his own hands if he could; while the duke, in return, would abandon to the king the Dukes of Brittany and Guienne and their lordships for him to do with as he could.

The Duke of Burgundy swore to uphold this peace—I was present —and, representing the king, the lord of Craon and the Chancellor of France took the same oath. As the latter were about to depart, they advised the duke not to disband his army but rather to continue his military preparations so that the king their master would be the more inclined to deliver prompt possession of the two places aforementioned. On their return journey they brought with them Simon de Quingey, who was to witness the king's swearing to uphold the peace and his confirmation of what the royal envoys had negotiated. The matter was delayed for some days, and in the meanwhile occurred the death of the Duke of Guienne. The king therefore sent Simon back with empty words, having refused to take the oath. The Duke

E me veulx taire de plus vous ad uertir de ces faictz dangleterre iusques a ce qnil viengne a propos en quelque autre lieu. Le dernier endroit ou ie me suis teu de noz affaires de par deca a este au departement que feit le duc de bourgongne deuant Amyens Et aussi du Roy qui de son coste se retira en touraine Et le duc de guyenne son frere en guyenne Lequel ne laissoit de conti nuer la poursupte du ma riage ou il pretendoit auec la fille du duc de bourgogne comme iay dit cy deuant.

E dict Duc de bourgo gne monstroit tous iours y vouloir entendre mais iamais nen eut le

A request for the hand of Marie, daughter and heiress of the Duke
of Burgundy

of Burgundy, considering himself ridiculed and scorned, thereafter bore the king a fierce grudge.

In the course of this war, the duke's people, for this reason and for others you have been informed of, used incredibly villainous language about the king, and the king's people were hardly less uncomplimentary.

It could seem to those who will see this in time to come that these two princes were far from trustworthy or that I am speaking ill of them. Of neither would I wish to speak ill, and to our king I was deeply obligated, as everybody knows. But to continue with what you, my lord Archbishop of Vienne, have asked of me, I must record that which I know in the way that it happened. However, whoever compares the king and the duke with other princes, will find these two great and notable, and our king very wise, for he has left his realm enlarged and in peace with its enemies. . . .

[To recapitulate,] both the king and the duke had their armies ready and in the field. The king had by this time taken a number of places, and while negotiating this peace with the duke, he had pressed his brother hard. Already [Gilbert de Chabannes] the lord de Curton, Patrick Folcart [captain of the Duke of Guienne's guard] and several others had abandoned the Duke of Guienne and come over to the king. The royal army was stationed near La Rochelle. Having many secret connections within the town, the king's men were urgently bargaining to win it over, prompted partly by rumours of a peace treaty with Burgundy, partly by the reports of the Duke of Guienne's illness. I believe it was the king's intention, if he accomplished his enterprise, or most of it, or if his brother died, to reject the peace treaty, but if he encountered severe opposition, to accept the treaty and fulfill its articles in order to escape from his peril. He timed his campaign superbly and pursued his ends with marvellous diligence. You have learned how he kept Simon de Quingey dangling for a whole eight days, the Duke of Guienne's death occurring in the meanwhile. Now the king knew well that the Duke of Burgundy so coveted possession of Amiens and St Quentin that the duke would not dare affront him but would let fifteen or twenty days pass [in hope that the king would sign the treaty], as indeed the duke did, and during this period the king would take the measure of his opportunity.

Since we have spoken of the king and of his plans to deceive the Duke of Burgundy, we must speak of the duke's intentions in

K

regard to the king and how he would have observed his treaty obligations if the Duke of Guienne had not died. At the king's request, Simon de Quingey had instructions from his master, as follows: once he had witnessed the king's swearing to the peace and had received from him letters confirming what the royal ambassadors had said and done, he was to go to Brittany to signify the contents of the peace treaty to that duke and also to the ambassadors of the Duke of Guienne, there present, for them to inform their master who was at Bordeaux. The king had wanted it thus in order to instill all the greater fear in the Bretons upon their finding themselves abandoned by the one who was their main hope.

With Simon de Quingey was a courier of the Duke of Burgundy named Henry, a native of Paris and a clever and knowing fellow, who bore a letter of credence in the hand of the duke addressed to Simon. He had instructions not to deliver this credence until Simon had left the king and reached the Duke of Brittany's court at Nantes. Henry was then to deliver the credence and recite the message it authenticated—namely, Simon was to tell the Duke of Brittany that he need have no fear of the Duke of Burgundy's abandoning the Duke of Guienne or him, but rather that Simon's master would succour them in person and with all his resources and that he had made the treaty merely in order to recover Amiens and St Quentin, which the king had, contrary to his promise, taken from him in time of peace.

Simon was further to say that the duke his master would send a distinguished embassy to the king as soon as he had possession of the two towns, which he would achieve without difficulty, to request him to desist from the war and hostile designs he was prosecuting against these two dukes and not to take a stand upon the oaths that he, the Duke of Burgundy, had sworn, for he was resolved not to observe them, any more than the king had observed the Treaty of Conflans, signed before Paris [in 1465] nor the one he swore to uphold at Péronne and long after confirmed. For the king knew well that he had taken the two towns contrary to his word and in time of peace and therefore should accept the duke's recovery of them by similar means. As for the Count of Nevers and the Count of St Pol, Constable of France, whom the king had abandoned to him, he declared that, though he hated them as he had good cause to do, he wished to remit their offences and leave them untouched, requesting the king to do the like with the two dukes whom he had abandoned to him; and he further requested the king to be content that everyone live in peace and security, as had been promised at Conflans, when the king and all the lords had there held conference; if the king refused, the duke would succour his allies. At the hour Simon was to deliver this message, the duke would already have taken the field.

However, matters turned out otherwise. Thus man proposes and God disposes; for death, which arbitrates all things and alters all plans, effected a different outcome, as you have heard and will hear further. The king, in fact, did not deliver the two towns, and secured the Duchy of Guienne by the death of his brother, as was right and proper.

To return to the war of which I have spoken, and the cruel treatment meted out to a parcel of unfortunate franc archers who had been captured at Nesle, the Duke of Burgundy, on leaving that place, encamped [on 14 June 1472] before Roye, which had a garrison of fifteen hundred franc archers and a number of men of arms of the feudal levy. So fine an army the Duke of Burgundy had never had. The day after the duke arrived, the franc archers began to be frightened. A number of them jumped down from the walls and came to yield themselves to him. The following day, terms were agreed on: the garrison quitted the town, leaving behind [baggage, weapons] horses and harness, except that each man of arms was permitted to take with him a docked-tail horse. After garrisoning Roye, the duke then moved on Montdidier, the fortifications of which he intended to demolish. However, because of the affection which, he perceived, the people of this region bore him, he instead had the walls repaired and left a garrison there.

When he departed from Montdidier, he was aiming to march into Normandy. However, in passing by Beauvais, my lord des Cordes, who commanded the advance guard, raided the outskirts. Right off his men captured the suburbs facing the episcopal palace; the place was taken by a very greedy Burgundian named Jacques de Mont-martin, who commanded a hundred lances and three hundred archers of the duke's standing army. My lord des Cordes attacked the city from another side, but his scaling ladders were short and he had few of them. He emplaced his two artillery pieces to face the city gate, and with only two rounds of fire they blew a great hole in it; had he had stone cannon balls to continue the attack, he would unquestionably have entered the city. However, not having brought siege equipment, he was ill prepared for such an exploit.

At the beginning there were only townsfolk to defend Beauvais, except for Loyset de Balagny, who had some few troops of the feudal levy and was captain of the town, but could not possibly save it. God willed, however—and gave vivid evidences of His will— that Beauvais should not thus be lost. My lord des Cordes' men fought hand to hand at the breach that had been made in the city gate; des Cordes sent several messages to the Duke of Burgundy urging him to come up and assuring him that the town was as good as his. In the time that it took the duke to arrive, some of the townsfolk conceived the idea, and put it into execution, of bringing flaming faggots to hurl into the faces of the Burgundians attempting to break down the gate. So many of these torches were hurled that they set the gate afire, and the assailants had to withdraw until the fire was extinguished.

The duke, on his arrival, considered, like lord des Cordes, that the town was as good as captured, once the fire was extinguished, but this, however, was very fierce for the whole gate was aflame. Had the duke decided to station part of his army on the side towards Paris, the town could not have escaped his grasp for nobody would have been able to enter it. But God willed that he should become a prey to doubts and fears, though there was no reason to fear: it was because of a little stream his troops would have had to cross that he opposed the project. Afterwards, when Beauvais was stuffed with soldiers, he wanted to make this move which then would have imperilled his whole army, and only with the greatest difficulty could he be dissuaded. It was on [Saturday] 27 June 1472, that the attack on Beauvais began.

This fire of which I am speaking lasted the rest of the day. Towards evening ten lances of the standing army, but that was all, entered the town, as I was afterwards told, for I was still with the Duke of Burgundy. These lances were not seen by the Burgundians, for the latter were busy setting up their quarters and also there were no Burgundians on the side of the town at which the lances entered. At dawn the duke's artillery began to be moved nearer the walls. Soon after, we saw numbers of troops enter Beauvais, some two hundred men of arms at least; and I believe that if they had not arrived, it would have taken little to bring the town to terms. In any case, because of the rage that had gripped the Duke of Burgundy, as you have heard above, he wanted to take Beauvais by assault; and undoubtedly he would have burned the town had he so taken it, which would have been a calamity. In my view it was preserved by a true miracle and not otherwise.

After these royal troops had entered, the duke's artillery fired continually for fifteen days or thereabouts. The place was as badly battered as was ever any place thus softened up for assault. Nevertheless, since there was water in the ditches [beneath the walls], two bridges had to be built to one side of the burned gate, though on the other side it was possible to reach the wall without danger, save for a single artillery emplacement which could not be destroyed because it was very low.

It was extremely perilous and foolish to assault a town so strongly defended, especially since the Constable was there, as I believe (or encamped near the town, I don't know which) [actually, he was at Creil], and also Marshal Joachim [Rouault], Marshal Lohéac, Louis de Crussol, Guillaume de Vallée, Méri de Couhé, [John of] Salazar, Estevenot de Vignoles, each of them commanding a hundred lances at least. With these captains there were in addition men of arms of the standing army, numerous foot-soldiers and many men of rank.

Nevertheless the duke resolved to mount an assault; but he was alone in so deciding, for no one was of this opinion save himself. That evening, as he was stretched out on his camp bed, fully clothed or almost so, as was his custom, he asked some if they thought the defenders were looking forward to being attacked. He was told, yes they were, because of the great number of troops they had—indeed, had they only been sheltered by a hedge they were sufficient to defend it. The duke took the answer in joke and said, 'You won't find anybody there tomorrow'. At dawn [on 28 June] the Burgundians moved smartly to the attack. Beauvais was fiercely assaulted and still more fiercely defended. A great number of troops crossed the bridge; in the crush my lord d'Épiry, an old knight from the Duchy of Burgundy, was smothered, the man of highest rank to die in the assault. On the other side [of the burned gate] some attackers reached the top of the wall, but all of them did not return. Hand-to-hand fighting went on for a long time. Other companies were ordered forward to the assault. Seeing, however, that there was nothing to be gained, the duke ordered them to withdraw. There was no sally by the defenders, for they could see masses of troops ready to welcome them if they issued forth. About six score men were killed in this attack, my lord d'Épiry being the one of highest rank. Some believed that a great many more perished. At least a thousand men were wounded [Burgundian losses were probably somewhat heavier than this].

The following night [actually, in the early hours of 10 July] the defenders made a sally, but with few men; most of them were mounted and their horses became entangled in tent ropes. They had no profit from their enterprise and lost two or three gentlemen. They wounded a first rate military man of rank named Jacques d'Orsans, the duke's Master of Artillery, who died a few days later. Seven or eight days after this assault, the duke wanted to divide his army in two and encamp with one part before the Paris gate. No one else shared this sentiment, because of the powerful garrison now within Beauvais. It was at the beginning that he should have done this, for it was now too late. Realizing that there was no chance of success, the duke raised the siege [on 22 July], the army preserving excellent discipline as it marched away. The duke expected the garrison to make a sally in force and he hoped to inflict a defeat on them. However, they made no move.

The Duke of Burgundy then made his way into Normandy, for he had promised the Duke of Brittany to advance as far as Rouen; that duke had agreed to meet him there, but changed his mind because of the death of the Duke of Guienne and did not budge from his province.

The Duke of Burgundy came before Eu, which yielded to him, as did St Valéry, and he had the whole region laid waste by fire to the gates of Dieppe. He took Neufchâtel-en-Bray and had it burned, as he did all of the Pays de Caux and most of the region to the gates of Rouen, before which he himself encamped. He lost many foragers and his army suffered severely from hunger. Then he withdrew because of the oncoming of winter. As soon as his back was turned, forces of the king retook Eu and St Valéry, gaining seven or eight prisoners by the terms of surrender.

About this time I entered the service of the king, who had taken in most of the servants of the Duke of Guienne. He was at Ponts-de-Cé, to which he had moved in his campaign against the Duke of Brittany.

There came to him some Breton ambassadors, and royal envoys likewise went to the duke. Among the Bretons were Philippe des

Essars, a councillor of the duke, and Guillaume de Soupplainville, a servant of my lord de Lescun. De Lescun had withdrawn into Brittany when he saw his master, the Duke of Guienne, near death—and thus took his departure in good time, quitting Bordeaux by sea for fear of falling into the king's hands. He brought with him the Duke of Guienne's confessor [Abbot Jourdain Faure] and one of his equerries [Henri de la Roche], to the pair of whom was imputed the duke's death. The two have spent long years as prisoners in Brittany.

The comings and goings between royal headquarters and Brittany having lasted a little while, the king decided to have peace on that side and to make such grants to the lord de Lescun as would secure his services and remove any desire on de Lescun's part to do him ill; for there was no intelligent policy or firmness of purpose in Brittany which did not proceed from him, and a duke so powerful directed by such a man was to be feared; but once the king came to terms with him, the Bretons would try to live in peace. And in truth most of them never desire anything else. In the realm there are always Bretons who enjoy honours and high place; and they have well served it in times past. I regard the treaty our king made with Brittany as a very wise move, though some criticized him for it who lacked his long view. He shrewdly judged the character of the lord de Lescun, saying that he saw no danger in putting into his hands what he put there. Further, the king esteemed him as a man of honour, because never during these past dissensions had he been willing to intrigue with the English nor consent that any place in Normandy be delivered to them, and this policy, being entirely of his own doing, was the cause of all the good things that came to him.

For these reasons the king had told the lord de Soupplainville to set down on paper everything that the lord de Lescun, his master, would want, both for the Duke of Brittany and for himself; and the king accorded all the demands. These were as follows: eighty thousand francs pension for the duke; for de Soupplainville's master, six thousand francs pension, the governorship of Guienne, the two seneschalships of Les Landes and the Bordelais, the captainships of one of the castles of Bordeaux, of Blaye, and of the two castles of Bayonne, of Dax and of St Sever, twenty-four thousand crowns in cash, the County of Comminges, and membership in the King's Order [of St Michael]. All was agreed to and accomplished, save that only half of the duke's pension was paid, and but for two years. In addition the king gave de Soupplainville six thousand crowns in cash, paid over a period of four years, as was his master's cash sum; de Soupplainville also received a pension of twelve hundred francs, the offices of Mayor of Bayonne and Bailli of Montargis, and some other little ones in Guienne. All these grants his master and he kept possession of until the death of the king. Philippe des Essars became Bailli of Meaux and Master of Waters and Forests of France and received a pension of twelve hundred francs and the sum of four thousand crowns. The Count of Comminges [de Lescun] remained a good and loyal servant of the king.

Soon after the king made peace with the Bretons he made his way to Picardy.

It was the custom of the king and the Duke of Burgundy to sign a truce as soon as winter was nigh, for six months or a year or more. Thus it was that they arranged one [on 3 November 1472]. To negotiate it on the duke's behalf there arrived [Guillaume Hugonet] the Chancellor of Burgundy, with other envoys. They were shown the final peace that the king had signed with the Duke of Brittany, in which that duke renounced his alliances with the English and the Duke of Burgundy; and the king therefore wished the ambassadors not to name him in the truce among the allies of Burgundy. To this they would not agree, saying that the Duke of Brittany had the choice of declaring himself on the king's side or theirs within the accustomed time. They added that in times past the duke had given formal notice of abandoning them and yet had not broken off the alliance and friendship; they considered the Duke of Brittany a prince managed by other wills than his own, but in the end he always came back to where his best interests lay.

In the negotiation of this truce there were complainings on both sides against the Count of St Pol, Constable of France. The king and his intimates had conceived a bitter hatred against the Constable. The Duke of Burgundy hated him still more—and with better cause, for I know the motives for hatred on both sides. The duke had not forgotten that the Constable had been responsible for the king's taking Amiens and St Quentin and regarded him as the cause and very engenderer of this war between the king and him, for in time of truce the Constable was all friendliness, but as soon as hostilities began he was his capital enemy. And he had sought to force the duke to bestow his daughter's hand, as you have seen before. There was still another sore spot: while the duke was before Amiens, the Constable had led a raid into Hainault, and, among his other

LA·SAVLT·DE·BEAVVAIS·

Partant de la
feist compte ti
rer en norman
die / mais paf
fant pres de beauuais alla
couure monff~ des cordes
deuant lequel menoit
lauantgarde. Oentree ~
ilz prindrent le faulxbourg
qui est deuant leuefche / et
le print vng bourguignō
trefauaricieux appelle

messire facques de mom
martin qui auoit cent lã
ces / et trois cens archiers
de lordonnance dud Duc.

Onff~ des cordes af
faillit dun autre co
ste mais fes efchelles eftoiēt
courtes et nen auoit que
res. Jl auoit deux canōs
qui tirerent au trauers
de la porte deux coups feŭ

The Siege of Beauvais: the opening assault on a northern gate

exploits, he burned a castle named Solre, which belonged to a knight named Baudouin de Lannoy. It was not then the custom for either side to burn places; and the duke used the Constable's action as a justification for the burnings that he was doing and had done in this season [of 1472].

Thus were begun the manoeuvrings as regards a way of destroying the Constable. Men on the king's side opened the subject to those Burgundians who were especial enemies of St Pol—the king's men being no less suspicious of him than was the duke, and each side said that the Constable was to blame for the war. The two parties then began to reveal all the propositions and approaches made by him to their respective masters, and so to plan his ruin.

If someone asks hereafter if the king could not have accomplished it himself, I reply that he could not, for the Constable's territories lay between those of the king and the duke. He held St Quentin in the Vermandois, a large and well fortified town. He had Ham and Bohain and other very strong places of his own, all of them near St Quentin and at any time he could station there men of either side as he pleased. He had from the king four hundred well paid men of arms [of the standing army], of whom he himself was the commissioner and audited the muster rolls, on which account he could pocket large sums since he did not keep his company up to the strength he reported. In addition, the regular income from his offices amounted to at least forty-five thousand francs; he exacted the tax of a crown on each cask of wine that passed through his territories on the way to Flanders or Hainault; and he possessed great lordships of his own and high connections in the realm of France and in the duke's domains, where he had many relatives.

The whole year that the Franco-Burgundian truce lasted, this bargaining to undo the Constable went on. The king's men addressed themselves to a knight in the duke's service, my lord de Humbercourt, of whom you have previously heard me speak, who had always bitterly hated the Constable. This hate had recently been exacerbated at a conference held at Roye at which the Constable and others represented the king and the Chancellor of Burgundy, the lord de Humbercourt, and others, the duke.

In the course of their discussion the Constable twice very foully gave the lie to the lord de Humbercourt. The latter made no reply except to say that if he endured this insult the Constable should not attribute this honour to himself but to the king, under whose safe

L

conduct de Humbercourt had come there to negotiate, and also to de Humbercourt's master, whose person he represented and to whom he would report the Constable's conduct.

This single outrageous insult, quickly spoken, afterwards cost the Constable his possessions and his life, as you will see. . . .

As well as with the lord de Humbercourt, the king's men also were constantly consulting with the Chancellor of Burgundy, because he had had some part in those words spoken at Roye and was likewise a close friend of the lord de Humbercourt. Negotiations proceeded so well that a conference on the subject was held at Bouvignes, near Namur. The king was represented by the lord de Curton, Governor of the Limousin, and Master Jean Héberge, later Bishop of Évreux; the duke, by the Chancellor of Burgundy and the lord de Humbercourt. This took place in the year 1474.

The Constable, warned that bargains were being struck at his expense, diligently plied both princes with embassies. He gave each of them to understand that he saw through the whole thing; and he succeeded in instilling in the king a suspicion that the duke intended to deceive him and draw the Constable over to his side. The king therefore sent word in great haste to his envoys at Bouvignes that they should conclude nothing against the Constable, for the reasons he gave them, but should, according to their instructions, prolong the truce, which was for a year or six months. I don't remember which.

When this message arrived, the agreement regarding the Constable had been concluded and the seals confirming it exchanged between the two parties the evening before. The ambassadors understood each other so well and were such good friends that the seals were given back. According to the articles of this treaty, the Constable was declared, for reasons given, the criminal enemy of both princes, who herewith swore to each other that which ever of them first could lay hands on him would put him to death within eight days or deliver him to the other to do with as he pleased; and he would be formally proclaimed the enemy of both parties, as would be all those who served or aided him. In addition, the king had promised to deliver to the duke the town of St Quentin and to give him, along with all the lordships the Constable held from the duke, all the Constable's money and possessions to be found within the realm. Among other places, the king would give the duke Ham and Bohain, both very strong, and on an agreed day forces of the king and the duke were to come before Ham and besiege the Constable. Nevertheless, for the reasons I have given, this settlement was cancelled. Instead, there was arranged a day and place at which the Constable was to be able to speak with the king, his safety guaranteed—for he feared for his person since he knew all about the agreement that had been made at Bouvignes.

The chosen place [Fargniers], three leagues from Noyon in the direction of la Fère, was situated on a little river; and on the side of the Constable the fords had been made impassable. Upon a causeway [bridging the stream] a stout barrier had been erected. The Constable arrived there first, bringing with him all his troops, or almost all—for he had there a good three hundred men of arms—and he was wearing his cuirass under a loose gown. The king was accompanied by at least six hundred men of arms, his escort including the Count of Dammartin, Grand Master of the Household of France, a capital enemy of the Constable.

The king had sent me ahead to make his excuses to the Constable for keeping him waiting so long. The king arriving soon after, the two of them spoke together [at the barrier], each having five or six men with him. The Constable apologized for having appeared in arms, saying that he had done so for fear of the Count of Dammartin. It was agreed between them, in sum, that all past matters were to be forgotten and never again spoken of. The Constable then made his way to the king's side of the barrier; and he and the Count of Dammartin were reconciled. The Constable went to lodge with the king at Noyon and then the next day returned to St Quentin, all differences settled, as he said.

After the king had thought over the matter and listened to the grumbling of his people, he came to the conclusion that it had been folly to go and speak like that to a servant of his who had thus barricaded himself and brought troops, all of whom were his subjects and paid out of his treasury. In consequence, if the king's hatred had previously been bitter, it was now still more so. As for the Constable, his pride was in no way diminished.

To consider well the actions of the king, they proceeded from the great good sense that he applied to the situation; for I believe that the Constable would have been received by the Duke of Burgundy in return for the delivering of St Quentin, whatever promise there had been to the contrary.

But for so sagacious a lord as was this Constable to appear in such a guise before his king and master to whom belonged all the troops by which he was accompanied—he had little understanding of his situation, or God had deprived him of his capacity to judge it. Indeed his countenance revealed that he was embarrassed and dumbfounded. And once he found himself in the king's presence, with only a small barricade between them, he was not slow in having the barricade opened and joining the king. That day, he was in great danger.

I add it up that he and some of his intimates preened themselves on this interview, complimented themselves on the king's fearing them, and held the king for a timorous man. It is true that he was so, but only when he had good cause. He had extricated himself from the great wars he had fought with the lords of his realm by giving much and promising still more; he was entirely unwilling to put his affairs in hazard if he could find another way of achieving his purpose.

A great many people thought that it was mere timorousness that guided his policy, and a great many possessed of this delusion, who were emboldened to oppose him, found themselves deceived—like the Count of Armagnac and others, who fared ill as a result; for he understood very well whether or not it was time to be afraid. Indeed I venture to give him this praise (I don't know if I have done so elsewhere, but even if I have, it is well worth repeating), that never have I known a man so wise in adversity. . . . Such audacity as the Constable's often comes from a sense of having done good service, and people like that think that because of their merits princes should put up with a great deal from them and that they are indispensable. But princes, on the contrary, are of the opinion that good service is obligatory, and like to be so reminded, and desire only to get rid of those who act high handedly towards them.

I must again refer to our master who once made two observations to me on this subject. Speaking of those who render great services, he said (and he mentioned the name of the one who had told him this) that to serve too well is sometimes the ruin of people and that often great services are recompensed by great ingratitudes; but the fault can as well lie with those who have performed the services, whose good fortunes make them too arrogant both to their masters and their fellows, as with the prince who is ungrateful. The king furthermore said that, in his view of how to prosper at court, a man is much better off when the prince he serves has bestowed on him a benefit far greater than he deserves, whereby he remains deeply obligated, than the man would be if he performed so great a service that the prince was deeply obligated to him; for princes naturally like those who are indebted to them more than they do those to whom they are indebted. Thus, whatever a man's rank in society, it is no easy matter to make one's way in this world, and God bestows great grace on those to whom He gives a keen native intelligence.

This interview between the king and the Constable took place in the year 1474.

BOOK FOUR

The English Invasion of 1475

A bitter quarrel between Arnold, Duke of Gelderland (on the lower Rhine) and his son and heir, Adolph, gave the Duke of Burgundy an opportunity to acquire that Duchy. Imprisoning the son and taking the father under his protection, Duke Charles persuaded old Duke Arnold on his deathbed to bequeath him the Duchy. A short campaign in June and July of 1473 put all of Gelderland in his hands.

THE DUKE OF BURGUNDY RETURNED TO HIS DOMAINS, HEART swollen with pride because of his adding this Duchy to his crown. He now found the affairs of the German Empire to his taste, because the Emperor [Frederick III] was a mean-spirited ruler who put up with anything in order not to have to spend anything; and on his own, without the aid of the Empire, he could do little.

Thus [with his eye on the Empire] the Duke of Burgundy prolonged his truce with the king [until 1 May 1475]. Some of the king's advisers thought that their master should not agree to the prolongation, nor allow the duke such opportunity for aggrandizement. Good sense prompted their advice, but, from lack of experience and not having the long view, they failed to understand the situation. Some who had a better grasp of it than they and who had greater knowledge, derived from first-hand experience, counselled the king that he boldly take this truce and allow the duke to beat himself to pieces against the Empire (an institution almost unbelievably vast and powerful), saying, 'When the duke will have taken one place or brought one campaign to an end, he will undertake another, for he is not a man ever to give over an enterprise' (and in that he was the opposite of the king, for the more deeply the duke became involved in a situation, the more ardently did he entangle himself in it). They also said that the king could find no better way of being revenged upon him than to let him have his head and even provide him with a little assistance and afford him no reason to suspect that the truce might be broken; for, given the vast extent of the Germanies and the power they represent, the duke must soon exhaust himself and be entirely ruined, since the princes of the Empire, even though the emperor was a man of little character, would see to it. And, in the end, thus it came about.

In a conflict that had developed between two claimants to the archbishopric of Cologne, one being a brother [Hermann] of the Landgrave of Hesse and the other [Robert of Bavaria], brother to [Frederick] the Count Palatine of the Rhine, the Duke of Burgundy espoused the cause of Robert of Bavaria and undertook to install him by force in the archespiscopal office, hoping to secure some places [in the territory of the archbishopric] for himself. He laid siege to the town of Neuss [downstream from Cologne on the left bank of the Rhine, on 30 July 1474]. The Landgrave of Hesse was occupying the town with a considerable number of troops. The duke had so many projects in mind, and such vast ones, that it was impossible for him to manage them. At this very time he wanted King Edward of England to cross the Channel, the latter having made ready a powerful army for the purpose. The duke made great efforts to accomplish his German enterprise, which was, once he had taken Neuss, to garrison it strongly together with another place or two upstream from Cologne, and thereby force the city of Cologne to capitulate; he would then advance up the Rhine to the County of Ferrette [in the Alsace region], which he held; and thus the whole Rhine would be his all the way to Holland—the Rhine valley having a greater number of strongly fortified towns and strongholds than are to be found in any realm of Christendom, except perhaps France.

The duke's truce with the king had been prolonged for six months [actually, prolonged from 1 June 1474 to 1 May 1475], and already the greater part of that time had elapsed. The king solicited a further prolongation, which would give the duke a free hand in the Germanies, but the latter refused because of a promise he had made to the English [by the Treaty of London, July 1474, in which both parties agreed to attack Louis XI the following summer with the aim of dismembering France].

I would gladly say nothing about the siege of Neuss, for it is not within the compass of this Memoir since I was not there, but I am forced to speak of it because of its relevance to other matters. The Landgrave of Hesse had established himself in the town of Neuss with many of his kin and friends, as I was told, to the number of eighteen hundred horsemen, men of quality—and so they proved themselves —and also with sufficient foot-soldiers to meet the need . . .

When the Duke of Burgundy put siege to Neuss, he had the finest army he ever commanded, especially its cavalry; for, because of some designs he claimed to have in Italy, he had recruited some thousand Italian men of arms, good and bad, chief of whom was the Count of Campobasso from the Kingdom of Naples, a very untrustworthy and dangerous man. There was also Giacomo Galeotto, a gentleman from the same kingdom, an excellent man, and there were numerous others whom I pass over for brevity's sake. In addition, the duke had three thousand English, first rate soldiers, and large numbers of his own subjects, well mounted and armed, who for a long time had followed the trade of war, and a powerful artillery. All this force he had held ready to unite with the English, who were making their invasion preparations in all diligence.

But in England such things require time, for the king cannot undertake such an enterprise without summoning Parliament, equivalent to the French Three Estates, which is a just and hallowed institution, and kings who make use of such institutions for matters like these are the stronger and the better served. When lords and commons are assembled, the King of England declares his purpose in summoning them and asks for a financial subsidy from his subjects, for no such taxes are raised in England except for invading France or Scotland, or for like enterprises. Parliament very willingly and liberally grants these subsidies, especially for invading France. Indeed it is a stratagem that English kings employ when they want to amass money—that of appearing to raise forces in order to invade Scotland; but, having paid the soldiers' wages for three months only, they then disband the army; and thus—having received a subsidy sufficient to pay these forces for a year—they make a great profit. King Edward was a master of this stratagem and often used it.

It would take the English a year to make ready their army, as King Edward informed the Duke of Burgundy, who at the beginning of

M

the summer [of 1474] had besieged Neuss. The duke thought that in little time he would have put his man in possession [of the arch-bishopric] and would win some places, like Neuss and others, to achieve the ends that I have indicated to you.

I believe that this turn of events came from God, who looked with pity upon this realm—considering the army that the duke com-manded, which for years had marched up and down this realm, without being offered battle or finding any power to oppose it, except for the royal forces garrisoning towns. True it is that such was the king's strategy, who was unwilling to take risks; he acted thus not only out of fear of the Duke of Burgundy but also because of uprisings which, he suspected, could occur in his realm if he happened to lose a battle; for he did not consider himself to be popular with all his subjects, especially the princes. If I may venture to say the whole truth, he many times told me that he understood his subjects well and that he would encounter much treason if his affairs went badly. Therefore when the Duke of Burgundy invaded, he took no measures to oppose him except to garrison strongly the towns in the duke's path. By his so doing, the army of the Duke of Burgundy defeated itself without the king's imperilling his rule, a policy which seems to me to have been dictated by great intelligence.

Nevertheless, considering the power of the Duke of Burgundy and the fact that the English army might have invaded at the beginning of the campaigning season [of 1475], as it doubtless would have done except for the Duke of Burgundy's blunder in so obstinately main-taining his siege of Neuss, there is no reason to doubt that this realm would have had all it could do to survive. For, as it happened, never did a King of England cross the Channel with so powerful an army at one time nor one so eager to give battle. All the great lords of England, without a single exception, were there. The army num-bered at least fifteen hundred men of arms, a tremendous force by English standards, all extremely well equipped and well furnished with support troops, and fourteen thousand archers, all mounted and armed with bows and arrows, as well as many auxiliary foot-soldiers. In the whole army there was not one page [i.e. not a single noncombatant]. In addition, the King of England was to send three thousand men to Brittany to join with the army of that duke. I saw two letters written in the hand of my lord d'Urfé, afterwards Grand Equerry of France who then was a councillor of the Duke of Brittany, which were addressed, one to the King of England and the other to Lord Hastings, Grand Chamberlain of England. Among other things, these letters said that the Duke of Brittany would accomplish more in one month through his secret connections [within the realm] than the English and Burgundian armies would accomplish in six, however powerful they were. I believe that this would have been true, if matters had developed differently. But God, who has always loved this realm, guided events, as I will recount hereafter. The two letters aforementioned were bought by the king our master, whom God absolve, from an English secretary for sixty marks of silver.

The Duke of Burgundy already had his hands full with the siege of Neuss and found it a tougher nut to crack than he had supposed. The inhabitants of Cologne, four leagues upstream on the Rhine, spent each month a hundred thousand gold florins on the war against the duke because of their fear of him; and other towns above them on the Rhine had already put in the field fifteen or sixteen thousand foot-soldiers, who were encamped on the opposite bank of the river from Neuss with a powerful artillery, by which they sought to destroy the Duke of Burgundy's supply ships coming upriver from Gelderland.

The emperor and the prince-electors of the Empire, on assembling to consider this matter, resolved to raise an army. The king had several times already solicited them [to oppose the Duke of Burgundy]. Hence they sent him a canon of Cologne cathedral, of the House of Bavaria, and another envoy, who brought with them a list of the troops the emperor intended to raise, if the king, for his part, was willing to join in the war. They did not fail to receive a good response and a promise of all that they asked for; in addition, the king gave a solemn undertaking, to the emperor and to many of the German princes and cities, that as soon as the emperor had taken the field and reached Cologne, he would send him twenty thousand men under the command of my lord de Craon and [John of] Salazar. Thus an army was assembled by the Empire, a force of almost unbelievable size; for all the princes of Germany, both temporal and ecclesiastical, and the bishops contributed men to it, and all the communities as well, and in great numbers. I was told that the Bishop of Münster, not one of the most powerful lords, brought 6,000 foot-soldiers, 1,400 horsemen, all clad in green, and 1,200 wagons. True, his bishopric is near Neuss.

It took the emperor a good seven months to assemble the army, at the end of which time he marched against the Duke of Burgundy, encamping his forces half a league from the duke's position. According to what several of the duke's people have told me, the King of England's army and that of the Duke of Burgundy together did not amount to more than a third of the imperial host. In addition to that army there was the force of which I have told you, on the right bank of the Rhine opposite the duke's power, which greatly harassed his troops and his supply line.

As soon as the emperor and the imperial princes appeared before Neuss, they dispatched to the king a doctor who enjoyed great authority among them, Dr Hesler [Archdeacon of Cologne], later cardinal, whose mission was to solicit the king to send the twenty thousand men he had promised or otherwise the Germans would come to terms [with the Duke of Burgundy]. The king made him an encouraging answer, gave him four hundred crowns, and sent back with him to the emperor an envoy named Jean Tiercelin, lord de Brosse. The doctor, however, did not depart in a happy frame of mind.

Marvellous intrigues were carried on during the siege of Neuss. The king worked to secure a peace with the Duke of Burgundy, or at least to prolong their truce, so that the English would not invade. The King of England, for his part, bent every effort to make the Duke of Burgundy abandon the siege and keep his promise to join the English in waging war upon this realm, saying that the campaigning season was passing by. On this mission [Anthony Woodville] Earl Rivers, nephew of the Constable, a very noble knight, and several others came twice to the Duke of Burgundy.

The duke, however, was obstinate—God had troubled his sense and his understanding, for all his life he had worked to bring about an invasion by the English and now that they were ready and all things favourable to them, in Brittany and elsewhere, he obstinately persisted in an impossible enterprise.

With the emperor was a legate from the Holy See, who each day went back and forth between the imperial and Burgundian armies to negotiate for peace. The King of Denmark [Christian I] was also there, quartered in a little town near the two armies and likewise working for peace. Thus the Duke of Burgundy would have been quite able to secure honourable terms in order to join the King of England. To do so was beyond him; and he justified himself to the

English on the grounds that his honour would be abased if he raised the siege, and gave other flimsy excuses. However, these were not the English who had waged the old French wars in the time of the duke's father, but were all of them inexperienced and ignorant of conditions in France: and therefore the duke acted very unwisely if he hoped to make use of them in time to come, for what they needed on their first French campaign was for him to guide them step by step.

While the duke persisted in his obstinacy, hostilities were begun against him from two or three directions. The Duke of Lorraine [René II], hitherto at peace with him, sent him a declaration of war, as a result of the endeavours of my lord de Craon who wished to secure the Duke of Lorraine for the king's service and did not fail to promise that he would become a great man. Immediately they took the field and did great damage in the [Duke of Burgundy's] Duchy of Luxembourg, including the demolishing of a place named Pierrefort, two leagues from Nancy [the capital of Lorraine], which was part of the Duchy.

In addition, under the guidance of the king and some of his servants, a ten-year alliance was negotiated between the Swiss and the cities of the upper Rhine like Bâle, Strasbourg and others. Peace was also made between Duke Sigismund of Austria and the Swiss so that he might regain the County of Ferrette which he had pledged to the Duke of Burgundy for a hundred thousand Rhenish florins. One point only remained in dispute: the Swiss demanded free passage, for their troops as well as their people, through four towns of the County of Ferrette. This point was submitted to the arbitration of the king, who decided in favour of the Swiss. In these manoeuvrings you can perceive the enmities that the king secretly stirred up against the Duke of Burgundy.

As soon as the treaty between the Swiss and Duke Sigismund had been concluded, it was put into effect. One fine night Pierre de Hagenbach, Governor of the County of Ferrette for the Duke of Burgundy, was captured, along with a force of eight hundred men that he had. The latter were all released, but Hagenbach was brought to Bâle, where he was tried for certain illegal and violent acts he had committed in the County of Ferrette; and, to conclude, his head was cut off [on 9 May 1474, but at Brisach, where he was likewise captured and tried]. The entire County of Ferrette was put in the hands of Duke Sigismund of Austria; and the Swiss, beginning to wage war in the County of Burgundy, took Blamont [actually, in a campaign the following year, on 13 August 1475], which belonged to the Marshal of Burgundy, of the House of Neufchâtel. The Burgundians who sent to succour [the town of Héricourt, besieged by the Swiss] were soundly beaten [on 13 November 1474]. The Swiss did a great amount of damage in the county and then withdrew, for that time.

The truce between the king and the Duke of Burgundy expired [1 May 1475], to the great regret of the king, who had hoped for its prolongation. Nevertheless, seeing that his negotiations had failed, he took the field by laying siege to an insignificant little castle named Tronchoy. The weather was very fine, it being the beginning of the campaigning season. Tronchoy was taken by assault in a few hours. Next day, the king sent me to speak to the Burgundians at Mont-didier. They abandoned the place, under terms of being able to depart with their baggage. The following day, along with the Admiral, [Louis] Bastard of Bourbon, I went to speak to those at Roye, and they likewise yielded their place to me for they had no hope of succour. They would not have surrendered it if the Duke of Burgundy had been in the region. Despite our promises to the contrary, these two towns were burned.

The king then laid siege to Corbie, the garrison of which was expecting him. For three days the king's artillery bombarded the town while the army expertly pushed forward their approach works. Within were the lord de Contay [Louis, successor to old Guillaume previously mentioned] and several others, who yielded on terms of baggage saved and then departed. Two days later the poor town was pillaged and it was fired as the other two had been. The king then planned to withdraw his army, hoping to secure a truce with the Duke of Burgundy since the duke obviously needed one. But a woman whom I know well—I will not name her because she is still living—wrote to the king that he should turn his army against Arras and its neighbouring region; and he took her at her word since she was a woman of high rank. I do not praise her act, because she was not obligated to it [i.e. was not a subject of the king]. The king dispatched the admiral with a stout force, and they burned a large number of Burgundian places from the region of Abbeville to the environs of Arras. The inhabitants of that city, who for long had known no adversity and were very arrogant, forced the garrison to make a sally against the royal army. Their numbers were too meagre to challenge that force; they were so badly routed [on 27 June] that many of them were killed and captured, including all their chiefs—Jacques de Luxembourg [Lord de Richebourg], brother of the Constable, the lord de Contay, the lord de Carency, and others—among whom were many very close relatives of the lady responsible for this exploit. Thus that lady suffered great loss thereby; but in time the king, out of favour to her, made full recompense.

At this time the king had dispatched Jean Tiercelin, lord de Brosse, to work upon the emperor so that he would not come to terms with the Duke of Burgundy and to make the king's excuses for failing to send troops as promised. The envoy gave constant assurances that the king would send troops and would continue the successes he had achieved against the duke and the damage he had inflicted on him, both on the borders of Picardy and in the Duchy of Burgundy. In addition, the king's envoy made a new proposal—that the king and emperor severally agree not to make a separate peace or truce and that the emperor take, by declaring them confiscated, all the lordships that the duke held in fief from the empire, while the king would take those which were held in fief from the French crown, such as Flanders, Artois, the Duchy of Burgundy and several others.

Although this emperor had been all his life a man of little strength of character, he was, however, perceptive, and the length of time he had lived could certainly have endowed him with experience; and then these bargainings between us and him had lasted long. Also, he was weary of the war, although it cost him nothing for all these lords of Germany served at their own expense, as is customary when the interests of the empire are involved.

The emperor made reply as follows. Near a German town there lived a huge bear who did great harm. Three fellows of the town, tavern-haunters, asked a tavern-keeper to whom they owed money to let them add one more debt and, within two days, they would pay the whole sum, for they would capture this bear who was doing so much harm and whose skin was worth a great deal of money, not to mention the presents that everybody would give them. The tavern-keeper accepted their proposal, and when they had dined they went to the bear's haunts. As they approached his cave, they found him nearer to them than they had realized. In terror they took to flight. One climbed a tree; the second fled for the town; the third was seized by the bear, who then flattened the man under him, thrusting his muzzle near the man's ear. The poor man, stretched out on the ground, played dead. Now this creature is of such a nature that when it sees that whatever it is gripping, man or beast, is no longer moving, it lets loose its prey, believing it to be dead. Thus the bear left the poor man without having done him much harm and returned to his cave. As soon as the poor man saw that he was free, he leaped to his feet and headed for the town. His companion in the tree, who had beheld this strange occurrence, descended and ran after him crying for him to wait. The man did so. When they met, the one who had been in the tree demanded of his friend to reveal, on his oath, what had been secretly imparted to him by the bear, who for so long had held its muzzle against his ear. The friend replied, 'He told me that I should never sell a bearskin until the beast is dead'.

With this fable did the emperor pay the king in the king's own coin, without making further response to our man, as if his meaning was, 'Come here as you have promised and let us kill this man if we can, and then we shall share his possessions'.

You have heard how Jacques of Luxembourg and others had been captured before Arras, which capture greatly displeased the Constable for Messire Jacques was a loyal brother to him. This was not St Pol's only misfortune, for at the same time his son [Antoine] the Count of Roussy, Governor of the Duchy of Burgundy for the duke, was likewise captured, and the Constable's wife [Marie of Savoy] died. She was a good lady, a sister of the Queen [Charlotte], who had favoured her and forwarded her interests. [This aid had been of importance to her husband] for the bargaining to dispose of the Constable, which had almost been consummated at the conference of Bouvignes, was still going on. Never after did he feel secure, but nursed suspicions and fears of both sides, especially of the king because he believed that the latter now regretted having cancelled the agreement made at Bouvignes. The Count of Dammartin and others were quartered with the royal army near St Quentin. The Constable feared them as his enemies and remained within St Quentin, where he had placed some three hundred foot-soldiers from his own estates, because he completely mistrusted the royal troops under his command.

He lived under constant pressure, for the king was urging him in message after message to take the field in order to campaign on the border of Hainault and lay siege to Avesnes—this at the time that the admiral and his force had gone to raid the territory around Arras, as I have recounted to you. The Constable finally obeyed the king's command, but in great fear. He made a show of besieging Avesnes for a few days, keeping himself closely guarded, and then withdrew to his strongholds. He sent work to the king (for, at the king's command, I received his man's message) that he had raised the siege because he was reliably informed that there were two men in his army whom the king had charged to kill him; and the messenger instanced so much evidence to support the accusation that it was difficult not to believe it, and there were suspicions that one of the two men had said something to the Constable about which he should have kept silent. I do not wish to name anyone or to speak further of this matter.

The Constable sent many messages to the army of the Duke of Burgundy. I firmly believe that his object was to persuade the duke to abandon his folly [of continuing to besiege Neuss]. When his messengers returned, he then dispatched some word or other to the king that he believed would please him and gave him bits of information and concocted explanations for his messages to the duke, and thus thought to keep the king happy with him. Sometimes, in order to instill some fear in the king, he dispatched word that the duke's affairs were going very well. He himself was so frightened of being attacked that he asked the Duke of Burgundy to send him his brother Jacques (this being before Jacques' capture) and also the lord de Fiennes and other relatives of his. He said that he could put them and their men within St Quentin—they, however, not wearing the Burgundian emblem of the St Andrew Cross—and promised to hold the town for the duke and restore it to him some time afterwards and to deliver his sealed engagement to this effect. The Duke of Burgundy complied with this proposal.

Twice Messire Jacques and the lord de Fiennes and other relatives of the Constable approached within a league or two of St Quentin, ready to enter, but on each occasion the Constable lost his fears, repented of his engagement, and sent them back. Indeed he tried the same thing a third time, so ardently did he desire to remain in this ambiguous situation, steering his course between France and Burgundy, for he was wondrously afraid of both king and duke. I learned these things from several people, especially from the mouth of Jacques de Luxembourg, who thus recounted them to the king after Jacques' capture, only I being present at the interview. It was worth much to him that he answered frankly all the king's questions.

The king asked him how many men he had brought to St Quentin. He replied that the third time he had had three thousand men. The king then asked him whether, if his force had turned out to be stronger than the Constable's, he would have held the town for the king [*sic*; the Duke?—see below] or for the Constable. Messire Jacques answered that on the first two occasions he had come only to aid his brother, but the third time, since the Constable had twice deceived him and his master [i.e. the Duke of Burgundy], had he found himself the stronger he would have kept the town for his master—without, however, doing any violence to the Constable nor anything to his harm, except that he would have refused to leave the town if the Constable so ordered. Not long after that interview, the king released Messire Jacques from prison and gave him a command in the standing army and high position and made use of his services until his, the king's, death. And Jacques' replies were the cause of this advancement.

Since I began to speak of Neuss, I have interpolated a great many matters, one on top of the other. Thus did things happen in this time, for the siege lasted a year [30 July 1474 to 13 June 1475]. Two developments put extreme pressure on the Duke of Burgundy to raise the siege: one was the war that the king was waging in Picardy, during which he had burned three little towns and a quarter of the open country of Artois and Ponthieu; the second was the great army which the King of England was assembling at the duke's request and instigation—that English invasion which the duke had worked all his life to bring about and had succeeded in obtaining only at this hour.

The King of England and all the lords of his realm were marvellously displeased by the duke's persisting in his siege; and, in addition to urgent requests, Edward IV made use of menaces, because of the great expenses he was incurring and the passing of the campaigning season. The duke, however, regarded it as a great glory that this huge German army—princes, prelates, cities—which was larger than any such in the memory of living man or over a long span of the past, had been unable to budge him from the siege. This glory cost him very dear; it is he who enjoys the profit of war who has the honour of it.

Meanwhile, the papal legate of whom I have spoken continued to go back and forth between the two armies, and finally the emperor and the duke signed a treaty by which Neuss was put within the legate's hands, to do with it as the Holy See would ordain.

To what bitterness of feeling was the Duke of Burgundy then reduced—on the one hand, to see himself thus pressed by the war the king was waging against him and also pressed and menaced by his friend the King of England, and, on the other hand, to see the town of Neuss escape his grasp when it was in such desperate straits that famine would probably have forced it to unconditional surrender within fifteen days (within ten days, I was told by one of the captains defending it whom the king took into his service). For these reasons, then, the Duke of Burgundy abandoned the siege of Neuss in 1475.

Now I must speak of the King of England, who had brought his army to Dover in order to cross the Channel to Calais. It was the greatest army that any King of England had led to France—all mounted men, the best equipped and armed that ever invaded the Continent; and all, or almost all, the lords of England were there. This English host numbered fifteen hundred well mounted men of arms, most of them richly armoured and equipped in the French fashion, each accompanied by several horsemen; at least fifteen thousand mounted archers with bows and arrows; a great many foot-soldiers; and a large force of other troops to pitch their tents and pavilions—of which they had a great quantity—to service the artillery, and to fortify their encampments. And in all this army there was not a single page [i.e. noncombatant]. In addition, the English had assembled three thousand men to send to Brittany.

Had it not been God's will to distract the mind of the Duke of Burgundy and thus preserve this realm, on which He has more often bestowed His grace than on any other, can it be believed that the duke would have so obstinately persisted in the siege of Neuss? In all his life he had never before found the English willing and ready to invade France. Furthermore if he were going to make good use of them, he would have had to keep them under his eye for an entire campaigning season in order to train them in the military tactics required for waging war in this country; for there is nothing more stupid or maladroit than an English army when they first invade, but in a short while they prove themselves to be bold and accomplished warriors.

The Duke of Burgundy, however, did just the opposite—and, among other blunders, he made the English almost lose their minds [because of his actions]. As for himself, his army was so disorganized, so poor and ragged, that he did not dare let the English see it, for he had lost before Neuss four thousand of his mercenaries, among whom perished some of the best troops he had. . . .

While King Edward was at Dover preparing to cross the Channel, the Duke of Burgundy sent him from Holland and Zeeland at least five hundred flat-bottomed boats called scuts [i.e. barges], which are very useful for the transport of horses. Notwithstanding this great number of ships, and all the additional ones that the King of England was able to provide, it took more than three weeks [of June] for the English to cross from Dover to Calais [Edward arriving at the latter port on 4 July].

Behold then how difficult it is for a King of England to invade France: if the king our master had understood sea warfare as well as he understood land warfare, never would King Edward have crossed the Channel, at least in this season; but he had no understanding of it and those to whom he gave authority over naval matters understood it still less. While the King of England was taking three weeks to cross, one single warship out of the port of Eu captured two or three of his small transports.

Before King Edward sailed from Dover, he dispatched to our king a single herald named Garter-King-of-Arms, a native of Normandy. He brought to King Louis a formal letter of defiance from the King of England, written in such fine language and style that I believe no Englishman ever had a hand in it. Edward IV demanded that our king yield up the realm of France, his by right, so that he could restore to the church, the nobles and the people their former liberties and remove the great charges and burdens with which they were oppressed; and, in the accustomed form of such defiances, he announced, in case of refusal, the hostilities that would ensue.

Our king read the letter to himself, then withdrew, alone, to a small chamber, giving order for the herald to be summoned. He informed him that he well knew the King of England was not mounting an invasion of his own volition, but was forced to it by the Duke of Burgundy and by the English populace; King Edward could certainly see that the campaigning season was already almost over and that the Duke of Burgundy was returning from Neuss a beaten and quite powerless man; and as for the Constable, he, King Louis, was well aware that St Pol had been secretly intriguing with

entre les autres maulx il
leur fist presque perdre la
saison. Et au regard de luy il
auoit so armee si rompue /
si mal en point et si poure q̃l
ne losoit mõstrer deuãt eulx
Car il auoit perdu deuant
mez quatre mil homes pre
nans soulde / entre lesquelz
y mourut des meilleures gẽs
quil eust. Et ainsi verrez

que dieu le disposa de tous
pointz a faire contre la raiso
de ce que son affaire reque
roit / et contre ce quil sca
noit et entendoit meulx q̃
mil autre dix ans auoit.

Coment le roy Edouard
dangleterre passa en france
et descendit a Calaix pour
faire la guerre au roy / et
de ce qui en aduint.

Edward IV lands at Calais, July 1475

the King of England, who had espoused the Constable's niece [Elizabeth Woodville, daughter of Jacqueline of Luxembourg], but the Constable would deceive King Edward—at which point King Louis recounted the benefits the Constable had received from him, adding, 'He has no other thought but to live by these dissemblings and to promise everything to everybody and thus make his profit'. King Louis enumerated several other reasons why King Edward of England should come to terms with him; and with his own hand he gave the herald three hundred crowns in cash and promised him a thousand if a treaty was signed. In public our king ordered that the herald be given thirty ells of beautiful crimson velvet.

The herald replied that he would work to bring about a composition; he believed that his master would readily entertain terms, but no approach to King Edward should be made until he had crossed to France. Once he had arrived, he should be sent a herald to ask for safe conducts for French negotiators, and communications should be addressed to Lord [John] Howard or Lord [Thomas] Stanley as well as to himself for aid in arranging audience for the herald.

While the king was speaking in private with the herald, many people in the great hall were eagerly waiting to hear what he would say and to see what sort of attitude he would adopt when he emerged from the small chamber. On concluding his conversation with the herald, he summoned me and told me that I should stay with the herald every minute until he had been given an escort for his return journey, so that nobody could speak to him, and that I should see that he received thirty ells of crimson velvet. I did so. The king, on his entering the hall, spoke to this one and that one about the letter of defiance; he beckoned seven or eight people aside, had them read the letter. He showed a serenely confident countenance, with not a sign of fear, for he was very happy with what the herald had told him.

At this point a word must be said about the Constable. He was a prey to anxiety because of the trick he had played upon the Duke of Burgundy regarding St Quentin; and he believed that he was already in the king's black books, for his principal servants had left him, such as my lord de Genlis and my lord de Moy. The king had taken them into his service, though my lord de Moy still was in touch with him. The king was urgently pressing the Constable to come to him, offering certain recompenses for the county of Guise that St Pol was requesting and that the king had formerly promised him.

The Constable was very glad to come, provided that the king took an oath on the Cross of St Laud at Angers [on which Louis XI himself often required oaths and which supposedly punished perjurors by death within a year] that he would do no harm to the Constable's person or allow anyone else to do harm, the Constable claiming that the king could as well make such an oath to him as he had formerly done to the lord de Lescun. The king replied that he would never take this oath, but any other the Constable asked of him he would take. You can well understand under what great strain both the king and the Constable laboured, for not a day passed, during a certain span, that envoys did not go from one to the other on the business of this oath. And it may well be thought how miserable human existence is when two such as these shorten their days by the toils and anxieties of saying and writing so many things almost the opposite of their thoughts.

But if the king and the Constable suffered great travail of spirit, the King of England and the Duke of Burgundy were no less afflicted. The king crossed to Calais and the duke abandoned the siege of Neuss at about the same time. The duke, with but a small escort, hastened to join the king at Calais, having sent his shattered army to pillage the duchies of Bar and Lorraine and thus to secure supplies and refresh themselves. He did so because [René II] the Duke of Lorraine had defied and opened war on him while he was before Neuss. It was another great mistake of his to add to the ones he had already committed in regard to the English, who upon landing at Calais expected to find him there with at least 2,500 well equipped men of arms and large numbers of horse and foot. Such a force the Duke of Burgundy had promised, in order to persuade them to come, and he had also promised to begin a campaign in France three months before their arrival so that they would find King Louis the wearier and the more oppressed. But God provided for all, as you have heard.

The King of England, accompanied by the Duke of Burgundy, left Calais [about 18 July] and, passing through the Boulogne region, marched to Péronne. There the duke gave his allies a very cold welcome, for he established guards at the gates of the town and would allow only small parties of Englishmen to enter. Edward IV and his army encamped in fields [south of the Somme with the river at their backs]—as they were well able to do for they were handsomely equipped for such campaigning.

Once they had reached Péronne, the Constable sent a man of his named Louis de Sainville to the Duke of Burgundy to excuse himself for not having delivered St Quentin. He declared that had he done so he would no longer have been of use to the duke in the realm of France for he would have entirely lost his credit and his connections; now, however, since he saw the King of England so close at hand, he would do whatever the Duke of Burgundy wished. In order to carry conviction, he included a credence, addressed to the King of England, which gave the duke a blanket authorization to speak in his name. In addition he sent a sealed engagement in which he promised to serve and succour the duke and his friends and allies, the King of England among them, under any and all circumstances. The Duke of Burgundy gave the credence to King Edward, and then, in speaking for the Constable, considerably fattened up the latter's promises; for he assured the King of England that the Constable would give him entry to St Quentin and all the Constable's other strongholds. King Edward immediately took this promise at its face value, for he had espoused the Constable's niece and also the Constable seemed to be in such great fear of the king that he would not dare go back on what he had promised the Duke of Burgundy. But neither the Constable's anxieties nor his fear of the king had yet brought him to that point; instead he chose to continue dissembling, as was his custom, in order to placate the King of England and the duke, and to put forward such plausible explanations that they would accept them without forcing him to declare himself.

King Edward and his people had little experience in dealing with French affairs; they practised a rather crude and simple form of statecraft. Hence it was that they were rather slow at seeing through the deceptions that are used here and elsewhere. The fact is that Englishmen who have never left England are, by nature, very choleric, as are all peoples living in a cold climate. Our own country, as you know, is situated between peoples of cold and of warm climate: we have Italy and Spain and Catalonia to the east [*sic*], England and Flanders and Holland to the west, and we also join with the Germanies everywhere along the borders of Champagne. Thus we are related to the hot regions and also to the cold, on which account our people are of two temperaments. In any case, it is my opinion that in all the world no region is better situated than that of France.

The King of England, who was overjoyed by this news from the Constable (though he could already have had some such intimations, but nothing so positive) left Péronne, accompanied by the Duke of Burgundy, who had no troops with him for they had all been sent to the duchies of Bar and of Lorraine as I have told you. As they neared St Quentin, a great crowd of English hastened ahead—not many days later, I heard them talking about it. They were expecting to be greeted by the ringing of the church bells and by a welcoming procession bearing crosses and holy water. When they approached the town, however, artillery began to fire and skirmishes ensued, involving both foot and horse. Two or three Englishmen were killed and some captured. All this occurred in a heavy downpour; and it was under these sorry circumstances that they returned to their army, bitterly fuming against the Constable and calling him a traitor.

The following morning the Duke of Burgundy announced that he was taking his leave—a very odd thing to do, considering that it was he who had persuaded the English to undertake this expedition. He explained that he wished to rejoin his army in the Duchy of Bar, promising that he would do great things. The English, who are a suspicious people and who were entirely new to the situation here and bewildered, could not reconcile themselves to his departure nor believe that he had any troops in the field. For his part, the Duke of Burgundy was unable to explain away the conduct of the Constable, notwithstanding that he told them the Constable had so acted from entirely worthy motives. The English were also dismayed by the approach of winter, and it seemed indeed, to hear them talk, that in their hearts they were more inclined to peace than to war.

As the duke, on the point of departing, was making these excuses for the Constable, there was captured by the English a servant of a gentleman of the king's household, one of the twenty-crowns-a-month men, named Jacques de Grassay. This servant was immediately brought before the King of England and the Duke of Burgundy, who interrogated him, after which he was put in a tent. The Duke of Burgundy then took leave of the King of England and made his way to Brabant in order to go to Mezières, where a part of his forces was quartered. The King of England ordered this servant of de Grassay to be freed since he was their first prisoner. As he was leaving, my lord Howard and my lord Stanley gave him a noble [a gold coin] and told him, 'Commend us to the good grace of the King your master, if you can manage to speak to him'. The servant hastened to the king, then at Compiègne, in order to repeat these words. The king was at first very suspicious of him, fearing that he was a spy because Gilbert de Grassay, brother of the servant's master, was then in Brittany enjoying high favour with Duke Francis II. The servant was put in irons that night and closely guarded. Nevertheless, by the king's command, many people talked with him; they reported that he spoke very convincingly and they thought that the king should hear him.

Early the next morning the king spoke with him. After hearing what the servant had to say, he ordered him to be unshackled but still kept under guard. The king then went to have a meal, pondering several possibilities, especially the alternatives of whether or not to communicate with the English. Before seating himself at table, he murmured some words to me—for, as you know, my lord of Vienne [Angelo Cato, Archbishop of Vienne], our king often spoke very intimately to those who were closest to him, as I was then and others were afterwards, and he liked to whisper in people's ears. There came to his mind the words that the English herald had said to him, namely that he should not fail to send a request for safe conducts so that a French embassy could then be dispatched to the King of England as soon as he had crossed the Channel and that such request be addressed to Lord Howard and Lord Stanley.

After he was seated at table and had pondered for a little [probably muttering to himself], as you are aware that he used to do—a habit that seemed very odd to those who did not know him (for any who did not know him would have judged him to be of feeble intellect, but his accomplishments eloquently proved the opposite to be true) —he whispered in my ear that I should leave the table and send for a certain servant of my lord des Halles, son of Jean Mérichon of La Rochelle; then, while I was eating in my chamber, I should, in secret, ask him if he would venture to undertake a mission to the English army, wearing a herald's costume.

I immediately did what the king had commanded me, and was very much astonished when I saw the servant, for it did not seem to me that his stature or demeanour was suitable for such an enterprise.

N

However, he had good sense, as I afterwards realized, and spoke with fluency and grace. Never had the king spoken to him but once. The servant was overwhelmed when he heard what I had to say, throwing himself down on both his knees before me as if he believed himself already dead. I heartened him as best I could and promised him an office of tax-collector in the Isle of Ré and some money. To hearten him further, I told him that the English had asked for this mission, and then I had him eat with me, only the two of us and a serving man, and little by little I disclosed to him what he would have to do.

It was not long before the king sent for me. I told him about our man and named others that I thought more suitable; but he would have no other and came himself to speak to the servant. He heartened him more with one word than I had done in a hundred. The king was accompanied only by my lord de Villiers, then Grand Equerry and now Bailli of Caen. When the king felt that our man was ready for the mission, he sent the Grand Equerry to procure a trumpeter's banner from which to make a herald's tabard—for the king had no use for ceremony and had neither trumpeter nor herald in his train, as many princes do; and so the Grand Equerry and one of my people fashioned this tabard as best they could. Then the Grand Equerry went to procure an enamelled escutcheon from a little herald of the Admiral named Open Road, which enamel was fastened to [the tabard of] our man. Then his riding boots and clothes were secretly fetched, his horse was brought and he was mounted on it, without anyone's knowledge. His herald's tabard was stowed in a handsome leather bag attached to his saddle; and, thoroughly instructed in what he was to say, he rode straight for the English army.

On his arrival, clad in his herald's tabard, he was immediately arrested and brought before the tent of the King of England. When asked his business, he replied that he had come as a representative of the king to speak to the King of England with orders to address himself to Lords Howard and Stanley. He was taken into a tent and given dinner, and was very well treated. When the King of England, who had been dining at the time the herald arrived, finished his dinner, he had the herald brought before him and heard his message, the essence of which was as follows: the king had long desired to have friendly relations with the King of England so that the two realms could live in peace. Never since he had become King of France had he waged war or undertaken anything against the king and kingdom of England—excusing himself for having formerly supported the Earl of Warwick by saying that he had done so only against the Duke of Burgundy and not at all against King Edward. The Duke of Burgundy, the king's message continued, had called the English into France only to secure better terms for himself from the king as a result of the invasion; and if others [i.e. other French lords like the Duke of Brittany or the Constable] had espoused the English cause, it was only to benefit themselves and their own interests. The interests of the King of England they did not care about, nor what happened to him, but sought merely to feather their own nests. The herald also pointed out, according to the king's instructions, that the weather was bad and winter was already approaching; the king well knew that Edward IV had expended great sums on this expedition and that there were many people in England, nobles and merchants, who favoured an invasion of France. If it should come about that King Edward were willing to consider making a treaty, the king for his part would go so far towards achieving it that the King of England and his kingdom would undoubtedly be satisfied with the terms. Finally, if in order to secure more information about this matter, King Edward wished to provide a safe conduct for a party of horsemen to the number of one hundred, the king would send him ambassadors with full instructions; or if the King of England preferred that envoys from each side should meet in some village midway between the two armies, the king would be quite satisfied with that arrangement and would dispatch the requisite safe conducts.

The King of England and a group of his intimates found these overtures very attractive. Our man was provided with safe conducts, as he requested, and given four nobles; and there came with him a herald to procure safe conducts from the king like the ones the English had furnished. The next day, in a village near Amiens, envoys from each side conferred. The king was represented by the Bastard of Bourbon, Admiral, [Jean Blosset] my lord de St Pierre, and the Bishop of Évreux named [Jean] Héberge. The King of England sent there my lord Howard, someone named [Thomas] St Leger, and a doctor named [John] Morton, who is today Chancellor of England and Archbishop of Canterbury.

Some people, I believe, might think that the king was humbling himself too much. But wiser folk may well perceive, from what I have previously pointed out, that this realm would have been in great danger had not God intervened. He disposed the king's mind to choose the sagacious course of action, while He distracted the mind of the Duke of Burgundy, who committed so many blunders in this situation, as you have seen, and who thus lost by his own fault what he for so long had desired. In France there were a great many secret intrigues among us, from which great evils would have come upon this realm, and soon (if this way of negotiation had not been found, and quickly), from the direction of Brittany and elsewhere; and I truly believe, as a result of the things I have seen in my time, that God holds this realm in special favour.

As you have heard, English and French envoys met on the very day after the return of our herald, for the two armies were but four leagues apart or less. Our herald enjoyed a warm welcome, and received his office in the Isle of Ré, his native place, and some money. A number of overtures were made by the ambassadors on both sides. The English began by claiming the crown of France, as customary; then demanded, as a minimum, Normandy and Guienne. Good attack; good defence. From this first meeting matters moved towards an agreement, for both parties greatly desired one. Our envoys came back and the others returned to their army. The king was told the demands of the English and their final position, which was as follows: a payment of seventy-two thousand crowns, in coin, before the English recrossed the Channel; the marriage of the present king [Charles VIII, then the five-year-old Dauphin] with the eldest daughter [Elizabeth, then ten years old] of King Edward who is today Queen of England [as the wife of Henry VII]; the revenues of the Duchy of Guienne for Elizabeth's maintenance or a yearly subsidy of fifty thousand crowns, paid at the Tower of London, for nine [actually, seven] years, at the end of which time the Dauphin and his wife were peacefully to enjoy the revenues of Guienne and, in return, our king was to be quit of his obligation to pay the subsidy. There were a number of other minor articles regarding trade relations which I pass over. This peace [i.e. truce] was to last for seven years. All the allies of both sides were included in it; mainly, by the King of England, the Dukes of Burgundy and of Brittany if they so wished to be. The King of England made a very strange offer indeed—to name certain persons who, he said, were traitors to the king and his crown, and to furnish proof in writing.

The king was marvellously overjoyed by what his envoys reported to him. He held council concerning the terms and I was present. Some were of the opinion that they represented only a deceit and trickery by the English. The king thought the contrary, pointing out the state of the weather and the lateness of the season, the fact that they did not hold a single place in France of their own, and the bad turns done them by the Duke of Burgundy, who had already left them in the lurch. The king was sure that the Constable would deliver no places to them, for every hour he was sending to the Constable to humour him and appease him and keep him from causing harm. The king also well understood the disposition of the King of England, who was devoted to pleasure and taking his ease. It thus appeared that the king spoke more wisely than anyone else at the council and had keener insight into the matters discussed. He concluded that this money demanded by the English must be procured in all haste; the manner of raising it was decided upon, and it was agreed that everyone should lend something so that it could be quickly amassed. In addition, the king said that there was nothing in the world he would not do in order to boot the English out of the realm, except that he would never consent to yield them any territory and, indeed, rather than permit it, would put all in peril and hazard.

My lord the Constable was beginning to be aware of these negotiations and was becoming apprehensive of being attacked on all sides, for he still feared the agreement which he believed had been concluded against him at Bouvignes; and for this reason he sent frequent messages to the king. At the moment of which I am speaking, there arrived at the royal headquarters a gentleman named Louis de Sainville, a servant of the Constable, and a secretary of his named [Jean] Richier, both of whom are still living. They spoke their credence to my lord du Bouchage [Imbert de Batarnay] and to me before the king, for so the king desired.

The message they brought greatly pleased the king when he was informed of it, because he had the intention of making use of it, as you shall hear. The lord de Contay, servant of the Duke of Burgundy, who had recently been captured before Arras as you have heard, was going back and forth, on parole, between the king and the duke—the king had promised to pay his ransom and give him a very large sum of money if he could negotiate a treaty. Furthermore he had returned to the king on the very day that the two envoys of the Constable arrived. The king had the lord de Contay hide behind a large old screen which was in his chamber, and I with him, so that he could hear and report to his master the language that the Constable and his people were using about the duke. The king sat on a stool by the screen so that we could hear what Louis de Sainville said. With him the king had only my lord du Bouchage. Louis de Sainville and his companion began to speak, saying that their master had sent them to the Duke of Burgundy to urge the duke to abandon his friendship with the English, and they had found the duke so enraged against the King of England that they had almost won him over, not only to abandoning the English but to aiding in attacking and undoing them on their retreat.

Thinking to please the king, Louis de Sainville on saying these words began to mimic the Duke of Burgundy, stamping his foot on the floor, swearing by St George, calling the King of England 'Blayborgne'—declaring that he was the son of an archer of that name—and mocking the duke as much as it is possible in this world to mock anyone. The king laughed heartily, told de Sainville to speak louder because he was becoming a little deaf, and bade him tell the tale again. De Sainville, nothing loath, began to repeat it with relish. My lord de Contay, with me behind the screen, was utterly amazed and would never have believed it, no matter what anyone could have said, had he not heard it with his own ears.

In conclusion, the Constable's men counselled the king that, to avoid all these great perils that he saw arrayed against him, he should take a truce; the Constable would, without fail, provide guidance; and in order to appease the English, they should be given just a small town or two for winter quarters—no matter how insignificant the towns were, the English would be satisfied with them. It seemed, though the Constable's men named no names, that they were referring to Eu and St Valéry. The Constable thought that by this means the English would be pleased with him and would overlook his refusal to let them enter any of his places.

The king, content with having played his game by which he had let the lord de Contay know of the language used by the Constable and his men about the Duke of Burgundy, made no harsh reply to the Constable's envoys but merely said to them, 'I will send to my brother and keep him informed of events'. He then gave them leave to depart. One of them swore an oath to me that if he learned anything of concern to the king, he would reveal it.

It had been hard for the king to dissemble his feelings when they advised him to deliver places to the English; but, fearing that the Constable might do worse, he did not wish to reply in such a way that they would perceive how ill he took their mission. Instead he sent an envoy to the Constable. The distance was short; a man could go and return in no time.

The lord de Contay and I came out from behind the screen after the others had left. The king laughed and was very genial. But the lord de Contay was like a man out of all patience, because of having heard such people thus ridicule his master, especially since the Constable was then treating with the duke; and every minute seemed an hour to him until he was galloping the road to recount the scene to his master the Duke of Burgundy. He was immediately sent off, bearing instructions written in his own hand and a letter of credence written by the king.

Our arrangement with England was already concluded, as you have heard, and all these dealings went on at the same time. . . . It was agreed by the French and English envoys that the two kings would meet and that after their interview and the taking of oaths to uphold the treaty, King Edward would return to England, first having received the seventy-two thousand crowns, and leave as hostages Lord Howard and his Master of the Horse, Sir John Cheyney, until he had recrossed the Channel. Sixteen thousand crowns in annual pensions, of varying amounts, were promised to the King of England's most intimate advisers and officers—two thousand crowns to [his Grand Chamberlain] my lord Hastings (that one was never willing to give a receipt for the payments); two thousand crowns to [Thomas Rotherham, Bishop of Lincoln] the Chancellor; and the remainder to Sir Thomas St Leger, [Sir Thomas] Mongomery, and others. And a great deal of money and valuable plate was distributed to the servants of King Edward's household.

As soon as the Duke of Burgundy, in Luxembourg [actually, at Valenciennes], heard this news, he rode in great haste to the King of England, arriving with an escort of only sixteen horse. Edward IV, astonished at his sudden appearance, asked why he had come—the king could see full well that his visitor was enraged. The duke replied that he had come to speak to him. The king asked if he wished to converse in private or in public. Then the duke asked him if he had made peace. The King of England replied that he had concluded a truce of seven years in which the duke was included [as his ally] and the Duke of Brittany too; and he begged him to accede to it. The duke, his anger mounting, began to speak in English (for he knew the language). He cited many renowned feats of arms performed by English kings who had invaded France and the trials they had undergone to acquire honour there; and he vehemently denounced this truce, declaring that he had not sought the English invasion for any need that he had of it, but merely that they might recover what belonged to them. So that they could see that he had no need of their coming, he would not sign a truce with our king until the King of England had been back in his realm for three months. After these words, he went off whence he had come [on 20 August, in actuality the second day of stormy interviews between king and duke]. The King of England and the members of his council were very much offended by what the Duke of Burgundy had said; but others who disapproved of the truce, praised the duke's words.

To put the finishing touches on the truce, the King of England [and his army] moved to the vicinity of Amiens, encamping half a league [downstream on the right bank of the Somme] from that city [Louis XI having arrived there the day before, 25 August]. The king, who had been able to see them approaching from afar, stationed himself at the city gate. In truth, the English appeared to have little experience in the art of campaigning, and they rode in disorder. The king sent the King of England three hundred wagons loaded with the best wines that could be found; the wagon train seemed to be an army almost as large as that of England. It being a time of truce, many Englishmen came into Amiens. They behaved foolishly and showed little respect for their king. They came fully armed, and in large companies; and had our king wished to act in bad faith, never could such a quantity of men have been destroyed so easily. But the king thought only of making them good cheer and establishing a peace with England that would last his lifetime.

He had ordered two huge tables to be set up outside the town gate, one on each side; they were laden with all kinds of things to eat that provoke thirst and with the best wines obtainable, and there were people to serve. Of water, there was no news. At each of the tables the king had seated five or six men of rank, large and fat men, in order to create an atmosphere of conviviality. My lord de Craon was there and the lord de Bricquebec, the lord de Bressuire, the lord de Villiers, and others. As the English approached the gate, they beheld this array; people took their horses' reins, saying that they should run a course in the lists there, and brought them to the tables, where they were treated to all that the scene offered; and they were very happy with the programme.

Whatever place they chose to enter, once they had gone within the town, they paid nothing. There were nine or ten taverns well stocked with the needful, where they went to eat and drink; and whatever they asked for was served them without charge. This situation lasted three or four days.

You have heard how this truce displeased the Duke of Burgundy, but it was still more displeasing to the Constable, who saw that he was imperilled on all sides and had trapped himself. He therefore sent his confessor to the King of England with a letter of credence that ran as follows—for the love of God, the king should put no faith in the promises or words of the King of France, but instead should seize Eu and St Valéry and establish quarters there for part of the winter, for, before two months had passed, the Constable would see to it that he had very good quarters indeed. The credence offered no other assurances but held out great hopes. Also, in order that King Edward have no cause to accept miserable terms for the sake of a little money, the Constable offered to lend him fifty thousand crowns and made a great many other proposals. Already our king had had these two places burned because the Constable had advised him to deliver them to the English, and the King of England was informed of their being burned. King Edward made reply to the Constable that, the truce having been concluded, he would make no change in his plans and that if the Constable had kept his word, he would not have made this treaty. Then was our Constable entirely reduced to desperation.

You have heard how these English were enjoying themselves in Amiens. One evening my lord de Torcy came to tell the king that there were large numbers of them in the town and the situation was very dangerous. The king flew into a rage against him. Everyone therefore fell silent. The next morning was the day of the week on which the Commemoration of the Holy Innocents [observed on 28 December] had occurred the previous year [i.e. on Wednesday, which must have been Wednesday, 30 August]. On that day of the week the king would not speak of affairs; he regarded it as very bad luck if anyone spoke to him about them; and he became very angry if any of his intimates, who knew about his observance, did so speak.

Nevertheless, on the morning to which I refer, as the king rose and was saying his hours, someone came to tell me that there were at least nine thousand English in the town. I decided to take my chances on informing him, and went back into his private chamber. I said to him, 'Sire, notwithstanding that it is the day of the Innocents, I must tell you what I have just been told'; and I recounted the report to him at length—the number of English in the town, more still coming, and all armed, and the fact that nobody dared refuse them entry for fear of offending them.

The king was not at all obstinate. He immediately left off saying his hours, telling me that it was not necessary to observe the ceremony of the Innocents that day, and ordered me to mount horse and try to speak with some of the English captains to see if we could get the English out of the town. I should invite the captains, if I met any, to come speak to the king, who would at once go to the gate after me. I did so. I spoke to three or four English captains whom I knew, explaining the matter as the situation called for. For every Englishman they ordered out of the town, however, twenty entered it. The king sent after me the lord de Gié, now Marshal of France. In order to investigate, we entered a tavern—a hundred and eleven servings had already been chalked up and it was not yet nine o'clock in the morning. The house was full: some were drunkenly singing and some were in drunken slumber. When I perceived the situation, it seemed to me that there was no danger and I so sent word to the king, who came immediately to the gate with a large escort. He secretly ordered two or three hundred men of arms to station themselves, armed, in the houses of their captains and some he placed at the gate by which the English were entering. The king had his dinner brought to the gate-keepers' lodge and had several Englishmen of rank dine with him.

The King of England, informed of this disorder, was ashamed of it. In a message to the king he asked that orders be given for none of his men to be admitted. The king made reply that this he would never do; however, if the King of England wished to, he should send some of his archers to take over the guarding of the gate and admit whomever they pleased. Thus was it done. And a great many English left the town by order of the King of England.

It was then decided that, to bring all matters to an end, a place must be chosen where the two kings would meet and men must be appointed to make the selection. My lord du Bouchage and I represented the king on this mission and my lord Howard, a man named St Leger and a herald acted for the King of England. After we had inspected the banks of the Somme river, we agreed that the best and most secure place for the meeting was Picquigny, three leagues [downstream] from Amiens, a stronghold belonging to the Vidame of Amiens, though it had been burned [in 1471] by the Duke of Burgundy. The town lies low on the river Somme, which is not fordable and, at this spot, is not wide.

On the route the king would take to come there [along the left bank], the countryside was handsome and open. On the other side, where the King of England would come to Picquigny, the country was also very attractive, except that at the approach to the river opposite Picquigny, there was a causeway, more than two arrow flights long, which had marshes on both sides. For anyone not going there with sincere assurances of his safety, it would have been a very dangerous route. There is no question, as I have said elsewhere, but that the English lack the subtlety in negotiation that the French have; whatever anyone can say, they conduct their affairs very crudely. However, one must have a little patience and not fall into angry debate with them.

The place for the interview having been chosen, orders were given to construct a stout bridge of good size—we furnished the carpenters and the materials. In the middle of the bridge was constructed a strong wooden lattice, like the kind used in making cages for lions. The spaces between the bars were just large enough to permit extending an arm through one with ease. For protection against rain there was erected a roof of planks of sufficient size to shelter ten or a dozen persons on each side of the barricade, which spanned the whole width of the bridge so that no one could pass from one side to the other. On the water there was only a single little boat, manned by two rowers, for those who wished to cross the river.

I want to explain what motivated the king to arrange for the interview in this way; it might be useful, in time to come, for someone in a similar situation. During the youthful years of Charles VII, the realm was severely oppressed by the English. King Henry V was besieging Rouen and held the city closely beleaguered [from July 1418 to its capitulation in January 1419]. Most of those within were partisans of Duke John [the Fearless] of Burgundy. Between this Duke and [Louis] the Duke of Orléans there had developed a bitter quarrel, and most of this realm was split between these two factions [of the Burgundians and the Armagnacs, the latter so called because Duke Louis' heir, Charles of Orléans, captured at the battle of Agincourt, 1415, had married a daughter of the Count of Armagnac, Constable of France]. This dissension in no way benefited the governing of the realm. Such factionalism never takes hold of a country but in the end it causes great harm and is difficult to extinguish.

This quarrel had already resulted in the murder of the Duke [Louis] of Orléans at Paris eleven years before [in 1407]. Duke John of Burgundy had amassed a large force with the intention of raising the siege of Rouen. The better to accomplish this end by assuring himself of the support of the king [Charles VII, then actually Dauphin], he had arranged for an interview with the king at Montereau. A bridge was there erected with a barricade in the middle. There was a little wicket in the barricade, locked on both sides, by which one could pass from one side to the other, if the parties on each side so wished. The king stationed himself on one side of the barricade and Duke John on the other, both accompanied by numbers of troops, though the duke's escort was the larger. They began to converse. The duke had only three or four persons close by him. Whether the duke was invited to do so or desired to humble himself before the king, he unlocked the wicket on his side and it was unlocked on the other, and he and his three companions passed through the barricade. The duke was immediately killed, as were those with him. This assassination engendered a host of evils, as everyone knows.

This piece of history is not relevant to my subject and I will therefore say no more about it. But the king, in arranging for his interview with Edward IV, recounted it to me just as I have reported it to you. He said that had it not been for that wicket in the barricade, there would have been no opportunity to invite the duke to pass to the other side, and this catastrophe would not have occurred, which was the work of some servants of [Louis] the Duke of Orléans, who had been murdered as I have told you, and these men were among the chief officers of the Dauphin Charles.

The bridge and its barricade having been completed, as you have heard, the two kings arrived there the following day, which was [Tuesday] 29 August 1475. The king, who had about eight hundred men of arms with him, was the first to appear. On the King of

England's side of the river his whole army was drawn up in battle array; and although we did not think we could see all, there seemed to us to be an amazingly large number of horsemen massed together. What we had on our side could not compare, but then a quarter of our army was not there. It had been arranged that each of the kings would have a dozen men with him, those of highest rank and their most intimate advisers, who had been ordered in advance to station themselves at the barricade. On our side we had four of the King of England's men to keep watch on our proceedings and we had the like number on the King of England's side. As I have told you, our king had arrived first and was at the barricade; and there were twelve of us with him, including the late Duke John of Bourbon and his brother [Charles, Archbishop of Lyons and later] the cardinal. It was the king's pleasure to have me dress like him that day. It had long been his custom to have someone dress like him on frequent occasions.

The King of England approached along the causeway I have mentioned, splendidly attended and looking every inch a king. With him were his brother [George] the Duke of Clarence, [Henry Percy] the Earl of Northumberland, and some other lords, his [Great] Chamberlain named [William] Lord Hastings, his Chancellor and others, of whom only three or four were clad in cloth of gold like their king. Edward IV wore a black velvet cap adorned with large jewelled *fleur-de-lis*. He was a most handsome prince, and tall, but he was beginning to grow fat, and when I had seen him previously he was even handsomer, for I do not remember ever having seen a more handsome man than he was at the time the Earl of Warwick drove him from England [in September 1470].

As he came within four or five feet of the barricade, he removed his cap and half knelt. Our king, who had already leaned against the barricade, did him a similar courtesy, and they then half embraced, their arms thrust through the spaces in the wooden lattice, and the King of England made an even deeper bow. Our king began the conversation by saying, 'Monsieur my cousin, you are most welcome indeed. There is no man in the world I so much long to see as you. Praise be to God that we have met here for this good purpose.' The King of England replied to this greeting in quite good French.

Then the Chancellor of England began to speak. He began with a prophecy—with which the English are never unprovided—which said that at Picquigny an important treaty of peace between France and England would be concluded. Then were brought forward the letters that the king had delivered to the King of England regarding the treaty. The Chancellor asked the king if he had ordered them thus drawn up and if they were satisfactory to him. The king said that they were, as were the letters which had been delivered to him from the King of England.

Thereupon the missal was produced, and each of the kings, extending one hand above it and touching with the other a cross containing a sliver of the True Cross, swore to maintain what they had promised each other—that is, the truce of seven years, including the allies of both sides, and the agreement for the marriage of their children as set forth in the treaty.

After this oath had been taken, our king, who had a ready tongue, said jokingly to the King of England that he would have to come to Paris; our king would offer him entertainments with ladies present and would give him as confessor the Cardinal of Bourbon, who would quickly absolve him of his sins, if he committed any—for King Edward well knew that the cardinal was a *bon compaignon*.

After the conversation on this subject, or similar, had lasted a little while, the king, who demonstrated that his was the commanding voice at this interview, bade us retire, telling us that he wished to speak with the King of England in private. The King of England's men withdrew likewise, without waiting to be told. After the two kings had conversed a little, the king summoned me and asked the King of England if he knew me. He replied that he did, naming the places where he had seen me and mentioning former occasions when I had undertaken to be of service to him at Calais, in those days when I was with the Duke of Burgundy.

The king asked what the King of England would like him to do, should the Duke of Burgundy refuse to accept the truce—he having already so arrogantly disdained it, as you have heard. King Edward replied that he should offer it to him once more and that if the duke still refused, he, King Edward, would leave it to the two of them. After that, the king brought up the subject of the Duke of Brittany— the real reason for his initiating this line of conversation—and asked him the same question. The King of England replied by asking him not to make war on the Duke of Brittany and declared that in his need he had never found so true a friend. The king said no more on the matter. With the most gracious and amiable words he could find, having recalled the escorts on both sides, he took leave of the

King of England, not neglecting to make some cordial remark to each one of that king's attendants. Thus at the same moment, or almost so, the kings withdrew from the barricade and mounted horse. Our king returned to Amiens and the King of England to his army; the latter was provided, from the king's household, with everything he could need, even including torches and candles.

The Duke of Gloucester [Richard, later Richard III], the King of England's other brother, and some others showed their discontent with this treaty by absenting themselves from this interview. But afterwards they came round; the Duke of Gloucester soon paid a visit to the king at Amiens, and the king gave him very handsome presents, such as valuable plate and horses with trappings.

As the king was returning to Amiens from the interview, he spoke to me along the road about two aspects of it. He had found the King of England very eager to come to Paris, a fact that had not pleased him. 'He's a very handsome king', he said. 'He's crazy about women. He could find some clever sweetheart in Paris who would say such nice things to him that she'd make him want to come back.' King Edward's predecessors, he added, had been all too often in Paris and Normandy; he had no desire for his presence on this side of the Channel; but, as long as he stayed on his own side, the king did want him for a good brother and friend.

The king was still worried by the fact that he had found King Edward somewhat rigorous when he had spoken to him about the Duke of Brittany; the king had been very eager to win over the King of England to giving him a free hand to make war in Brittany. He had my lords du Bouchage and de St Pierre sound that king again on the subject; but when King Edward realized that he was being pressed, he said that if there were any hostilities against Brittany he would again cross the Channel to defend it. Having learned this response, our king said nothing more to him about the matter.

As the king was going to supper after his return to Amiens, there arrived to sup with him three or four of the King of England's people who had aided in bringing about this treaty. My lord Howard began to whisper in the king's ear that if the king so wished, he would find the means of persuading his master to come to Amiens, perchance even to Paris, to make good cheer with the king. Though this offer was anything but pleasing, King Louis kept a very amiable countenance and, saying little in reply, began to wash; but he whispered in my ear that just what he had prophesied had come about, namely, this offer. The English spoke of it again after supper, but as adroitly as possible we scotched this enterprise, saying that the king would have to depart immediately in order to go against the Duke of Burgundy.

Although these matters were of the gravest importance and those on both sides took all pains to manage them sagaciously, there occurred some amusing things which are worth preserving. No one should be astonished, considering the great evils the English have visited upon this realm, and recently, that the king spared neither money nor energy to expel them from it in amiable fashion, so that he could keep them as friends in the future or at least avoid their making war on him.

The day after our interview [Wednesday, 30 August, the day of the Holy Innocents that Commynes has already described], a great many English came to Amiens. Some of them told us that the Holy Ghost had brought about this treaty—for with them everything is founded on prophecies and omens. What made them say this was that a white pigeon had perched on the King of England's tent the day of the interview and, despite the noise in the camp, had refused to budge. Some were of the opinion, however, that since it had rained a little and then the sun shone bright, the pigeon had perched on the royal tent, the highest elevation, in order to dry its feathers. This view was expressed to me by a Gascon gentleman named Louis de Bretaylle, a servant of the King of England, who was very much discontented with this treaty. Because he had known me a long time, he said to me privately that we would ridicule the King of England. I asked him how many battles that king had won. He told me nine, at which he himself had been present. I then asked him how many his master had lost. He said that the English king had lost but one—this one that we were making him lose. He added that, in his view, the shame King Edward had incurred in thus being sent home outweighed the honour he had achieved in winning the other nine battles.

I recounted this conversation to the king, who said to me—he's a rascal, that one, and must be prevented from talking like that. The king sent him an invitation to dinner and had him dine at the royal table. He offered him all sorts of benefits and opportunities if he were willing to remain in France. When he saw that de Bretaylle was unwilling to do so, he gave him a thousand crowns in coin and promised to favour the brothers of de Bretaylle living here; and I whispered an entreaty in his ear that he do all he could to further the friendship which had been established between the two kings.

There was nothing in the world our king feared more than that he would let slip some remark which would lead the English to think they were being mocked. As it happened, on this day following the interview, as the king was in his private chamber with but three or four of us, he let slip some joking remark about the wines and gifts that he had sent to the English army. [According to an interpolation in the *Chronique Scandaleuse*, Louis said that he had driven out the English more easily than his father had done, for he had driven them out by having them devour venison pastries and drink good wine.] Then, on turning his head, he saw a Gascon merchant, resident in England, who had come to ask for permission to export a certain quantity of Gascon wines from Bordeaux without paying duty—a concession that could be immensely profitable to the merchant if it was granted him. The king was very much amazed at the sight of the merchant and at the fact that he had gained entry to the chamber. He asked him what the name was of his native town in Guienne, and then whether he had married in England. The merchant said that he had, but did not possess much of value there. With that, even before the merchant left the chamber, the king provided him with an escort, a man who conducted him to Bordeaux. On the king's command, I spoke to him; and he received a very good office in his native town and the concession he was seeking for export of wines and a thousand francs in coin to defray the costs of having his wife join him. So that he need not go himself to England, a brother of his was sent there to fetch her. Thus the king adjudged himself guilty in paying this 'fine', acknowledging that he had talked too freely.

On this day, the one following our interview, the Constable sent a servant of his named [Jean] Rapine, on whom the king afterwards conferred benefits; he was a faithful servant to his master. He brought letters to the king, who designated [Jean de Daillon] my lord du Lude and me to hear his credence.

My lord de Contay had now returned to the king after the practice against the Constable which I have described above. The Constable no longer knew to which saint to vow himself and considered himself lost. Rapine's relation to us [i.e. his credence] was very humble. His master, Rapine said, knew well that many charges had been

o

levelled against him, but the king could well realize, from experience, that the Constable had knowingly committed no fault. To better assure the king of his good intentions, he outlined some scheme of persuading the Duke of Burgundy to aid the king, if he so wished, in giving a beating to the King of England and his crew. It appeared indeed, from Rapine's way of speaking, that his master had lost all hope. We told him that we had achieved a good accord with the English and had no desire to stir up strife. My lord du Lude, who was with me, was brash enough to ask Rapine if he knew where his master kept his store of coin. I was astonished that this question (undoubtedly reported by Rapine, a very faithful servant) did not prompt the Constable to perceive the truth of his plight and what was being prepared for him and take flight—given also the peril in which he had found himself only a year before. But then in my lifetime I have known of few people, either in France or elsewhere, who had the sense to flee in time. Some are completely without hope of a secure asylum in neighbouring countries, while others are too much attached to their possessions, their wives, and their children. For such reasons many men of high position have lost their lives.

When we had made our report to the king [of what Rapine had said], he summoned a secretary. At the moment he had with him only my lord Howard, who knew nothing of what was in store for the Constable, and my lord de Contay, just returned from the Duke of Burgundy, and we two [Commynes and lord du Lude] who had spoken with Rapine. The king dictated a letter for the Constable, in which he reported the signing of the truce the day before, said that he was involved in many great affairs and needed a good head like the Constable's to aid him. Then he turned to the Englishman and my lord de Contay and observed to them, 'I do not mean us to have the body, but only the head—the body can stay where it is'. This letter was delivered to Rapine, who found it very encouraging: he thought it kind of the king to say that he had need of such a head as his master's—Rapine not perceiving the underlying meaning of the sentence.

The King of England sent our king the letters of credence the Constable had written him, along with all the messages he had dispatched to Edward IV. Thus can you behold the situation in which the Constable had put himself among these three mighty rulers, all of whom wished him dead.

After the King of England had received his money, he headed straight for Calais by forced marches, for he feared the hatred of the Duke of Burgundy and of the people of the countryside; and, in truth, when his soldiers straggled, one of them invariably remained lying in the bushes. He left as hostages, as he had promised, my lord Howard and Sir John Cheyney, Master of the Horse, until he recrossed the Channel.

You have heard, at the beginning of this narrative of the English invasion, how King Edward had little heart for the enterprise. For as soon as he arrived at Dover, in England, and before taking ship to cross, he had entered into quasi-negotiations with us. He invaded France for two reasons: first, the pressure exerted by his whole people, who desired the invasion, as is their custom, and the pressure put upon them by the Duke of Burgundy; and second, the opportunity of keeping for himself a large part of the subsidies he had raised in England to mount the invasion. For the kings of England have no revenues but those of the royal domain, except when they raise money for waging war in France.

Another clever device King Edward had employed, this one to [help] prevent grumbling by his subjects if he failed to make war. He had brought with him ten or a dozen men, big fat ones, some from London and some from other towns, who were leading figures of the English commons and who had done much to promote the invasion and raise [funds for] the army. King Edward had them quartered in handsome tents, but campaigning was not at all the sort of life they were used to and they quickly wearied of it—three days after they had landed at Calais they were worrying that there would be a battle. The King of England stimulated their doubts and fears and thus prompted them to look favourably upon the peace, so that when the army had recrossed to England, they would help him in extinguishing the objections which might be raised because of the way the king had returned. For never did the King of England, since King Arthur, bring so many men, in a single expedition, to this side of the Channel. He returned very quickly, as you have heard; and there remained in his coffers a great deal of the money he had raised in England for the payment of his troops. Thus did he achieve the greater part of his aims. He did not have the temperament to endure the toils required of a King of England who hopes for a career of conquest in France. As for our king, he had well provided on this occasion for the defence of the realm, though he would not have been able to defend himself against the enemies he had everywhere, for he had too many.

Another ardent desire cherished by the King of England was the accomplishment of the marriage of King Charles VIII who reigns today [then Dauphin] with his daughter [Elizabeth]; and for the sake of this marriage he afterwards closed his eyes to many things, which proceeding resulted in great gains for our king.

After the English had recrossed the Channel, save for the hostages who were with the king, the latter moved towards Laon, halting at a small town named Vervins near the borders of Hainault. In [the border town of] Avesnes were the Chancellor of Burgundy [Guillaume Hugonet] and other ambassadors, along with the lord de Contay, representing the Duke of Burgundy. The king desired, for this time, a complete pacification. This great number of English had put fear in him, for in his lifetime he had seen what they had done in the realm and had no wish for them to return.

The king received a request from the Burgundian Chancellor to dispatch his envoys to a bridge half way between Avesnes and Vervins, where the Burgundian representatives would meet them. The king sent word that he himself would come there, although there were some whom he consulted who were not in favour of his going. Nevertheless he went there, taking with him the English hostages. They were present when the king received the Burgundian ambassadors, who came splendidly escorted by archers and other soldiers. At that audience they had no other words with the king except those of greeting, and they were then given dinner.

One of the English [hostages] began to regret the [Anglo-French] treaty. He told me, as we were together at a window, that if his countrymen had seen an army of such soldiers (as those accompanying the Burgundian envoys) with the Duke of Burgundy, perhaps they would not have made peace. My lord [Jean de Foix, Viscount] of Narbonne, who today is called my lord [Count] of Foix, heard this remark and said to him, 'Were you so simple-minded as to suppose that the Duke of Burgundy did not have great numbers of such troops? He had merely sent them off to refit. But you were so eager to return home that six hundred casks of wine and a pension that the king is giving you sent you back very quickly to England.'

The Englishman, angered, retorted, 'This is just what everybody told us, that you would ridicule us. Do you call the money that the king is giving us a pension? It is tribute. And, by St George, you could go on saying so much about it that we might return.' I interrupted this talk, treating it as a joke; but the Englishman was not mollified and he mentioned it to the king, who flew into a rage against the lord of Narbonne.

The king said little to the Chancellor of Burgundy at this time; it was arranged that his embassy would come to Vervins, and so it did, journeying there with the king. Once arrived at Vervins, the king commissioned Tanneguy du Chastel, Pierre Doriole the Chancellor of France and others to carry on negotiations. Both sides began with recriminations and with justifications of their positions. Our representatives made their report to the king, declaring that these Burgundians were using arrogant language but that they themselves had nailed them right to the floor, and they repeated the replies they had made. The king, dissatisfied with their conduct, told them that all such responses had been made many times and that there was no question of a final peace; it was a matter of a truce only, and he forbade them to use any more language like that and said that he himself would deal with the Burgundians. He then summoned the Chancellor and the other envoys to his chamber, having with him only the late Admiral, the Bastard of Bourbon, my lord du Bouchage and me. He concluded a truce good for nine years, based on the *status quo*. The ambassadors, however, begged the king not to have the truce immediately proclaimed, in order to save the oath of the duke, who had sworn not to take a truce until the King of England had been outside the realm for a certain period [three months—see above, p. *168*], in order that there be no appearance of his having subscribed to the Anglo-French treaty. [In fact, the duke signed the truce on 13 September, only two weeks after the English army departed from Amiens.]

The King of England, who was extremely irritated by the duke's refusal to be included in his truce and had been informed that the king was negotiating a separate treaty with him, sent a knight named Thomas Mongomery, one of his chief intimates, to the king at Vervins, Mongomery arriving as the king was negotiating the treaty with the Burgundian envoys. Sir Thomas requested the king not make any other truce with the duke than the one provided for in the Treaty of Picquigny. He also asked him not to deliver St Quentin to the duke. He then offered that, if the king wished to continue at war with the duke, King Edward would recross the Channel at the next campaigning season in order to aid him, provided that the king recompensed the King of England for the loss he would incur because the duties collected by the Wool Staple at Calais [where English wools were sold to Burgundian merchants] would be worth nothing (these duties sometimes bringing in 50,000 crowns [about £10,000] annually), and provided that the king also paid half the costs of the English army, King Edward paying the other half. The king expressed profound thanks to the King of England for this offer and presented Sir Thomas with a gift of valuable plate. He made excuses for not continuing the war, saying that the truce with Burgundy was already agreed upon and that it was the same that the two kings had signed with the same duration of nine years [the English truce was actually for seven], but that the duke had wanted a separate document. Thus the king explained away the matter as best he could in order to satisfy the English envoy, who then returned to England and the two hostages with him.

The king was greatly amazed at these offers that the King of England had made him—I was the only one present to hear them. He considered that it would have been a very perilous proceeding to have the King of England recross the Channel. It does not take much to put French and English at odds when they are together, and the English might well have again allied themselves with the Burgundians. Thus the king became even more desirous of concluding the truce with the Duke of Burgundy.

Once the truce was concluded, negotiations regarding the Constable were resumed; and, to put it briefly, the arrangements made at Bouvignes, which I have previously mentioned, were taken up again, each side delivering to the other its agreement, signed and sealed, on the matter. The bargain that was thus struck gave to the duke St Quentin, Ham and Bohain and everything that the Constable owned in the Burgundian domain and all his movables, wherever they were; and it set forth the way in which the Constable was to be besieged within Ham, where he then was, with provision that the first one [the king or the duke] who could capture him was to have him executed in eight days or yield him up to the other.

This bargaining immediately aroused fears; and most of the Constable's chief adherents, like my lord de Genlis and several others, began to desert him. The Constable, who knew that the King of England had turned over his letters and had revealed what he knew of him, and that his enemies had been negotiating a truce, became terror-stricken and sent a message to the Duke of Burgundy begging him to provide a safe conduct so that the Constable could go speak to him about matters that greatly concerned him. At first the duke evaded the issue, but in the end he provided a safe conduct.

This powerful man, the Constable, had already had long thoughts about the right direction in which to flee, for he was informed of everything and had seen a copy of the documents drawn up at Bouvignes to dispose of him. On one occasion he addressed himself to some adherents of his who were from Lorraine: he deliberated fleeing with them into the Empire and taking a large sum of money —for the road was quite safe—in order to buy a place on the Rhine and remain there until he had come to terms with the king or the duke. Another time he decided to hold out in his stronghold of Ham, the fortification of which had cost him so much, for he had accomplished it in order to save himself in just such a necessity as this; and indeed Ham was as completely furnished with provisions and munitions as any castle that we had knowledge of. Yet he did not find to stay there with him people whom he trusted, for all his servants were natives either of France or of the Burgundian domain. Perhaps he lived in such fear that he did not dare to confide sufficiently in them; for I certainly believe he could have found men who would not have abandoned him, and a goodly number of them. He had less cause to fear being besieged by the two princes than by only one, for it would have been impossible for the French and Burgundian armies to co-operate.

His last resort was to head for the Duke of Burgundy, trusting in the safe conduct. This he did, taking with him but fifteen or twenty horse, and went to Mons in Hainault, where dwelt the lord of Aimeries, Grand Bailli of Hainault, the Constable's dearest friend. And there he sojourned, awaiting word from the Duke of Burgundy. The latter had begun war against the Duke of Lorraine because that duke had declared war on him when he was besieging Neuss and had wrought great destruction in his province of Luxembourg.

As soon as the king learned of the Constable's departure, he decided to take steps to prevent the Constable's regaining the friendship of the Duke of Burgundy. He hastened to St Quentin with seven or eight hundred men of arms he had assembled for the purpose, well aware of the situation within the town. As he approached St Quentin, some of the inhabitants came forth to give him an obedient welcome. The king commanded me to enter the town and arrange for quarters. I did so, and the troops then entered; and after them the king made his entrance, warmly received by the citizens. Some of the Constable's men withdrew into Hainault.

The king himself immediately sent word to the Duke of Burgundy of the taking of St Quentin, in order to destroy any hopes he might have of regaining the town through the agency of the Constable. As soon as the duke received this news, he dispatched an order to my lord of Aimeries to have the town of Mons so well guarded that the Constable could not slip away, and to forbid the Constable to leave his quarters. The Bailli of Hainault, not daring to refuse, carried out the order. Nevertheless, the town was not so closely guarded that a single man could not have escaped from it, had he wished to flee.

Commynes muses that that deceitful goddess Fortune had indeed turned a baleful countenance upon the Constable. Yet Fortune is but a poetic fiction. The Constable was, in truth, abandoned by God as a punishment for his having constantly worked with all his power to keep the king and the duke at war with one another—no difficult task since they were so opposite of temperament.

With the Constable thus under house arrest, the king requested the Duke of Burgundy either to deliver up the prisoner or else fulfill the agreement [i.e. execute him]. The duke, sending word that he would do so, had the Constable brought to Péronne under close guard.

The Duke of Burgundy had already captured several places in the Duchies of Lorraine and Bar and was besieging Nancy [the capital of Lorraine], which, however, defended itself stoutly. The king had a strong force in Champagne, which made the duke fearful, for there was no provision in the truce allowing him to destroy the Duke of Lorraine, who had withdrawn to the king. My lord du Bouchage and other royal envoys strongly pressed the duke to make good what he had promised. He kept saying that he would do so; and thus the limit of eight days within which he was obliged to deliver up or execute the Constable was exceeded by more than a month. Meanwhile the duke remained under great pressure from the royal ambassadors and in constant fear that the king might prevent the conquest of Lorraine that he longed to achieve in order to secure passage from Luxembourg to the County and Duchy of Burgundy and thus have all his territories united (for, once he possessed the little Duchy of Lorraine, he could go from Holland to the vicinity of

Lyons without setting foot outside his domains). For these reasons, he dispatched a directive to his Chancellor and the lord de Humbercourt, both enemies of the Constable, that they should proceed to Péronne and, on a day that he named, should deliver the Constable to those whom the king would send there—for the Chancellor and de Humbercourt had full power to act for the duke in his absence—and the duke likewise ordered my lord of Aimeries to deliver the Constable to them.

Meanwhile, the duke hotly bombarded Nancy. There were first rate troops within, who defended it valiantly. One of the duke's captains, the Count of Campobasso, a native of the Kingdom of Naples, from which he had been banished for supporting the House of Anjou there [against Alfonso V of Aragon], had already established a secret connection with the Duke of Lorraine. (For my lord of Lorraine, who was a close relative and heir of the House of Anjou [being the grandson, on his mother's side of René, Duke of Anjou and Lorraine, titular King of Naples], had found the means of winning him over; and it was also the count's devotion to the House of Anjou which led him to betray his master in serving the Duke of Lorraine.) Campobasso promised to draw out this siege and to see that military equipment necessary for the capture of the town would be unavailable. He could indeed accomplish what he promised, for he was then the chief commander of the Burgundian army—and the evil star of his master, as I shall hereafter explain. All this was but a foretaste of the disasters that were to fall upon the Duke of Burgundy.

I believe that the duke expected to capture Nancy before the day appointed for delivering up the Constable, in which case he would not have kept his word. For the king's part, it can be that if he had had the Constable in his hands, he would have done more for the Duke of Lorraine than he did; for he was informed of Campobasso's connection with that duke, but he did nothing about it. On several counts, he was under no obligation to allow the Duke of Burgundy a free hand in Lorraine, had he not wished to; and he had large forces near that Duchy.

The Duke of Burgundy was unable to capture Nancy before the day on which his people, on his orders, were to deliver up the Constable. Consequently, when that day had passed, they carried out the command of their master, and gladly, for they hated the Constable. At the gate of Péronne they put him into the hands of the

Bastard of Bourbon, Admiral of France, and of my lord de St Pierre, who brought him to Paris. Some have told me that three hours after he was surrendered, messengers came posting from the duke to countermand his order; but he acted too late.

In Paris, the trial of the Constable was immediately begun, the king putting great pressure on the Parlement of Paris. People were appointed to conduct the trial; the evidences against him turned over by the King of England were examined; and finally the Constable was condemned to suffer death and the confiscation of his possessions.

The Duke of Burgundy's surrender of the Constable was strange indeed. I do not say this to excuse the Constable's faults or to blame the duke, for St Pol had done the duke much wrong. But there was no need for the Duke of Burgundy, a prince so great and of a House so renowned and honourable, to give him a safe conduct in order to seize him; and it was very cruel of the duke to deliver him up, out of greed, to certain death. Once he had committed this shameful act, it was not long before he was afflicted with troubles. Judging from the things that God has brought to pass in our time and brings to pass every day, it appears that he is unwilling to leave any wrong doing unpunished—and it can be seen openly that these strange happenings are of His doing, for such sudden punishments are out-side the realm of natural phenomena. They are directed especially against those who are violent and cruel—and these usually cannot be insignificant persons but rather the very great, either rulers or men in high authority with a prince.

For long years this House of Burgundy had flourished; during the century or thereabouts in which four of its dukes had reigned, the House was as highly reputed as any in Christendom—for others greater than it had suffered afflictions and adversity whereas it had enjoyed happiness and prosperity.

The first great ruler of this House was Philip the Bold, brother of King Charles V, who espoused [Margaret] the heiress of the Count of Flanders and hence Countess of that region and also of Artois and of Burgundy [i.e. Franche-Comté], Nevers and Rethel. The second was John [the Fearless, murdered on the bridge of Montereau in 1419]. The third was Duke Philip the Good, who annexed Brabant, Luxembourg, Limbourg, Holland, Zeeland, Hainault and Namur. The fourth has been this Duke Charles, who, upon the death of his father, was one of the richest princes of Christendom, possessing

more magnificent jewels and plate [of silver and gold], tapestries,
books and linens than could be found in three greater Houses. Other
Houses, it is true, had richer treasuries of coin, for Duke Philip the
Good had not levied taxes for a long time. Nevertheless, on Philip's
death, Duke Charles found more than 300,000 crowns in his coffers,
and he found his domain at peace with its neighbours, though that
peace did not last long. I do not, however, mean to attribute to him
the starting of the wars, for others were equally responsible.

His lordships, immediately after the death of his father, accorded
him an annual subsidy for ten years—and did so very willingly and
with little urging, each acting on its own—which subsidy could well
amount to 350,000 crowns a year, not including the sum contributed
by the Duchy of Burgundy. At the time the duke delivered up the
Constable, he was raising more than 300,000 crowns; in addition, he
had more than 300,000 crowns in coin in his treasury. And all the
Constable's possessions he received were not worth 80,000 crowns,
for in coin he had only 76,000. Thus the grounds for committing so
great a wrong were insignificant.

God raised up against the duke an enemy who had very little
power (it was the Duke of Lorraine) and was very young and of
small experience in affairs. God brought it about that an officer of the
duke [of Burgundy], whom he then trusted more than any other,
became treacherous and evil and He caused him to be suspicious of
his subjects and his loyal servants. Are there not here the very same
portents that God, in the Old Testament, visited upon those whose
fortunes he wished to alter from good to bad? The duke's heart,
hardened in pride, never softened, but to the very end he believed
that all his good fortunes were due to his own intelligence and
talents.

Even before delivering up the Constable, he had become ex-
ceedingly mistrustful of his subjects or held them in great contempt;
for he had sent into Italy to recruit a thousand lances, and at the siege
of Neuss there were large numbers of Italian men of arms with him.

Of these the Count of Campobasso commanded four hundred or
more. After he lost his lands in the Kingdom of Naples, as a result of
serving the House of Anjou in the wars there, he had then been in
Provence with René of Anjou [who was Count of Provence] or with
[René's grandson] Duke Nicolas [of Lorraine], son of Duke John.
Upon Duke Nicolas' death, the Duke of Burgundy had taken into
service a number of his men, especially all the Italians, like the

aforementioned count and Giacomo Galeotto, a very valiant, honourable and loyal gentleman, and many others.

The Count of Campobasso, when he went into Italy to recruit his company of soldiers, received from the Duke of Burgundy a subsidy of forty thousand ducats. In passing by Lyons, he made the acquaintance of a physician named Master Simon of Pavia, through whom he sent word to the king that if the king met certain conditions, he would, on his return from Italy, deliver the Duke of Burgundy into the king's hands. Campobasso said the same thing to my lord de St Pierre, then in [the Duke of Savoy's province of] Piedmont as a royal ambassador. After the count had returned, quartering his troops in the county of Marle, he again made his offer to the king, declaring that as soon as he joined his master in the field, he would without fail either kill him or take him prisoner. He even described how he would do this: the Duke of Burgundy, he said, often made a tour of his camp riding a small horse and accompanied by few people—which was true—and at such a time the count would not fail to kill or capture him. Campobasso made still another proposal, offering, if one day the armies of the king and the duke were ranged against each other for battle, to come over to the king's side with his troops, provided certain conditions were met.

The king had nothing but contempt for Campobasso's treachery; and, deciding to be completely open with the Duke of Burgundy, he made known all this to him through my lord de Contay. The duke, however, put no faith in this revelation, choosing to believe that the king had acted from ulterior motives, and cherished the count more than ever. You can therefore see that God had clouded the duke's mind, on this occasion, so that he ignored the clear evidences that the king sent him.

Giacomo Galeotto, on the other hand, was as good and loyal as the count was wicked and treacherous; and at the end of a long life he died in great honour and renown.

BOOK FIVE

The Downfall of Burgundy
1476–77

AFTER THE DUKE OF BURGUNDY HAD CONQUERED ALL OF
Lorraine and received from the king the Constable's movables and
St Quentin, Ham and Bohain, he entered into negotiations with the
king about settling their affairs by an interview at Auxerre, the two
of them to meet on a bridge over a river like the one that had been
constructed at Picquigny for the interview of the king and King
Edward of England. Envoys went back and forth on this mission.
The duke wanted to rest a part of his army, which was in very bad
shape as a result of the siege of Neuss and the war in Lorraine, and
send the remainder to garrison some places near the Swiss towns of
Berne and Fribourg, most of which belonged to the Count de
Romont [Jacques, a son of the Duke of Savoy, and one of Duke
Charles' chief officers]. He intended to make war on Berne and
Fribourg because they had invaded the County of Burgundy when
he was besieging Neuss, and had helped to deprive him of the
County of Ferrette, as you have heard [see p. *149*], and had seized
part of the lands of the Count de Romont. The king urgently
solicited the duke to agree to this interview and also to leave in peace
these poor Swiss folk and rest his army.

The Swiss, realizing that the duke was pressing close to them, sent
him an embassy with an offer to restore what they had taken from
the Count de Romont. That count, on the other hand, was urging the duke to come succour him in person. The duke refused to heed
the prudent counsel—which was on all counts the best, considering
the season of the year [midwinter] and the condition of his army—

and decided to march against the Swiss. By an exchange of letters it was agreed between the king and him that they would not come to blows over Lorraine [the king having given him the option of taking all the Constable's possessions or keeping the places in Lorraine that he had won, and the duke choosing the latter alternative].

The duke, setting out from Lorraine with his army, entered the Duchy of Burgundy, where ambassadors from this old German league called the Swiss Confederation came to meet him with much more attractive proposals than before. They offered, in addition to restoring the Count de Romont's places, to abandon all their alliances of which he disapproved, especially the alliance with the king, and to become his allies and serve him against the king with six thousand men at modest wages, any time he should so require. The duke, however, would listen to no offers, being already in the grip of his unhappy fate.

What are called in their own regions the New Alliances consist of the cities of Bâle and Strasbourg and other imperial towns along the Rhine, which, for long, had been enemies of the Swiss and had supported Duke Sigismund of Austria at the time he was at war with them. Since then, they had made an alliance with the Swiss for ten years, as had also Duke Sigismund [the celebrated League of Constance, concluded in 1474]. This league was accomplished under the auspices of the king and by his guidance and at his expense—as you have seen previously, at the time that the Duke of Burgundy was deprived of the County of Ferrette and Pierre de Hagenbach, the duke's governor there, was put to death, Hagenbach's brutality and extortions having been the cause of this disaster, a major one for the duke because all his other reverses originated from it.

This alliance that the king had brought about turned to his great advantage, a greater advantage than most people realize. I believe that it was one of the wisest things he ever did, and the one that wreaked the most harm upon his enemies. For after the Duke of Burgundy was overthrown, never was there a man who dared raise his head against the king or gainsay his will—I mean those who were his subjects and in his realm—for all the others had only steered their course in the wake of the duke. It was therefore a master stroke to create the alliance of Duke Sigismund of Austria and the New Alliance with the Swiss, who for so long had been enemies; and it was not accomplished without great expense and many embassies.

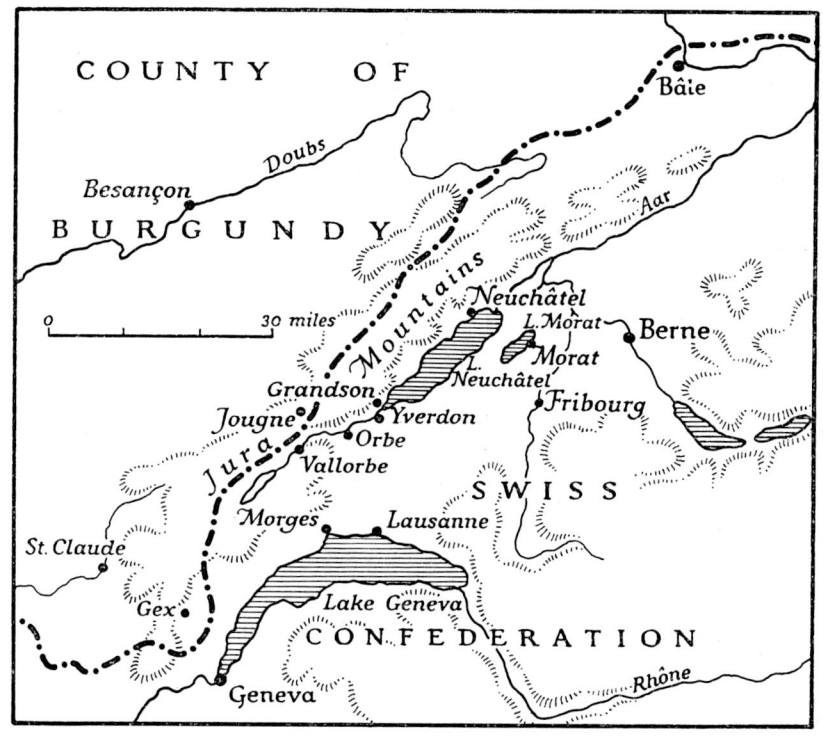

GRANDSON AND MORAT

After the Duke of Burgundy had destroyed the hope of the Swiss envoys of being able to come to terms with him, they returned to inform their people and to make ready to defend themselves. The duke and his army marched for the Pays de Vaud in Savoy [now a part of Switzerland: see map] which the Swiss had taken from my lord de Romont, as has been said; and the duke captured three or four places belonging to the lord de Châteauguion [an adherent of the duke] which the Swiss held but only weakly. The Duke of Burgundy then went on to besiege a place called Grandson [near the southwestern tip of Lake Neuchâtel], which also belonged to the lord de Châteauguion. The Swiss had garrisoned it with seven or eight hundred picked men, for the town lay close to their territories and they intended to defend it stoutly.

The duke had a very large army, for every hour it was swelled by troops from Lombardy and natives of the Duchy of Savoy. Duke Charles preferred these aliens to his own subjects, and he was able to recruit plenty of such mercenaries, and good ones—indeed, the death of the Constable had increased his mistrust of his own people and stimulated other suspicions of his about them. The duke possessed a large and powerful artillery; he lived with great pomp in his camp in order to impress the embassies coming from Italy and Germany; and he had with him all his best jewels, a great display of gold and silver plate, and numerous other ornaments. His head teemed with ambitious visions concerning the Duchy of Milan, in which he intended to establish a following.

After he had besieged and bombarded Grandson for some days, the defenders surrendered unconditionally [28 February 1476] and, on his order, were all put to death. By that time the Swiss had assembled an army—not a large one, however, as I have heard several of them relate; for they do not raise as many troops from their territories as is thought and they raised still fewer then than now because since that time most of them have left their fields in order to become mercenaries. Their army had few contingents from their allies, for they were forced to mobilize in haste in order to succour Grandson. Just as they were taking the field, they learned of the deaths of their comrades there.

The Duke of Burgundy, against the counsel of those whose opinions he asked, decided to march to meet the Swiss at the foot of the mountains, where they still were. By this decision the duke deprived himself of a great advantage, for his camp was situated in a very good place for awaiting the enemy, being enclosed by his artillery and, on one side, by a lake [Neuchâtel]; and it did not appear that the Swiss had the slightest chance of making a successful attack.

He had sent ahead a hundred archers to secure the entrance to a certain mountain pass, and they encountered the Swiss [on 2 March 1476]. He himself then moved forward, while the greater part of his army was yet in the plain. The troops nearest the Swiss sought to turn back in order to unite with the main body. The soldiers at the rear thought that those in front were fleeing, and they took to flight. Thus little by little this advance force began to retreat towards the camp, some men valiantly doing their duty. Finally when they reached the army, there was no attempt to make a stand; instead the whole mass of troops began to flee. The Swiss won the duke's camp and his artillery and all the tents and pavilions and infinite spoils, for the Burgundians escaped only with their lives. All the magnificent jewels of the duke were lost, but as to soldiers, he lost on this occasion only seven men of arms. All the remainder fled, and he with them. It were better said of him, that he lost both honour and possessions this day, than of King John of France who, fighting valiantly, was captured at the battle of Poitiers [1356].

Here was the first calamity and misfortune that the Duke of Burgundy had ever experienced. In all his other enterprises he had won the honours or the profit. What harm befell him this day for consulting only himself and scorning counsel! What harm his House received from this disaster, and in what pitiful state it is still—and likely to be for a long time! How many kinds of people became the duke's enemies, and so declared themselves, who only the day before had treated with him deferentially and feigned to be his friends! And what cause provoked this war? It was a wagon load of sheep-skins that my lord de Romont seized from a Swiss passing through his lands!

If God had not forsaken the duke, it is not comprehensible that he would have put himself in peril for so insignificant a matter, con-sidering the offers the Swiss had made him and the impossibility, if he fought them, of gaining either profit or glory. For at that time they did not have the high repute they enjoy today, and no people were poorer. I have heard from a knight of theirs, who had been on the first embassy they sent to the Duke of Burgundy, that he had told the duke, in the course of their attempts to dissuade him from this war, that he could hope to gain nothing by it for their country

P

was poor and barren and those taken prisoner would be lean pickings —the spurs and bridles of the duke's cavalry, he believed, were worth more than the sum of the ransoms that captured Swiss could pay.

Coming back to the battle of Grandson—the king was soon informed of what had happened [about 9 March], for he had numerous spies and messengers throughout the region, most of them dispatched by my hand. He was overjoyed by the news, his only regret being the small number of Burgundians killed. He maintained his headquarters at Lyons, in order to receive reports more quickly and be in a position to take immediate action to counter the Duke of Burgundy's moves, whatever they might be. For the foresighted king feared lest the duke force the Swiss to ally with him. The House of Savoy he disposed of as his own; the Duke of Milan was his ally; King René of Naples [René of Anjou] wanted to put his county of Provence in the duke's hands. If the duke had succeeded in his enterprise, he would have been the master of a territory stretching from the North Sea to the Mediterranean, and, had he so willed, the inhabitants of France could have gone beyond its borders only by sea, since he would have held Lorraine, Savoy and Provence.

The king was dispatching messengers in all directions. One whom he sent to was his sister [Yolande], the Duchess of Savoy, a partisan of the duke. Another was his uncle King René, who, however, hardly listened to his messengers but reported everything to the duke. The king sent to the Swiss Confederation, but his men had great difficulty getting through because the roads were guarded. He therefore had to employ beggars and pilgrims and such folk. The Swiss towns replied arrogantly: 'Tell the king', they said, 'that if he does not declare himself [against the Duke of Burgundy], we will come to terms with the duke and then declare against him.' The king feared that they might do so. He had no intention of declaring himself against the duke, and so he continued to fear that the duke might find out about his network of spies and messengers.

We must now see how the world changed after this battle, and how people sang a different tune, and how our king managed everything wisely. And it will be a fine example for those young lords who foolishly rush into enterprises without realizing what can happen to them and without having any experience and who scorn the counsel of those whom they should consult.

First of all, the duke himself sent the lord de Contay to the king as the bearer of humble and gracious words--quite contrary to his nature. Behold then how a single hour changed him! He requested the king to maintain their truce loyally, excused himself for not having met with the king at Auxerre, and gave assurances that he would, in a short time, come to Auxerre for their interview, or anywhere else that was designated. The king gave the lord de Contay a hearty welcome and granted all his requests—for he did not yet think it time to do the opposite. He was fully aware of the fundamental loyalty of the duke's people and knew that [should he show himself the aggressor] they would all rally to the duke's cause; and he wanted to see the end of this adventure, which meant not providing any motive for the duke and his dissident subjects to fall into accord. Whatever the good cheer that the king made the lord de Contay, however, the latter could not help hearing the ridicule heaped on the duke throughout the city of Lyons, for songs in praise of the conquerors and in derision of the vanquished were being chanted in the streets.

As soon as the Duke of Milan, Galeazzo-Maria Sforza [son and successor to Louis XI's great ally, Francesco Sforza], had news of Grandson, he was overjoyed, notwithstanding that he was an ally of the duke [by the Treaty of Moncalieri, January 1475, a gross desertion of his alliance with Louis XI]; for he had made the alliance out of fear engendered by the high favour the other Italian states showed the Duke of Burgundy. In great haste the Duke of Milan dispatched to the king a most unimpressive envoy, a townsman of Milan [Giovanni Bianchi, whose dispatches bear out Commynes' judgement]. Through an intermediary he addressed himself to me and brought me letters from the duke. The king, when I informed him of the envoy's arrival, ordered me to hear him; for he was very much displeased with the duke, who had deserted his alliance to ally himself with the Duke of Burgundy, even though his wife [Bona of Savoy] was the sister of the Queen [Charlotte]. The ambassador's official statement ran as follows: his master the Duke of Milan had been informed that the king and the Duke of Burgundy were going to sign a final peace and alliance, which would greatly displease the duke his master. He gave some flimsy reasons why the king should not do so and finally said that if the king would bind himself to make neither peace nor truce with the Duke of Burgundy, the Duke of Milan would give him a hundred thousand ducats in coin.

Having heard from me the substance of the envoy's mission, the king had him summoned to a chamber, no one else present except me, and said to him tersely: 'Here is my lord d'Argenton, who has reported to me on your mission. Tell your master that I have no desire for his money—my annual revenues are three times greater than his. As for the question of peace and war, I will do as I wish. However, if he regrets having deserted my alliance to ally himself with the Duke of Burgundy, I am content to return as we were.'

The ambassador very humbly thanked the king—it seemed to him that the king was indeed far from avaricious—and begged him to have the alliance, in its old form, proclaimed immediately, saying that he had full powers to guarantee his master's adhesion. The king agreed to do so; and, after dinner, the alliance was proclaimed, and an ambassador was at once dispatched to Milan, where the alliance was proclaimed with great fanfare [Commynes here confuses a first Milanese mission, after Grandson, which was rejected, with a second, after the battle of Morat, which resulted in the renewal of the Franco-Milanese alliance on 9 August 1476, and its proclamation in Milan on the 25th]. Here already is another link in the chain of Burgundian adversities and the example of a powerful man [the Duke of Milan] changing attitude—he who had sent so splendidly impressive an embassy to the Duke of Burgundy to conclude an alliance, only three weeks before [actually, more than a year before, in January 1475].

King René of Naples was treating to make the Duke of Burgundy his heir and to put Provence in his hands. My lord de Châteauguion [brother of the lord killed at Grandson] was then in Savoyard Piedmont, *en route* to take possession of Provence in the name of the Duke of Burgundy, accompanied by others who were to raise troops there; they had with them twenty thousand crowns in coin. When the news of Grandson arrived, this mission barely escaped capture, and the Count of Bresse [Philip, a son of the Duke of Savoy], who happened to be in Piedmont, seized the money. The Duchess of Savoy, as soon as she had news of this battle, transmitted it to King René, making light of the defeat and of the loss of the money. Her messengers, natives of Provence, were intercepted [by the French], and thus was revealed King René's intrigue with the Duke of Burgundy.

The king immediately dispatched troops to the borders of Provence, and ambassadors to the King of Naples; the mission of the envoys was to request King René to come to their master, assuring him of finding a warm welcome, and to say that, should he refuse, the king would use force to settle the matter. King René was quickly persuaded to join the king at Lyons, where he was received with the greatest honour and cordiality [in April 1476].

I was present at the first exchange of words between the king and King René. In the course of it, Jean Cossa, Seneschal of Provence [a Neopolitan follower of the House of Anjou and chief confidant and adviser to René], a man of rank and of good lineage, native of the Kingdom of Naples, spoke up, as follows: 'Sire, don't marvel that my master, the king your uncle, offered to make the Duke of Burgundy his heir; for so was he counselled to do, especially by me, seeing that you, the son of his sister and his own nephew, had done him such great wrong in taking over the castle of Angers and castles in the Duchy of Bar and had so badly treated him in all his other affairs. We wished to push this bargaining with the Duke of Burgundy so that you had word of it, in order to prompt you to do us right and recognize that the king my master is indeed your uncle; but we never had any intention of bringing matters to a conclusion.' The king [a connoisseur of good service] very cordially—and wisely —accepted this explanation; and Jean Cossa spoke truly, for he had managed the Burgundian negotiations. Within a few days all differences were well settled; and the King of Naples, and all his servants too, received money; and the king fêted him with entertainments graced by the ladies and saw to it that he was given additional entertainments and treated to splendid occasions that approximated as closely as possible the kind of ceremony he so loved. The king and King René were now good friends and nothing more was said about the Duke of Burgundy, whom René completely renounced. Here is yet another link in the chain of that duke's adversities.

The Duchess of Savoy, who for a long time had been on very bad terms with the king her brother, sent a secret messenger, the lord de Montagny, who addressed himself to me in order to seek a reconciliation with the king. He set forth reasons why she had alienated herself from her brother and explained the fears that she had of him. However, she was a very clever woman—a true sister of the king our master—and was not being sincere in her talk of separating herself from the Duke of Burgundy and his friendship; and it appeared that she was seeking to temporize and to re-establish some kind of connection with the king. Through me, the king made her a very encouraging reply, coupled with a warm invitation to come to him; and then her ambassador was sent back. Here is another ally of the Duke of Burgundy who is intriguing to cut loose from him.

In all parts of Germany people began to declare against the duke, as did imperial cities like Nuremberg, Frankfurt and many others, who allied themselves with the Old and New Alliances against the duke—one would think that doing him a bad turn guaranteed remission of sins.

The spoils of Grandson greatly enriched these impoverished Swiss, who at first did not realize the value of what they had in their hands, especially the more ignorant ones. One of the costliest and most splendid pavilions in the world was cut into several pieces. Some sold a great quantity of silver plates and bowls for two silver coins apiece, thinking they were made of tin. The duke's great diamond, one of the largest in Christendom, from which hung a pearl, was carried off by one of the Swiss, who then put it back in its case and tossed it under a wagon; then he came back and picked it up and offered it to a priest for a florin. The latter sent it back to the [Swiss] lords, who gave him three francs for it. The Swiss also won for themselves three matched rubies called The Three Brothers; another great ruby called The Pack and another named The Ruby of Flanders, which were the largest and most beautiful to be found anywhere; and infinite other precious objects; all of which have since taught the Swiss what such things are worth. Their victories and the high esteem in which the king held them from then on and the benefits he lavished on them have combined to make them very rich indeed.

Henceforth, every ambassador of theirs who came to the king received great gifts of money from him. It was by this means that he kept the Swiss satisfied with his not declaring for them; he sent their envoys home, purses full and bodies clad in silk. He also promised pensions, which he did afterwards pay, but not until he learned the result of the second battle [Morat]. He undertook to disburse 40,000 Rhine florins every year, 20,000 for the towns and the other 20,000 for the individuals who governed those towns. I don't believe I exaggerate in thinking that, from this first battle of Grandson until his death, these Swiss towns and individuals enriched themselves through the king to the extent of a million Rhine florins—and I refer only to four towns: Berne, Lucerne, Fribourg and Zurich, and the Swiss cantons, all mountainous country, of which one, Schwyz, is only a village. I have seen its mayor among the Swiss envoys, in very humble dress.

To return to the Duke of Burgundy—he reassembled troops, gathering them on every side; and, three weeks after the battle of Grandson, he had more men under his command than on the day of the battle. He established quarters at Lausanne in Savoy, where you, my lord Archbishop of Vienne, served him with excellent medical advice in a serious illness, which was engendered by his morbid brooding on the ignominy of his defeat—and, to tell the truth, I do not believe that he ever afterwards had as clear a mind as he had had before that battle.

Concerning this new army he had mustered, I speak by the report of the Prince of Taranto [Frederick of Aragon, second son of King Ferrante of Naples], who recounted the story to the king when I was present. This prince, about a year before, had come to the duke with a splendid retinue, hoping to secure his daughter and sole heiress [Marie]; and he indeed appeared every inch a king's son, in his own person, in his princely display, and in his train; and it was clear that his father, the King of Naples, had spared no expense. The duke, however, had put him off, since he was then giving the Duchess of Savoy hope for her son [as Marie's husband] and was encouraging other suitors as well. Hence the Prince of Taranto, ill content with the duke's evasions, as were the prince's counsellors, sent to the king a herald, an able man, who requested a safe conduct so that the prince could pass through the realm and return to his father, who had sent for him. The king readily granted it—such a departure on the part of the prince seemed to him to diminish the credit and renown of the Duke of Burgundy.

Before the herald returned, however, the Swiss cantons had already assembled their army, which was stationed near the Duke of Burgundy. The Prince of Taranto took leave of the Duke of Burgundy on the very eve of the impending battle; he was thus obeying his father's command [and not showing cowardice] for in the first battle he had proved himself a good soldier. Some say that he was also influenced by your advice, my lord of Vienne; for after he reached the king's court, I heard him say and affirm to the Duke of Atri, called Count Giulio, and to some others that several days before the first battle, and before the second, you had sent letters to Italy which recounted the outcome of them.

As I have said, by the time the Prince of Taranto took leave of the duke, the Swiss had marched to Morat [which they had garrisoned], a little town near Berne belonging to the Count de Romont, to raise the duke's siege of the place in giving battle. The Swiss forces, according to what I was told by some who were there, probably numbered 4,000 horsemen and 30,000 foot-soldiers, choice and well armed men—11,000 pikemen, 10,000 halberdiers [forming the celebrated Swiss phalanxes] and 10,000 hand-gunners. All the Swiss contingents had not yet arrived; only those I have mentioned took part in the battle, but they were more than sufficient. The Duke of Lorraine arrived in the Swiss camp with a small force—and well did his coming turn out for him afterwards, for the Duke of Burgundy then held all his territory.

It also served the Duke of Lorraine well that one grew weary of him at our court; but then a man of power, when he has lost everything, usually wearies those who sustain him. The king had given him a little money and had had him escorted across Lorraine by a goodly number of troops, who, having taken him as far as Germany, then returned. The duke had lost not only his Duchy of Lorraine but also the County of Vaudemont and the greater part of Barrois, the king holding the rest of it. So there remained nothing of his; but what was worse, all his subjects had taken an oath of allegiance to the Duke of Burgundy, even his own household officers, and without being constrained to do so. It seemed, then, that there was little hope for his affairs. It is God alone, however, who judges these matters, when it pleases Him to do so.

After riding for some days, the Duke of Lorraine reached the Swiss only a few hours before the battle and with but few men. This journey brought him great honour and great profit, for had he not taken it he would have found small welcome anywhere. No sooner had he joined the Swiss forces than the two armies advanced against each other [22 June 1476], for the Swiss had already been encamped for three days, in a strong position, close to the Burgundians. After a feeble resistance, the Duke of Burgundy's army was overthrown and put to flight. Whereas in the previous battle the duke had lost but seven men of arms, this time he fared very differently. At Grandson the Swiss had had no cavalry, but here at Morat they had four thousand horsemen, well mounted, who pursued for a long distance the fleeing Burgundians; and also the Swiss phalanxes this time came to grips with the duke's foot-soldiers who were numerous. For, not counting his subjects and a goodly number of English with him, there had again joined his forces a great many men from Piedmont and from the Duchy of Milan, as I have said. The Prince of Taranto, after his arrival at the royal court, told me that he had never seen so fine an army and that he and his people, counting the troops as the army crossed a bridge, reckoned them at fully twenty-three thousand mercenaries, omitting camp followers and the men who serviced the artillery. This seems to me a very large figure, though many people think nothing of talking about thousands and thousands and thus exaggerating the size of armies.

The lord de Contay, who arrived at court soon after this battle, confessed to the king, when I was present, that the duke had lost eight thousand of his mercenaries and large numbers of common soldiers; and I believe, from what I was able to learn, that there were some eighteen thousand killed in all. It is easy to accept this figure, partly because of the large force of Swiss cavalry, which had been sent by several German lords, and also because of the Burgundians [who were trapped while still] maintaining the siege of Morat.

The duke fled all the way to the County of Burgundy, in a state of despair, as was to be expected; and he established himself at a place called La Rivière, where he reassembled whatever troops he could find. The Swiss pursued only until night fell and then withdrew without following up the victory.

This catastrophe drove the duke to desperation. He felt sure that all his friends would abandon him—having seen the signs of such desertion after his previous defeat at Grandson, which had occurred only three weeks [actually, three and a half months] before. Because of these fears, heeding some counsel given him, he had the Duchess of Savoy, and one of her sons who is today Duke of Savoy, seized by force and carried off to [the Duchy] of Burgundy. The eldest son [Philibert] was saved from capture by some servants of the House of Savoy, for those who carried out this abduction did so in fear and had to act hastily. The Duke of Burgundy ordered this exploit because he was afraid the duchess might withdraw to the king her brother, and he asserted that it was his willingness to succour the House of Savoy that had brought this whole disaster upon him.

The duke had her brought to the castle of Rouvres, near Dijon, where she was lightly guarded. Anyone could see her; and among her visitors were the present lord de Châteauguion, and the present Marquis de Rothelin. The duke had treated for the union of these lords with two daughters of the duchess—marriages which did not then take place but have been accomplished since.

Young Philibert, the Duke of Savoy [under his mother's regency], was brought to Chambéry [capital of the Duchy] by those who rescued him. There they put him and a little brother of his [Jacques Louis] called 'The Protonotary' into the hands of the Bishop of Geneva [Jean-Louis, one of Duchess Yolande's several brothers-in-law], a very rash man who was under the thumb of someone called 'The Commander of Ranvers'; and they also delivered up the castle of Chambéry and Montmélian to the bishop, who likewise held another castle containing all the treasure of the Duchess of Savoy.

As soon as the duchess, accompanied by all her ladies and numerous attendants, found herself at Rouvres and perceived that the Duke of Burgundy was busy assembling troops and that those who guarded her did not have the fear of their master that his servants had once had, she decided to send to the king her brother to treat for terms and to beg him to rescue her. Nevertheless she would have remained in great fear of falling into his hands, had it not been for the situation in which she saw herself, for the hate between them had been bitter and of long duration.

There arrived at court on the lady's behalf a gentleman of Piedmont named [Geoffroi de] Riverol, her majordomo. Someone directed him to me. After I had heard him and reported to the king what he had said to me, the king heard him. When he finished, the king told him that he would not fail his sister in her need, notwithstanding their past differences, and that, if she was willing to ally with him, he would have her fetched by the Governor of Champagne, Charles d'Amboise, lord de Chaumont. Taking leave of the king, Riverol returned to his mistress with all speed. She was overjoyed at his report. However, she dispatched a second man, as soon as she had heard the first, to beg the king that he give surety for his allowing her to return to Savoy. She also begged him to see to it that she regained possession of the duke her son and her other little boy and her castles also, and to help her maintain her rule in Savoy. In return, she was happy to renounce all her alliances and take only his. The king agreed to all that she asked and immediately sent an express courier to the lord de Chaumont with order to carry out the rescue.

This feat de Chaumont accomplished very neatly. Without doing any damage, he and a goodly force made their way to Rouvres, and then returned across the border with the Duchess of Savoy and her whole retinue.

When the king sent back this last messenger of the duchess, he had already left Lyons, where he had remained the space of six months in order subtly to thwart the Duke of Burgundy's enterprises without breaking their truce. Indeed, to grasp the situation of the duke—the king waged far more effective war against him in giving him his head and secretly stirring up enemies against him than if he had openly declared himself; for as soon as the duke had seen such a declaration he would have abandoned his enterprise, on which account that which happened to him would not have happened.

The king, after leaving Lyons, took ship on the Loire river at Roanne and thus came to Tours. As soon as he arrived there, he learned of the rescue of his sister, which overjoyed him; and he immediately requested her to join him, giving order for payment of the expenses of the journey. As she approached Tours, he sent numbers of people to greet her and he himself went to the gate of Plessis du Parc [his favourite dwelling, on the outskirts of the town] to receive her. With a genial countenance he said to her, 'Madame the Burgundian, welcome!' She realized, by his smile, that he was only joking, and replied very prudently that she was a good French-woman and ready to obey any command the king wished to give her.

The king escorted her to her chamber and saw to it that she was honourably treated. True it is that he longed to be rid of her. She, for her part, was very sagacious; the two of them understood each other perfectly, and she was even more eager than he for her departure. I was ordered by the king to take the necessary steps: first, to find money for her expenses at court and for those of the return journey to Savoy; then to procure some silks for her; and finally to draw up the treaty of alliance and the articles governing their future relationship.

The king wanted her to cancel the marriage plans which I have mentioned for her two daughters; but she put the responsibility for them on the daughters, who, she said, were determined to make the marriages. In truth, the girls did have their hearts set on these suitors. When the king realized how they felt, he gave his consent. After the duchess had sojourned at Plessis seven or eight days, the

king and she swore an oath together to be good friends for the
future and the appropriate documents were exchanged. Then the
lady took leave of the king, who had her escorted all the way home;
and he saw to it that her children and all her places and her treasure
and everything of hers were delivered to her. Both of them were
overjoyed to see the last of each other, and they remained good
brother and good sister until death.

To continue my account, I must now speak of the Duke of Burgundy, who, after the rout of Morat, had gone just within the
border of the County of Burgundy, to a place called La Rivière.
There he sojourned for more than six weeks, still having the heart to
try to reassemble an army. Nevertheless he accomplished little, and
kept apart from everyone. His first defeat at Grandson had so deeply
distressed him and troubled his spirits that he fell gravely ill [as has
been mentioned]. Before then, his choleric disposition and natural
heat had been so intense that he drank no wine, but in the morning
ordinarily drank herb tea and took rose-hip syrup to refresh himself.
His turmoil of mind so altered his disposition that his physicians had
to have him drink very strong wine, unwatered; and in order to
draw his blood back to the heart, containers of burning oakum were
applied to his chest. About this subject, you, my lord of Vienne,
know much more than I, as one who helped to cure this illness and
had him shave his beard, which he had allowed to grow. In my
opinion, never since that illness were his faculties as sound as before,
his mind being permanently affected. Such are the passions of those
who have never previously experienced adversity and can find no
way to remedy it, especially princes swollen with pride.

 For in these cases one's first refuge is to return to God and to
consider whether one has in any way offended Him and to humble
oneself before Him, acknowledging one's misdeeds; because He
determines the course of events—and none can say that He ever errs.
Then, one should use the curative power of confiding one's troubles
to a friend and openly expressing one's woes, being quite unashamed
about showing one's grief before a special friend; for that relieves
and comforts the heart, and one's spirits revive. It is inevitable, since
we are men, that deep griefs stir violent passions, which must be
given vent or be suffered in private. Therefore one should not take
the road followed by the duke in hiding himself away from people
like a hermit. And then too, since in his wrath he was so terrible to

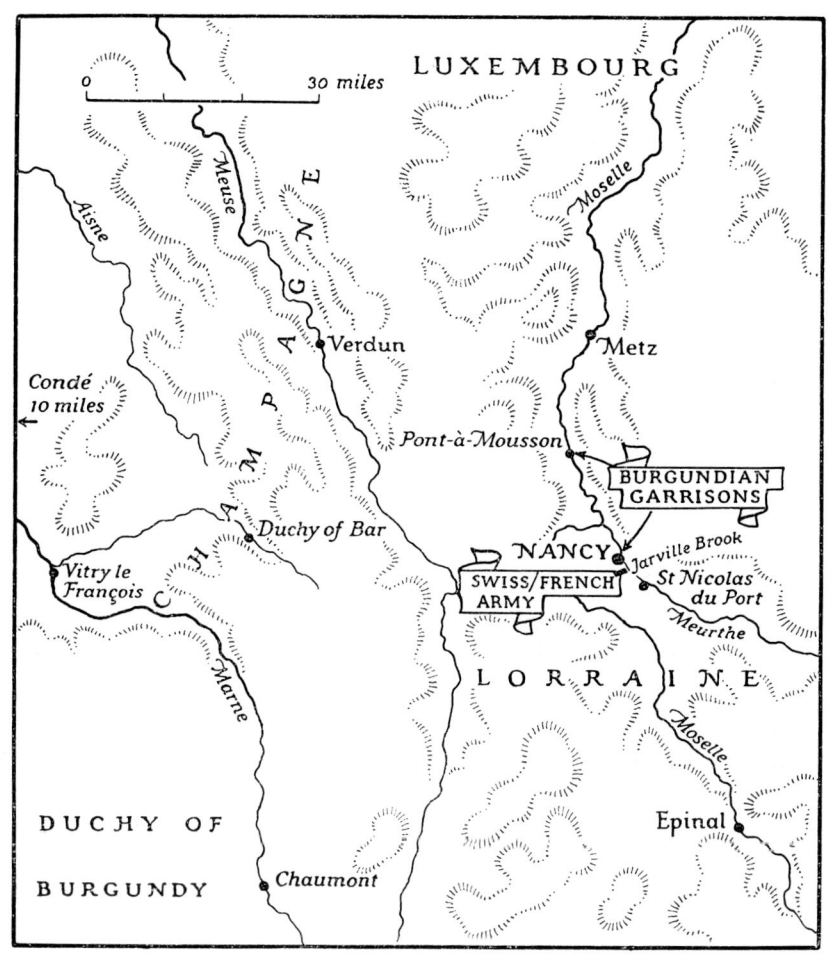

NANCY

his people, none dared put himself forward to offer comfort or counsel; but they left him to his own devices out of fear that if they made any remonstrance, they would pay for it.

During these six weeks, or thereabouts, in which he hid himself at La Rivière with but few attendants—no marvel that he did so after suffering two such disastrous defeats—many new enemies declared themselves, friends grew cold and his subjects, beaten down and ruined, began to talk against their master and hold him in scorn —as is the way of the world after such adversities.

Several little places were recaptured from him in Lorraine, like Vaudemont and Épinal and, later, still others. On all sides people began to take arms in order to attack him; and the most insignificant were the boldest. On getting word of this situation, the Duke of Lorraine gathered a small force and came to lay siege to Nancy—he held most of the little towns in the vicinity. However, a Burgundian garrison still occupied Pont-à-Mousson, about four leagues from Nancy.

The commander of the Burgundian force defending Nancy was a member of the de Croy family named [Jean] lord de Bièvres, a good, loyal knight. He had first rate troops, among them an Englishman named [John] Colpin, a very valiant man of low degree, who had come, with other Englishmen, from the garrison of Guines [one of the castles defending English Calais] to serve the Duke of Burgundy. At Nancy, Colpin had about three hundred English under him. Though the siege was not being pressed or any approach-works constructed, they were annoyed that the Duke of Burgundy was so slow in coming to relieve them. In truth, he made a great mistake in not moving on Nancy; for where he was, he was far from Lorraine and accomplishing nothing useful there. It was much more needful for him to defend what he had than to [attempt to] prepare another attack upon the Swiss in the hope of avenging his defeats; and his refusal to heed any counsel but his own cost him dear, for, despite urgent appeals to succour the garrison of Nancy, he remained at La Rivière about six weeks for no reason at all. Had he acted differently, he would easily have raised the siege, for the Duke of Lorraine had almost no men; and the Duke of Burgundy, as long as he kept the Duchy of Lorraine, had free passage from [the Low Countries and] Luxembourg to the County and Duchy of Burgundy. Therefore, if he had been able to think as clearly as he formerly did, he would have managed matters differently.

While those within Nancy were awaiting succour, Colpin was killed by a cannon ball. This was a severe loss for the Duke of Burgundy, for a single man is sometimes the cause of preserving his master from catastrophe—though he be not of his House or even of high rank but simply an intelligent and forceful person. In this respect the king our master, I have realized, was especially wise, for never was prince more fearful than he of losing his men.

As soon as Colpin was killed, the English under his command began to become disaffected and to despair of succour—they were unaware of how small the Duke of Lorraine's force was and of what great resources the Duke of Burgundy had for raising troops. But then, since the English for long years had waged no wars outside their realm, they had no understanding of the technique of sieges. The upshot was that they began to demand a parley with the enemy, and they told my lord de Bièvres, commander of the garrison, that if he did not become to terms, they would make terms without him. Though he was a loyal knight, he lacked strength of character, and he used appeals and remonstrances; whereas, it seems to me, had he answered the English more boldly and firmly, he would have done much better—unless God had thus ordained matters, and this I believe, for had they held out for but three days longer, they would have had their succour. However, in sum, he yielded to the English and surrendered Nancy to the Duke of Lorraine, with proviso for the garrison to depart unharmed with their baggage.

The next day, or, at the most, two days later, the Duke of Burgundy arrived before Nancy with a force strong enough to have relieved the city, for reinforcements from his other lordships had joined him via Luxembourg. His forces and those of the Duke of Lorraine confronted each other. However, nothing much happened, for the Duke of Lorraine could not afford to give battle.

Thus the Duke of Burgundy began to chase after the ball, too late, by putting siege to Nancy. Had he been willing to listen to advice and strongly garrison the little places in the vicinity of Nancy, he would have quickly recovered the city, for it was poorly provisioned and he had more than enough men to establish a tight blockade. He would thus have been able to rest and refit his army; but he grasped the wrong end of the stick.

While he persisted in this siege—a misfortune for him and for all his subjects and even for many who were entirely uninvolved in the cause—a number of his people began to engage in intrigues against him. Already, as I have said, enemies had risen on all sides, and, among them, Count Nicolas of Campobasso, who had previously sought to betray his master [see p. *188*]. Now once again, seeing his master in adversity, he began to intrigue, both with the Duke of Lorraine and with some officers of the king who were stationed on the border of Champagne near the Duke of Burgundy's army.

Campobasso promised the Duke of Lorraine to see to it that the siege did not progress and that essential equipment for the approach-works and the guns was lacking. He was well able to fulfill this promise, for he was the principal commander and enjoyed complete authority under the Duke of Burgundy. To our men his promises were more vivid: he constantly offered to murder or capture his master, demanding in return the subsidizing of his four hundred lances, twenty thousand crowns in coin and a county with good revenues.

While he was carrying on these intrigues, a band of the Duke of Lorraine's gentlemen attempted to make their way into Nancy. Some succeeded in entering. Others were captured, including a gentleman of Provence named Syffred de Baschi [a Neapolitan follower of the House of Anjou], who had handled all the bargaining between the Count of Campobasso and the Duke of Lorraine. The Duke of Burgundy ordered Syffred to be hanged immediately, asserting that, once a prince has established his siege and opened a bombardment of a place, anyone attempting to enter in order to assist the garrison is liable to execution according to the laws of war. In fact, such is not the usage in our wars, which are otherwise much more cruel than warfare in Italy or Spain where the custom is observed, but the duke none the less insisted upon the gentleman's death. Syffred, realizing that there was no help for it and that he was to be led to execution, said that he wanted to speak with the Duke of Burgundy in order to disclose something that concerned the duke's person.

The gentlemen to whom he said these words reported them to the duke. It happened that the Count of Campobasso was in the duke's presence, where, indeed, having learned of Syffred's capture, he had stationed himself on purpose out of fear that Syffred might reveal what he knew, for Syffred had full knowledge of the count's dealings on both sides, everything having been communicated to him, and it was those dealings that he meant to disclose.

The duke replied to the gentlemen reporting Syffred's words that the condemned man was only trying to save his life and that anything he had to communicate he should tell them. The count strongly seconded this answer—except for a secretary, who was writing, he was the only adviser there with the duke, for he had entire charge of military operations. The prisoner said that he would make his disclosure only to the duke himself. On being so informed, the duke ordered him hanged forthwith, which was done. On the way to execution, Syffred asked several people to intercede for him with the duke, saying that he would reveal things which if it cost their master a Duchy he would want to know. Several who were acquainted with him took pity and went to the duke's quarters determined to urge the duke to hear the man. But this wicked count had stationed himself at the door of the wooden house in which his master lodged, in order to prevent anyone from going in; and he refused entry to these people, saying, 'My lord says that the hanging should be carried out at once'. And the count then sent messengers to the provost-marshal to get on with it. Finally Syffred was hanged, which turned out very badly for the Duke of Burgundy. Better for him would it have been had he not acted so cruelly but instead had heard the gentleman. If he had done so, perchance he would still be alive and his House unimpaired—indeed, probably even greater, considering what has since happened in this realm. But it is to be believed that God had ordained otherwise.

You have heard earlier in these Memoirs of the disloyal act perpetrated by the duke, a little while before, against the Count of St Pol, Constable of France. . . . Just as in this very place, besieging Nancy, he had committed that crime, so now, in this same place, having just laid siege to Nancy again and had Syffred executed, he was himself betrayed by the one he most trusted and thus perhaps appropriately punished for what he had done to the Constable. . . .

The Duke of Burgundy was besieging Nancy in the dead of winter with but few troops, and those poorly armed and infrequently paid, and a great many of them sick. All were in general complaining and condemning what the duke was doing, as is customary in time of adversity, as I have often said before. But no one plotted against his person or his government except the Count of Campobasso; among his subjects there was no disloyalty.

During the first campaign of the Duke of Lorraine, he was treating

Q

with the Old and New Alliances, which I have heretofore mentioned, in order to procure troops and thus be able to give battle to the Duke of Burgundy. All the towns of these Alliances very much wanted to help; it was only a question of finding money. The king, through his ambassadors to the Swiss, urged this aid, and also furnished the Duke of Lorraine with forty thousand francs to help him pay for the German troops he was requesting. In addition, my lord de Craon, the king's lieutenant in Champagne, was quartered in the Duchy of Bar with seven or eight hundred lances and a force of franc archers under the command of excellent captains.

Aided by the backing and the money of the king, the Duke of Lorraine succeeded in enlisting a large number of Germans [i.e. Swiss and Germans of the imperial cities allied with them], both foot and horse; for in addition to those in his pay, they provided some contingents at their own expense. He also had with him many gentlemen from this realm; and then there was the king's army quartered in the Duchy of Bar, which did not wage war but was waiting to see who would be the victor. It was in these circumstances that the Duke of Lorraine moved to St Nicolas-du-Port, near Nancy, where he and his Germans encamped. . . .

On the day that the Duke of Lorraine and his army advanced from St Nicolas to give battle to the Duke of Burgundy, the Count of Campobasso came over to them, with about eight score men of arms, in order to achieve his designs. He was displeased that he had not been able to do a worse turn to his master. Those within Nancy had been informed of the plotting of the Count of Campobasso, which helped encourage them to hold out. Now, a man succeeded, by casting himself into the defensive ditch outside the walls, in entering the city in order to assure the garrison of succour—otherwise, they would have been on the point of surrendering. Had it not been for the treachery of the count, they would not have held out this long. But God willed the fulfillment of His mysterious ways.

The Duke of Burgundy, informed of the approach of the Duke of Lorraine, held a council of sorts, though such was by no means his custom, for he usually did everything out of his own head. Several expressed the opinion that he should withdraw to Pont-à-Mousson, close by, and leave garrisons in the places he held around Nancy; then, as soon as the Germans had revictualled the city, they would go home; the Duke of Lorraine, his money gone, would not be able to gather new forces for a long time; the fresh supplies in Nancy would not last half the winter and the garrison would then be in as desperate straits as it now was; and meanwhile the Duke [of Burgundy] would have assembled a large army.

For I have heard, from those who claimed to know, that he did not have four thousand men, and of those he had, but twelve hundred were fit for combat. The duke possessed plenty of money, for he had in the castle of Luxembourg, not far away, at least 450,000 crowns and could have raised many troops. But God did not grant him the grace of heeding this wise counsel nor of taking account of how many enemies surrounded him. Making the wrong choice—and talking like a man out of his wits—he insisted upon awaiting battle with his handful of frightened soldiers, notwithstanding that time and again he had been informed of the great number of Swiss with the Duke of Lorraine and of the king's army quartered nearby in the Duchy of Bar.

When the Count of Campobasso joined the Duke of Lorraine, the Swiss let him know that he was to quit the army, for they wanted no traitors with them. So he retired to Condé, where there was a castle overlooking a narrow passage, which he fortified as best he could in the hope that if the Duke of Burgundy and his men fled [by the passage] he would have his share of the slaughter, as indeed he did.

This count's main intrigues had not been with the Duke of Lorraine; for with some others he had plotted, before he deserted the Burgundians, that, since he could not see a way of laying hands on the Duke of Burgundy, he would go over to the other side when the hour of battle arrived. The count wanted to turn his coat at the last minute, so that his departure would create the greatest possible panic in the duke's army, but he gave assurances that if the duke took to flight he would never escape alive for the count would leave behind a dozen or fourteen men he could trust, some to lead the flight as soon as they saw the Swiss advancing, and others to keep their eyes on the duke in order, if he fled, to kill him fleeing. There was no slip up in this plot, for I have made the acquaintance of two or three of those who remained behind to kill the duke. Having thus plotted this great betrayal, the count then, when he saw the Germans advancing, turned against his master. On learning that the Swiss would not have him with them he went to Condé, as has been said.

With the advancing Swiss were large numbers of French horsemen who had been permitted to join the Duke of Lorraine. Many soldiers established themselves in ambushes in the vicinity of the duke's lines in order, should the Burgundians be routed, to snap up prisoners and other booty. Thus can be seen in what a sorry plight this poor duke had put himself through failing to heed counsel.

Of the two armies ranged for battle, the duke's had already been twice defeated and numbered few troops, and those in bad shape. They were immediately routed, all of them either killed or in flight. A large number escaped; the rest were dead or captive. Among others, there perished on the field the Duke of Burgundy. I do not wish to speak of how he met his death, for I was not there. However the manner of it was recounted to me by men who saw him hurled to the ground. They could not aid him because they were prisoners. They did not actually witness his death. He was set upon by a crowd of soldiers, who killed him and despoiled his body without recognizing him. This battle was fought on 5 January 1477, the eve of Epiphany. [Two days later, the duke's naked corpse, frozen to the ice of a pond, was identified: the head had been split to the chin by a Swiss halberd, the body many times pierced by Swiss pikes.]

I afterwards saw at Milan a seal incised in a cameo which I had many times observed hanging from the Duke of Burgundy's doublet—the seal showed his coat-of-arms along with a lamb and flint-and-steel [the former signifying the Burgundian Order of the Golden Fleece and the latter being the emblem of the ducal House]. It had been sold for two ducats in that city. The person who had taken it was a base *valet de chambre.* I many times saw the duke being arrayed in the morning and disrobed at night with reverential ceremony, and by high personages. And at this last hour, all his honours had vanished. He perished, he and his House, in the place, as I have said, where out of avarice he had consented to yield up the Constable, and his death occurred but a short time after. May God pardon his sins! The time has been when I saw him a great and honourable prince, as much esteemed and sought after by his neighbours as—perchance more esteemed and applied to than—any prince in Christendom. . . .

No prince ever surpassed him in his desire to maintain a numerous and highborn retinue, and to enforce upon his lordly court a rigid discipline. He was sparing of rewards, for he wanted everyone to appreciate to the full what he bestowed. No prince was ever more generous in giving audience to his officers and his subjects. During the time I was with him, he was not cruel; but he became so before his death, which augured ill for a long life. He was most splendid of dress and in everything else, a little too much so. He treated ambassadors and other distinguished foreigners with the greatest of honour—they were handsomely lodged and magnificently entertained at his court. He longed for glory, and it was this desire more than anything else that prompted him to wage his wars: he wished to resemble and to share the renown of the Great Captains of history. He was as tough and bold as any man who lived in his time.

And now his dreams are done, all his ambitions transformed into his destruction and his ignominy—for those who win in this world gain the honours as well as the rewards.

I do not know towards whom Our Lord showed Himself more angered—towards the duke, who died a sudden death in the field, without lingering pain, or towards the duke's subjects, who continually have either been forced to fight wars against enemies whom they lack the resources to resist or have among themselves engaged in cruel and deadly civil strife. What has made their lot harder to bear is that those defending them were foreigners, and people who had formerly been their foes, namely the Germans. [Commynes is alluding to the marriage, in August 1477, of the duke's heiress, Marie, to Maximilian of Austria, son of the Emperor Frederick III, which led the Burgundian domain, shorn of much territory, to engage in a fruitless struggle with France and also in internecine hostilities between Maximilian and his subjects.]

In effect, since the duke's death, there has never been a man, no matter who aided them, who wished them well—and, indeed, in view of their actions, it appears that they were as distracted in mind as their prince; for, a little before his death, they had cast aside all good, sound counsel and sought out the very ways that were to do them harm. And the way they are going at present, their troubles are certain to be renewed in a short time, or, at least, they have good reason to fear that they will be.

I endorse an opinion that I heard someone else express: it is that the kind of prince God provides for subjects is determined by whether or not He wishes to punish them; and the kind of subjects— and their willingness to obey—He gives the prince is determined by whether He wishes to raise him up or abase him. . . .

To continue with my subject—the king, who had previously established a postal system (and before that, there had never been any such), was very quickly informed [by a network of couriers who, in relays, speeded royal messages on their way] of the overthrow of the Duke of Burgundy. At every hour he had been expecting the news, for he had earlier been informed of the arrival [near Nancy] of the Duke of Lorraine's Swiss and of all the other circumstances indicating an impending battle. A great many people had their ears stretched wide in order to be the first to hear the news and report it to him, for he was very free in giving a reward to anyone—not forgetting the couriers too—who brought him grand tidings. He liked to talk about such news before it arrived, saying, 'I will give such-and-such to the one who brings it to me'. My lord du Bouchage and I together secured the first message of the battle of Morat, and together we repeated it to the king, who gave us each two hundred marcs of silver.

My lord du Lude, who slept outside the palace of Plessis [on the outskirts of Tours], was the first to learn of the arrival of the courier who brought the letters about the battle of Nancy. He demanded them from the courier, who did not dare refuse for du Lude enjoyed great authority with the king. Very early in the morning—it was hardly daylight—this lord banged on the door of the king's chamber. On being admitted, he delivered the letters, which had been written by my lord de Craon and others. They contained no certainty about the duke's death, for some of the writers said that he had been seen to flee and had escaped.

The king was at first so overcome by joy at this news that he hardly knew how to react. On the one hand, he feared that if the duke were captured by the Swiss, they might be willing to settle for a huge ransom, which the duke could easily furnish. On the other hand, the king was anxious about whether, should the duke have thus escaped destruction for the third time, he should take over the Duchy of Burgundy or not. He thought that he could easily do so, considering that almost all of the men of rank in the Duchy had been killed in these battles. Concerning this point, he resolved (and I believe few people besides me have known of this) that, should the duke have escaped with a whole skin, he would order his army then stationed in Champagne and the Duchy of Bar to enter the Duchy of Burgundy immediately and seize the province at this moment of greatest panic; and as soon as he had possession of it he would inform the duke that he had acted thus in order to preserve the Duchy for him and prevent the Swiss from destroying it (because the Duchy was held in fief from him, the king, and he would never let it fall into the hands of the Swiss); and that what he had taken into his hands, he would render again to the duke. Without difficulty the king could have carried out this resolve, though people would be unwilling to believe so; and also few knew the motive which had prompted his decision. However, the king changed his mind as soon as he learned of the death of the duke.

As soon as he had received these first letters of which I have spoken—which said nothing positive about the duke's death—he sent into the town of Tours to summon all his captains and several other high officers who were there; and upon their arrival he showed them these letters. They all put on the appearance of being overjoyed. It seemed, however, to those who were watching closely that, for most of them, the pleasure was forced, and that notwithstanding their demeanour, they would have much preferred the duke's fortunes to turn out otherwise. The cause could be the deep fear which the king inspired: these men were afraid that if he no longer had outward enemies to deal with, he might decide to make changes at home, especially in estates and offices—for there were many in that company who during the War of the Public Weal [1465] and the later conflict with the king's brother, the Duke of Guienne [1471–72], had been against him.

After he had talked with them for a while, he heard Mass and then ordered a table set up in his chamber and had them all dine with him, among them being the Chancellor [Pierre Doriole] and some members of his council. Throughout the meal he spoke of these matters. You may be sure that I, and others, carefully noted the kind of appetite the company showed in dining—in truth, I do not know whether it was from joy or sorrow, but not a single one, it seems, ate even half his fill. They could not have been embarrassed by finding themselves at the king's table, for every one of them had dined with him often.

On rising from the table, the king moved apart from the company [for private conversations with this one and that]; and to some he gave lands possessed by the Duke of Burgundy, on condition that the duke had indeed perished. He dispatched the Bastard of Bourbon, Admiral, and me [to Picardy, but not until about 11 January] with powers necessary to accept the allegiance of all who were willing to go over to the king; and he ordered us to set out at once and to open all the letters carried by couriers and messengers whom we

encountered on our journey in order to learn if the duke were alive
or dead.

We made very good time, notwithstanding that the weather was
the coldest I have ever experienced. We had not ridden half a day
before we met a messenger, whose letters we opened. These letters,
from my lord de Craon, informed the king that the duke had been
found among the dead on the field by an Italian page and by his
physician, one Master Lope, a Portuguese, who had then certified
to the lord de Craon that the body was that of the duke his master.

Having read the letters, we continued our journey and came to the
outskirts of Abbeville [one of the Somme towns still held by
Burgundy]. We were the first ones to inform the duke's adherents in
that region of his death. We discovered that the townspeople were
already treating with my lord de Torcy, to whom they had been
devoted for a long time. The Burgundian garrison and ducal officers
opened negotiations with us through a messenger whom we had sent
ahead to them. As a result of the terms we proposed, they dismissed
from the town the four hundred Flemish troops they had; but
as soon as the people saw that the Flemings had left, they opened their
gates to my lord de Torcy—an event which was very unfortunate
indeed for the duke's captains and other officers of the town, for to
seven or eight of them we had promised money and pensions, having
such authority from the king, but now they received nothing because
they were not the ones who delivered up the town.

Abbeville was one of the Somme towns yielded by Charles VII
[to Duke Philip of Burgundy] by the terms of the Treaty of Arras
[1435], which towns were to be returned to France on the death of
the last Burgundian male heir [or could be repurchased for 400,000
gold crowns, a deal consummated by Louis XI with Philip of
Burgundy in 1464 but annulled, as the price of the Treaty of Conflans, 1465, by Charles, then Count of Charolais]. Therefore it is no
marvel if the people of Abbeville so readily opened their gates to us.
From there the Admiral and I proceeded to Doullens and dispatched
a summons to Arras, capital of Artois, long the patrimony of the
Counts of Flanders, which at all times had been inherited by
daughters as well as sons [it being thus that the Counties of Flanders
and Artois had come to Duke Charles' great-grandfather, Philip the
Bold].

My lord of Ravenstein and my lord des Cordes [Antoine de

Crèvecoeur], who were at Arras, agreed to come and speak with us at Mont-St-Eloy, an abbey near that city, bringing with them representatives of the citizenry. It was decided that I should go there, and some others with me; for it was feared that we might encounter a rebuff and the Admiral therefore held aloof.

Soon after I reached the abbey, my lord of Ravenstein and my lord des Cordes arrived, along with other men of rank and some townsfolk of Arras including their chief official and spokesman, Master Jean de la Vacquerie, who later became First President in the Parlement of Paris. At this meeting we demanded, in the king's name, that they open their gates and receive us in the city, saying that the king claimed both Arras and Artois by right of confiscation. Should they refuse, we continued, they would be in danger of being taken by force, considering that their lord had been overthrown and killed and that the region had been stripped of defenders because of the three battles the duke had lost.

Replying for the lords, Jean de la Vacquerie said that the County of Artois belonged to Mademoiselle [Marie] of Burgundy, daughter of Duke Charles, and came to her by true descent from [her great-great grandmother] Marguerite, who was Countess of Flanders, of Artois, of Burgundy, of Nevers and of Rethel, and had married Philip the Bold, first Duke of Burgundy, son of King John [captured at Poitiers by the English in 1356] and a younger brother of Charles V. The lords also addressed to us the request that the king maintain the truce between him and the late Duke Charles.

The representations we made were moderate, for we had expected their reply; and the main purpose of my coming there was to have some private words with certain individuals among their delegation in order to win them over to the king. I spoke to some, who soon afterwards were loyal servants of the crown.

We found the region to be in a panic, and not without cause; for I believe that, given eight days, they would not have been able to muster eight men of arms, nor were there any other troops in that whole part of the country except about fifteen hundred men, horse and foot, around Namur and in Hainault, who had escaped from the battle of Nancy.

The tone and language of these people had greatly changed; for they spoke very softly and very humbly—I do not mean that in the past they had spoken arrogantly, but true it is that, during the years I was among them, they regarded themselves as so mighty that they did not speak to the king nor of the king with such reverence as they have since used. If people were always as prudent as they should be, they would be so moderate in their language in times of prosperity that they would have no need of changing their tone in time of adversity.

On returning to the Admiral to make my report, I learned that the king was on his way northward. He had taken to the road soon after we had, and had dispatched many letters, some in his own name and others in the name of various officers of his, which were designed to win over people through whom he hoped to reduce the Duke of Burgundy's lordships to his rule.

The king was very joyous, thus to find himself victorious over all his hated enemies. On some he had revenged himself, like the Constable and the Duke of Nemours [executed in August 1477] and others; the Duke of Guienne, his brother, was dead and the duke's estates were in his hands; of the House of Anjou, his uncle, the Count of Maine, and Duke John and John's son, Nicolas of Calabria, were dead [and his uncle King René and his cousin, the Count of Maine, were now powerless]; the Count of Armagnac had been killed at Lectoure [March 1473]; and the king had gathered in [or, as in the case of the House of Anjou, would by 1481 gather in] all their provinces and possessions. The House of Burgundy was greater and more powerful than these others—with the aid of the English it had waged uninterrupted war for thirty-two years against his father Charles VII, its territories pressed upon the borders of France, and its subjects were always ready to attack King Louis and his realm. Therefore, so much the greater was the pleasure that the king took and the profit that he gained in the downfall of the Duke of Burgundy. And he believed that for the rest of his life he would find none to gainsay him in his realm or among his neighbours. He was at peace with the English, as you know, and he made every effort to see that that peace was maintained.

On which account, since he was relieved of all fears, God did not permit him to resolve this great question of the Burgundian succession as he should have managed it. For by means of a marriage, and using the way of friendship, he could easily have annexed to the crown all these great Burgundian lordships, over which he could not otherwise claim any rights. All his desires he would have accomplished through the agency, and under the terms, of this marriage because of the chaotic condition, poverty and weakness of these Burgundian lordships. He would then have strengthened and enriched his realm by long years of peace during which he could have in many ways lightened the burdens of his people, especially in the reform of the troops of the standing army, who, in the past and at the present, have trampled the realm from one end to the other, often with no real need for them to do so.

While the Duke of Burgundy was still alive, the king several times talked to me about what he would do if the duke met his death, and what he said made great good sense. He said that he would seek to marry the Dauphin Charles, our present king, to the daughter of the duke, afterwards Duchess of Austria. Should she refuse the match (because the dauphin [six years old] was much younger than she [almost twenty]), he would try to have her marry some young lord of this realm in order to maintain friendly relations with her and her subjects, and thus recover, without strife, what he claimed to be his. The king was still of this mind eight days before he learned of the death of the duke; but on the day that news came, and at the moment he dispatched the Admiral and me to Picardy, he was already beginning to change this wise resolve. However, he said little on the subject, but to some people he promised lands and lordships.

While the king was riding northward, after us, pleasing news came to him from all directions. The castles of Ham and Bohain were yielded to him. The inhabitants of St Quentin submitted without waiting to be summoned, and welcomed [a royal official] who was their neighbour. The king was quite sure of the town of Péronne, held by Guillaume Bische [who had once acted as liaison between the king and the duke] and he had hope, because of reports from us and others, that my lord des Cordes would come over to him. He had sent to Ghent his barber [the famous Master Olivier le Daim], native of a village near that city, and to other towns he had dispatched other emissaries—all of them buoying his optimism, for several served better in words than in deeds.

As the king approached Péronne, I joined him [on 3 February 1477]. Master Guillaume Bische and others came to signify the allegiance of the town, which made him very happy; and that day he lodged there. I dined with him, as I was accustomed to do, for he liked to have seven or eight persons at least at his table daily and

sometimes a great many more. After he had dined, he drew apart.
[Speaking to me] he indicated that he was displeased with the petty
exploit of the Admiral and me: he had dispatched Master Olivier his
barber to Ghent, who would secure for him the allegiance of that
city, and Robin d'Oudenfort to St Omer, who had friends there and
they were the kind of people to take the keys of the town and admit
his men. He had sent still others, whom he named, to other large
towns. The king then had my lord du Lude and others argue with
me in favour of this proceeding. It was not my place to dispute with
him nor speak against what he willed. However, I told him that
I feared Master Olivier and the others he had named would not
succeed so easily with these great towns as they thought.

What made our king speak to me thus was that he had changed
his plans; and this good fortune he was having at the beginning gave
him hope that everything would be yielded to him on all sides. He
was advised by some—and was himself disposed—to destroy completely this House of Burgundy and distribute its lordships among
several people. He named the persons to whom he meant to give the
counties, like Namur and Hainault, which are situated near him; the
other great provinces like Brabant and Holland he intended for
certain German lords, who, their friendship thus secured, would help
him to achieve his designs. He chose to tell me all these things
because when I had spoken with him formerly I had counselled him
to take the other road, which I have explained above; and he wanted
me to understand his reasoning and the causes for his change of
mind and why this new way was more useful for his realm, which
had suffered severely because of the power of this House of Burgundy
and the great lordships it possessed.

In worldly terms, what the king said was very persuasive; but
judged by conscience, it seemed to me the contrary. Nevertheless,
the intelligence of our king was so great that neither I nor others of
his entourage were capable of the insight into his affairs that he had;
for without any question he was one of the most sagacious and subtle
princes of his time. But in these grand matters God disposes the
hearts of kings and mighty princes, whom He holds in His hand, to
follow such courses as will lead to the results that He intends to
bring about later. For had it been God's will that our king carry out
the plan that he had himself devised before the death of the duke
[to bring about the marriage of Marie of Burgundy and the dauphin],
the wars which have since occurred and are continuing, would not

have happened. But we, French and Burgundians both, were not yet worthy, in our attitude towards God, of being given this long peace; and from that fact proceeded the error that the king made, and not at all for lack of intelligence because, as I have said, his was great.

I write of these matters at length in order to demonstrate that, before undertaking a great enterprise, one should consult about it and discuss it thoroughly in order to be able to choose the most effective course; and, above all, one should commend oneself to God and pray to Him to point out the best road; for from God come all things, as is evidenced in writings and by experience. I do not mean to blame our king in saying that he had erred in this matter, because perhaps others who had greater knowledge and insight than I would be—and were then—of his opinion, although he did not put the matter to discussion either at Péronne or elsewhere.

Chroniclers usually record only the favourable things about those of whom they write, and they omit many things or sometimes, out of ignorance, report them inaccurately. I am resolved to write only the truth and to recount only what I have myself seen or have learned from personages so great that they are worthy of credence, without regard for flattery. For it is good to realize that there is no prince so wise that he does not err a number of times—quite often, if he lives long. Thus would the facts turn out, if the truth were always told. The greatest deliberative bodies and councils that have ever been or exist now have frequently been wrong, and seriously wrong, as can be seen in the past and is seen every day.

When the king was preparing to make his entry into Péronne, he drew me aside, as he was about to set forth, and ordered me to Poitou [of which Commynes was Seneschal] and to the Breton frontier there. He whispered in my ear that if Master Olivier's mission failed and my lord des Cordes did not come over to his side, he would have a part of the County of Artois burned, namely a region named 'L'Allœuë' on the south bank of the river Lys [a very fertile area], and then would immediately go back to Touraine. I recommended to him some men who had come over to his side because, in his name, I had promised them pensions and other rewards. He had their names put in writing, and he made good to them what I had promised. Thus, for that time, I left him.

As I was about to take horse, my lord du Lude came up to me. A man who made himself very agreeable to the king in certain ways, he ardently pursued his own profit and never feared to deceive anybody; he was also credulous and thus was himself often deceived; he had been brought up with the king in their youth, knew perfectly how to entertain him, and was a very amusing man. He said, in mockery of me but pretending to speak seriously, 'Now then, are you going off at the one moment when, if ever, you should be making your fortune—in view of the great things falling into the king's hands which he can use to advance and enrich all those whom he loves? As for me, I expect to be Governor of Flanders and turn myself into gold!'—and he gave a great laugh. I had no desire to laugh, because I feared that the king might have put him up to saying this, and I replied merely that I would be delighted if thus it came about and that I hoped the king would not forget me. With that, I took my departure.

Not half an hour before, a knight of Hainault had come to me, bringing word from several others to whom I had written asking them to come over to the king's service. This knight and I are related, and he is still living, on which account I do not wish to name him nor those from whom he brought word. In brief, he had proposed to deliver the chief places and towns of Hainault. In taking leave of the king I had outlined this offer to him. Immediately he sent for the knight, then told me, about him and the others I named to him, that these were not the sort of people he needed. One of them displeased him for one reason, another for another, and, in sum, it seemed to him that their offers were worth nothing and that he would gather in everything without them. After I departed, he ordered my lord du Lude to speak with this knight. The latter was astonished at du Lude's attitude and he left very soon without saying much about the bargain; for lord du Lude and he were far indeed from any understanding since the knight had come in the expectation of enriching himself, whereas lord du Lude demanded to know, right off, what the towns would give him for managing the matter.

I still think that the king's contemptuous rebuff of these knights was God's doing; for I afterwards saw the time when he would have prized them very highly if he had had the opportunity of dealing with them. However, Our Lord perchance did not wish him to achieve all his desires, for reasons I have mentioned, or was unwilling for him to usurp the possession of Hainault, an imperial fief, both because of his having no title to it and because of the long-standing alliances and oaths that exist between the emperors and the kings of

France. Later, the king himself showed that he knew he had no just claim, for having taken possession of Cambrai, and Le Quesnoy and Bouchain in Hainault, he yielded up the places in Hainault and restored Cambrai, an imperial town, to its accustomed neutrality.

Although I was not with the king, I was informed how affairs were going; I had no difficulty understanding them because of my knowledge and experience of both sides [French and Burgundian]; and I afterwards had my understanding confirmed by word of mouth from those who were, on each side, managing these matters.

[The king's barber] Master Olivier, as you have heard, had gone to Ghent with letters of credence addressed to Mademoiselle of Burgundy, daughter of Duke Charles. He bore instructions to set forth some matters to her in private so that she might agree to put herself in the king's hands. This was not his principal mission, for he feared that it would be well nigh impossible for him to speak with her alone, and even if he did thus speak with her, there was little hope that he could persuade her to accept his proposal. His main purpose was to bring about in the city of Ghent a revolutionary uprising. He knew that the city is always inclined towards revolt and that under Dukes Philip and Charles it had been ruled by a regime of fear, having been forced to surrender some of its privileges [in July 1453] in order to terminate a war it had [unsuccessfully] waged against Duke Philip. Another privilege, concerning municipal jurisdiction, had been taken away [in 1467] by Duke Charles because of an offence against him which the inhabitants had committed on the occasion of his first entrance into the city as its new duke. . . . For all these reasons Master Olivier, the king's barber, was greatly emboldened to pursue his aim. He spoke to some who, he thought, should be willing to lend ear to what he desired; and he offered to see to it that the king restored the privileges they had lost, and promised other things. However, he did not confer publicly with these people in the town hall, for he wished first to see what he could accomplish with this young princess. Still, he knew something about the situation in the city.

After Master Olivier had been in Ghent a few days, he was sent for [by the Burgundian court] to present his credentials. He came into the presence of the princess, much more splendidly clad than befitted him, and delivered his letter. The young lady was seated in a chair of state with the Duke of Clèves, the Bishop of Liége and other great personages about her and many people in the hall of audience. After she had read his letter, he was bidden to explain his mission. He replied that he was instructed to speak only privately with the lady. He was told that such was not the custom, especially in regard to this young lady, as yet unmarried. He went on repeating that he would speak only to her. He was then told that he would be made to speak, and he became frightened. I believe that at the moment he presented his letter he had not given a thought to what he was to say, for this audience was not his chief mission, as you have heard.

Some of the princess's council held him in derision, because of his insignificant status and the kind of language he used; the people of Ghent ridiculed him even more, because he was a native of a little village near the city, and treated him to open mockery. Then, suddenly, he fled from Ghent, for he was informed that if he did not do so, he was in peril of being drowned in the river. And I believe the peril was real.

Master Olivier, who had himself styled Count de Meulan, a little town near Paris of which he was captain, fled to Tournai after leaving Ghent. That town is neutral [being a French enclave in Burgundian territory], but it is devoted to the king, being his, and pays him ten thousand Paris livres a year; but otherwise it enjoys complete freedom, and foreigners of all nationalities are welcome there. It is a splendid town, and very strongly fortified, as everyone in this region well knows. All the landed property and revenues of the churchmen and townsmen of Tournai were in Hainault and Flanders, for it borders both those counties. For this reason the people of Tournai had always been accustomed, during the old wars between Charles VII and Duke Philip of Burgundy, to give Duke Philip ten thousand livres a year, and I have seen them give as much to Duke Charles. At the time Master Olivier entered Tournai, it paid nothing and enjoyed great prosperity and peace.

Although Master Olivier's mission was too much for him, he was not nearly so much to blame as those who charged him with it; and the failure of the mission was inevitable. However, he showed intelligence and enterprise in what he did. For he knew that Tournai was right there between Hainault and Flanders, and thus well situated to do great damage to both, provided that he could introduce into the town the troops whom the king had stationed nearby (to which entry the townspeople would under no circumstances have consented, for they never took sides but remained neutral between

Le dit Duc de bourgongne aduertir de ceste venue tant quelque peu de conseil combien quil ne lauoit point fort acoustume, mais vsoit communement de son propre sens/ La fut lopinion de plusieurs que il se retirast aupont a mousson pres de la et laissast de ses gens es places quil tenoit enuiron nancy disans que des ce que les alemans auroient auitaille Nancy sen iroient/et seroit largent failly au duc de loraine qui de long temps ne rassembleroit tant de gens. Et lauitaillement ne scauroit estre si grant quauant que la moytie de liuer fust passe quilz ne fussent aussy a destroit comme ilz estoient lors. Et que cependant led

Defeat and death of the Duke of Burgundy in the Battle of Nancy,
January 1477

Burgundy and France). Master Olivier therefore sent secretly to my lord de Moy—whose son was royal bailiff of the town (but he did not exercise his office there)—to bring his company of troops, which was at St Quentin, and some others who were in the region. The lord de Moy came, at the hour designated, to a gate of the city, where he found Master Olivier with some thirty or forty men. Master Olivier had much ado to [make the guards] open the barrier—he managed the matter half by persuasion and half by force, and thus introduced the royal troops into the city. The people as a whole were quite happy about it, but not so the governors of the town. Master Olivier sent seven or eight of the latter to Paris, who did not dare leave their exile [which, to them, in view of Tournai's virtual independence, was what it was] until the king died. Following these troops, there entered others, who have since done a marvellous amount of damage in Hainault and Flanders, pillaging many handsome estates and country houses—more to the harm of the burghers of Tournai than of any others, for the reasons I have explained [i.e. because their properties were located in those counties]. The destruction was so great that the Flemings, releasing the Duke of Gelderland from prison, to which Duke Charles had consigned him, in order to make him their war-chief, came before the walls of Tournai. They did not stay there long; for [attacked by the royal troops] they were routed and fled in great disorder, losing many men. Among them, there perished the Duke of Gelderland, who had put himself at the head of the rearguard in order to protect the retreat. But he was poorly supported and there died. Thus came this honour to the king by the agency of Master Olivier, and the king's enemies suffered great loss. A much wiser and greater personage [than the barber] might well have failed to bring off this success.

I have said enough about the mission which was given by this sagacious king to this insignificant person who was quite incapable of handling so great a matter. It appears indeed that God had, in this instance, blurred the king's intelligence; for, as I have said, had the king not been under the illusion that he could easily achieve his aims and had he checked his emotions and his desire for vengeance upon the House of Burgundy, he doubtless would have today the entire Burgundian domain under his control.

. . . After Péronne had been yielded to the king, he received there an embassy from Mademoiselle of Burgundy, consisting of the greatest

R

personages [at her court and in her towns] who could help her. It was not wisely done to send so many important people on one mission; but the desolation and fear of the Burgundians were so overwhelming that they knew not what to say or do.

The embassy included their Chancellor, Guillaume Hugonet, a distinguished and sagacious man who had enjoyed great credit with Duke Charles and received great rewards from him; the lord de Humbercourt, often mentioned in these memoirs—I don't remember to have ever seen a wiser gentleman nor one more capable of managing great affairs; the lord de la Vere, a great noble of Zeeland; the lord [Louis de Bruges] de la Gruthuse; and several others, lords and churchmen and town officials. Our king, before giving them formal or informal audience, took great pains to win over each one of them. And he was treated to humble words and great reverence, as was to be expected from people so frightened. Nevertheless, those who believed that their lands were situated beyond reach of the king were unwilling to commit themselves to him, except in agreeing to the marriage of the dauphin, his son, to Marie of Burgundy.

On the other hand, the Chancellor and the lord de Humbercourt, who had long enjoyed great power and wanted to keep it and whose estates were on the borders of France, the one in the Duchy of Burgundy and the other at the edge of Picardy, near Amiens, lent ear to the king and his offers; they gave indication of being willing to serve him in bringing about this marriage and, once it was accomplished, of openly taking service with him. Although this was the king's best opportunity, nevertheless it did not please him; and he was annoyed with them and by the fact that they were unwilling, right then, to commit themselves unreservedly to him. He concealed his feelings, however, for he wanted to make as much use of them as possible.

The king had already achieved a good understanding with my lord des Cordes, chief and master within Arras; and, by the advice of that lord, he asked the Burgundian ambassadors to arrange to have the citadel of Arras opened to him by the lord des Cordes; for there was then a wall with ditch between the town of Arras and the citadel, with the gates closing against the citadel. Now it is the opposite, for the citadel can close itself against the town. After it had been several times pointed out to the ambassadors that such a step would be for the best and that peace could more easily be attained if they made this acknowledgement of the king's authority, they gave their consent, the chancellor and my lord de Humbercourt taking the lead. They delivered letters of discharge to lord des Cordes and their consent that he yield the citadel of Arras, which he did at once. As soon as the king entered the citadel [4 March 1477], he had earthworks constructed to face the town gate and at other locations near the town. By the terms of this agreement, my lord des Cordes and his garrison withdrew from the town, each one going wherever he wished and taking whatever side he choose.

My lord des Cordes, thus regarding himself discharged from the service of his mistress, decided to take the oath of allegiance to the king and to become his servant—considering also that his family name and coat-of-arms were on this side of the Somme near Beauvais; for his name is Philippe de Crèvecoeur. Moreover, the towns and lands that, in accordance with the Treaty of Arras [1435], the House of Burgundy had occupied in the lifetimes of Dukes Philip and Charles, reverted without any question to the king by the terms of that treaty; for they were delivered to Duke Philip for him and his male heirs only, and Duke Charles left but this daughter, of whom I have spoken. Thus Philippe de Crèvecoeur saw no reason why he should not become a king's man. He would have been unquestionably within his rights in taking service with the king, had he not sworn allegiance to Marie of Burgundy and acknowledged her overlordship of his Burgundian property. The matter has been spoken of and will continue to be spoken of in divers ways; and therefore I leave it at whatever the truth is. I do know that he had been brought up, advanced and given great estate by Duke Charles, that his mother was partly in charge of Marie of Burgundy's rearing, that at the death of Duke Charles he was that duke's Governor of Picardy, Seneschal of Ponthieu, Captain of Crotoy, Governor of Péronne, Roye and Montdidier, Captain of Boulogne and of Hesdin, and at present he holds these same positions from the king, in the form and manner that the king our master bestowed them upon him.

After the king had done in the citadel of Arras what I have told you, he left there and went to lay siege to Hesdin, bringing with him lord des Cordes, who not three days before had himself held the place and whose men were still there. They gave the appearance of remaining loyal to Marie of Burgundy saying that they had sworn allegiance to her—and there was some artillery fire. However, they gave ear to their master (and in truth those within and those without understood each other very well), and thus the place was delivered

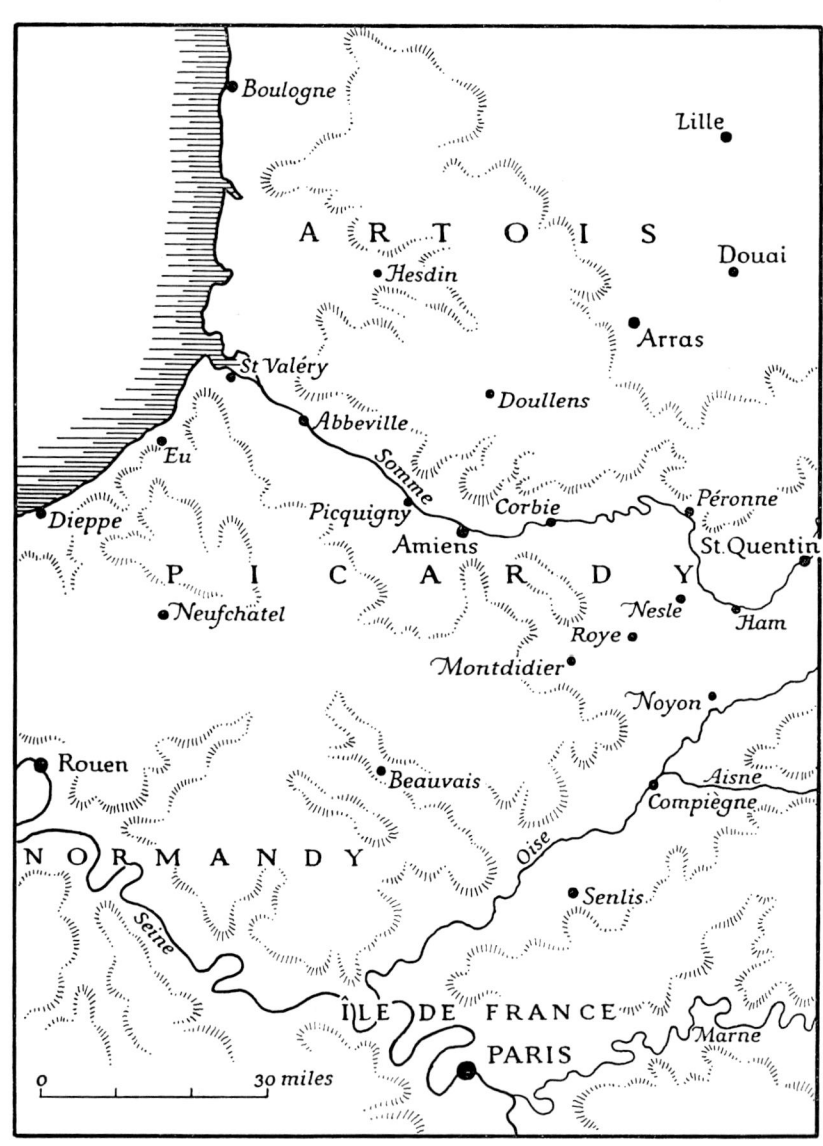

PICARDY AND THE SOMME TOWNS

to the king. He then went before Boulogne, where the same thing happened. The city held out, perhaps, for an additional day. Nevertheless, this delaying trick could have proved dangerous if there had been [Burgundian] troops in the region. The king, as he afterwards told me, was well aware of it; for there were people in Boulogne who understood the situation, and had they been able to find any troops in time, they would have introduced them into the city and defended it stoutly.

While the king was encamped before Boulogne—a time span of about five or six days—the people of the town of Arras had come to feel themselves betrayed because they were thus enclosed on all sides by a large force of soldiers and a powerful artillery. They therefore sought troops to garrison their town, writing to neighbouring cities like Lille and Douai. At Douai there were a few horsemen, among them the lord de Vergy and others whose names I do not remember. They were part of the troops who had come back from the battle of Nancy. Deciding to help defend the town of Arras, they assembled all the men they could—some two or three hundred horse, good and bad, and five or six hundred foot. The people of Douai, who at that time still had a little arrogance, insisted that these troops depart in broad daylight, whether they wanted to or not. Very foolish the inhabitants were so to insist, and it cost them dear. For the countryside beyond Arras is as flat as your hand, and this force had about five leagues to travel. If they had waited for nightfall, they would have carried out the enterprise as they intended.

While they were on the way, the king's men in the citadel of Arras, such as the lord du Lude, Jean du Fou and Marshal Lohéac's people, were informed of their coming, and decided to gamble everything and intercept them rather than allow them to enter the town, for they believed that lacking this force the town of Arras could not put up a defence.

It was a perilous enterprise but they carried it out boldly and crushed this band from Douai, killing or capturing almost all of them, among the captives being the lord de Vergy. The king, arriving next day, was overjoyed by this exploit and had all the prisoners turned over to him. He had a number of the foot-soldiers put to death, hoping thus to frighten the few Burgundian troops in the region. My lord de Vergy, who refused to take an oath of allegiance to the king, was kept long in prison, closely guarded and heavily fettered. In the end, however, following the advice of his mother after being a year and more in prison, he did as the king wished, which was the only wise thing to do. The king restored to him all the lands that he owned and all those that he claimed and made him the possessor of more than ten thousand livres in annual revenues and of attractive offices.

The few from Douai who escaped death or capture entered the town of Arras. The king had his artillery pieces, which were numerous and powerful, planted nearer the walls, and they opened fire. Neither the walls nor their defensive ditch was worth much. The bombardment was tremendous and frightened all the inhabitants; and they had almost no troops in the town. My lord des Cordes enjoyed important secret connections there. And then, since the king held the citadel, the town could not escape his grasp. Therefore, the inhabitants yielded the town, on terms which were very poorly observed, the lord du Lude being partly to blame. The king ordered the execution of a number of burghers and other people of importance. Lord du Lude and Master Guillaume de Cerisay profited greatly in the occupation of the town: du Lude told me that at that time he had gained 20,000 crowns and two marten pelts. The inhabitants made a loan of 60,000 crowns, much more than they could afford. I believe, however, that they were afterwards repaid, for the townspeople of Cambrai lent 40,000 crowns, which, I know for certain, was paid back to them.

At the time of this siege of Arras, Mademoiselle of Burgundy was at Ghent in the hands of those highly irrational folk, which caused loss to her and profit to the king—for one man's loss is another man's gain.

As soon as these people had learned of the death of Duke Charles they concluded that freedom was theirs, and they seized all the municipal officers, twenty-six of them, and put all or most of them to death—using as their excuse that these officials had, the day before, executed a man, but, notwithstanding that he well deserved the punishment, they possessed no such power because their authority had expired with the death of the duke who had appointed them. The people also put to death several great and worthy men of the town who had been friends and favourites of the duke, among them being some who in my time there and when I was present had helped to dissuade Duke Charles from destroying a large part of the town. The people forced Marie of Burgundy to confirm their former privileges, some of which had been taken from them by the

Treaty of Gavre [1453] they had made with Duke Philip, and others which had been taken from them by Duke Charles. These privileges served only to create trouble between them and their prince. Their main desire is to have their prince weak. They love no princes once they have become reigning dukes, but, as is natural, they love them as children before they attain sovereignty—as they had done with this young lady, whom they had carefully guarded and cherished until she became Duchess of Burgundy.

It is also important to understand that if, upon the duke's death, the people of Ghent had made no trouble and had sought to guard the country, they could have quickly garrisoned Arras and perhaps Péronne also; but their only thought was creating turmoil.

While the king was besieging the town of Arras, there came to him some ambassadors from the Three Estates of Marie of Burgundy's territory [the three Estates of Flanders]; for certain deputies representing the Three Estates were meeting in Ghent but, in fact, the people of Ghent did as they pleased in this assembly since they held the young lady in their hands. The king gave the envoys audience. Among other things, they said that their proposals, aimed at securing a peace, represented the will of Marie of Burgundy, who in all matters had decided to be governed by the advice of the Three Estates. In addition, they asked the king to suspend the war he was waging in [the county of] Burgundy and in Artois and agree to a conference for amicably settling terms of peace.

The king already had the upper hand and still believed that he could do even better, for he knew that many of the Burgundian troops were dead, that the rest were everywhere beaten down and that a great many had come over to him, especially my lord des Cordes. This lord he highly esteemed, and not without cause, for over many years he had not accomplished by force what, just a few days before, he had accomplished by secret understandings arranged through des Cordes, as you have heard. Therefore the king thought little of the requests made by these ambassadors. Furthermore he knew well that these people of Ghent were making so much trouble for their own side that they would be unable to plan or conduct a war against him. For no man of intelligence who had enjoyed authority under their former princes was consulted in anything, but rather such men were persecuted and in danger of death; and they especially hated those from the County and Duchy of Burgundy because of the great power they had had in the past. The king was well aware of all this; for in such matters he perceived as clearly as any man of his realm; and he knew that the people of Ghent have always wanted to see their prince enfeebled, provided that his weakness did not adversely affect them. He therefore decided that, since they had already begun to split into factions, he would put them still more at odds—for those with whom he was dealing were but brute beasts (and townsmen for the most part), especially in regard to the subtleties of statecraft that the king so well knew how to use. He therefore did what was indicated in order to bring his enterprise to a successful conclusion.

He interrupted the ambassadors after they had declared that their princess would do nothing without the advice and consent of the Three Estates. He told them that they were badly informed both on the subject of the princess' will and regarding some individuals; for he was sure that she intended to have her affairs governed by a certain few people who were opposed to peace, and the ambassadors would find themselves disavowed. These envoys were very much upset by the king's statement, being folk unaccustomed to dealing with such great affairs. They replied immediately that they were quite certain of what they were saying and that if necessary they would produce their instructions. They were answered that letters would be shown them, when the king so pleased, written in such hands that they would believe the contents, according to which the young lady of Burgundy intended to have her affairs managed by only four persons. The ambassadors repeated that they were very sure the contrary was true.

The king then had them shown a letter which the Chancellor and the lord de Humbercourt had brought, on the previous embassy at Péronne. The letter was written in three hands—partly by Marie of Burgundy, partly by the Dowager Duchess of Burgundy, Duke Charles' widow [Margaret], sister of Edward IV of England, and partly by the lord of Ravenstein, brother of the Duke of Clèves and a close relative of the young lady. The letter was written as if only in the name of Marie, but this style was used in order to give it greater weight. The letter consisted of a credence for the Chancellor and the lord de Humbercourt; in addition, Marie of Burgundy declared that she intended to have all her affairs governed by four people, namely, the Dowager her stepmother, the lord of Ravenstein, the Chancellor and de Humbercourt, and she begged the king that whatever negotiations he choose to have with her pass through their hands and that he address himself to them and have communication with them and no others.

On reading this letter, the envoys of Ghent and the other ambassadors were highly indignant, and the king's men who were dealing with them fanned the flames. In the end, the letter was given to them, and that was about the only answer they had—indeed, they were thinking only of their factional interests and of making a new world and did not look beyond their noses, although the loss of Arras should have been their prime concern. But they were people who had been taught nothing of state affairs—townsmen, most of them, as I have said.

They headed right back to Ghent. In that city Marie of Burgundy had with her, among others, the Duke of Clèves, now very old [he was fifty-eight], her close relative through his mother [Marie of Burgundy, who was her great-aunt] . . . and the Bishop of Liége [Louis of Bourbon], brother to Jean and Pierre, successive Dukes of Bourbon, a man of pleasure who had little awareness of affairs. . . . The Duke of Clèves was there in the hope of bringing about the marriage of his eldest son and the young lady, which seemed to him very suitable for many reasons. I believe that that match would have been made had the prospective bridegroom been to the taste of her and her advisers; for he was a scion of, and had been reared in, this very House, of which the Duchy of Clèves was a fief. Perchance it was seeing him and knowing him which spoiled his chances.

To come back to my matter—these ambassadors returned to Ghent. To hear their report, Marie of Burgundy's council was assembled and she seated upon her throne, with several lords attending upon her. They began to speak of the terms of the mission she had given them, emphasizing the point which was to serve their purpose. When, they said, they had duly told the king that she was entirely resolved to be governed by the advice of the Three Estates, he had replied to them that he was sure this was the reverse of true. When they had persisted in the statement, the king had offered to show them a letter. The young lady, suddenly agitated and angry, said immediately—it was false that any such letter had been written or seen. At once the spokesman, who was the chief magistrate of Ghent or of Brussels, drew from his bosom the letter in question and, in front of everybody, handed it to her. He showed that he was a very bad man and one of little honour in visiting this ignominy upon the young lady, on whom no such villainous trick should have been played; for if she had committed a fault, it was not his place to expose it in public.

There is no need to ask whether she was greatly humiliated, for to everyone she had said the opposite [of what the letter proved]. The Dowager Duchess [Margaret of York], the lord of Ravenstein, the Chancellor and the lord de Humbercourt [the four mentioned in the letter] were present. Hopes had been held out to the Duke of Clèves and others regarding the union of his son and the young lady; they were all infuriated, and thus the divisions within Marie of Burgundy's court grew sharper and began to show themselves. The Duke of Clèves had always, up to then, believed that the lord de Humbercourt was with him in the matter of the marriage; now, on learning the contents of the letter, he became de Humbercourt's enemy. The Bishop of Liége had no love for de Humbercourt, because of what had happened at Liége when that lord was its governor [for the Duke of Burgundy].

The Count of St Pol, son of the late Constable, hated the lord de Humbercourt and the Chancellor because at Péronne they had delivered his father into the hands of the king's officers, as you have heard at length. The people of Ghent hated these two also, not because they had committed any offence against the city but only because of the great authority they had enjoyed under Duke Charles. And surely they deserved their offices as much as did any who lived in their time, French or Burgundian; and they had served their master faithfully and well.

In the end, during the night following the morning on which this letter had been shown, the Chancellor and the lord de Humbercourt were seized by the people of Ghent, notwithstanding that the two of them had plenty of warning; but, unfortunately for them, like many others [including the late Constable] they could not bring themselves to take to flight. I believe indeed that their enemies, whom I have named, had a hand in their being seized.

With them was taken Messire Guillaume de Cluny, Bishop of Thérouanne (who would die Bishop of Poitiers), and the three of them were imprisoned together. The people of Ghent gave them a form of trial—not customary with those people when taking their vengeances—and appointed municipal officers to question them.

At the beginning they asked their prisoners why the latter had had my lord des Cordes yield up the citadel of Arras; but they spent little time on this, although it was the only real fault of which the men could have been accused. However, the hearts of the people were not in that question for it did not bother them, at least for the present, to see their lord deprived of such a town, nor did they have the foresight to realize what harm, as a result, could come to them in a short while. The interrogators settled upon two points. The first concerned certain gifts they accused the prisoners of having accepted, particularly in the case of a suit that the city had won against an individual, the Chancellor having given the verdict and he and de Humbercourt having accepted a gift from the city.

Concerning this whole charge of corruption they answered very well. As to the particular accusation of having sold justice in taking money from the city, they said the city had won its suit because its case was good and that, in regard to the money, they had not asked for it directly or indirectly, but when it was presented to them they accepted it.

The second point the interrogators settled upon was that during the time the accused had been with the late Duke Charles, and in his absence [from the Low Countries] were his lieutenants, they had done a number of things contrary to the privileges and dignity of the city, and any man who went against the privileges of Ghent should die. This case against the accused had no foundation what so ever; for they were not citizens of Ghent nor natives thereof and they had no power to annul the city's privileges. When Duke Charles and his father had deprived the inhabitants of some of their privileges, they had done so in accordance with treaties concluded after wars and revolts; and their remaining privileges, which are broader than is necessary for their welfare, had been carefully respected.

Notwithstanding the defence made by these two good and notable persons against the charges aforementioned (for nothing was said about the main charge which I spoke of earlier), the aldermen of Ghent, in their town hall, condemned the two to death, on the pretext that they were guilty of the two charges.

On hearing this cruel sentence, the two lords were utterly dumb-founded, as well they might be; and they saw no way out because they were in these people's hands. Nevertheless they drew up an appeal to the king as represented by the High Court of the Parlement of Paris, hoping that this device might at least delay their execution and that in the meanwhile their friends might be able to help them escape.

Before the sentence was passed, they had been severely tortured, without any legal justification; their trial lasted no more than six days; notwithstanding their appeal, their execution was immediately ordered, and they were allowed but three hours to be shriven and to give thought to their affairs. When the time expired, they were brought to the marketplace and put upon a scaffold.

The young lady of Burgundy, afterwards Duchess of Austria, on learning of this sentence of condemnation, went to the town hall to beg for the lives of the Chancellor and de Humbercourt; but it was to no avail. [The moving appeal Commynes describes below was indeed probably made in the marketplace, but occurred, like the foregoing scene in the town hall, on Easter Monday, 31 March 1477, three days before sentence was passed. Marie was not present at the execution on 3 April.] She then went to the marketplace, where all the people were assembled in arms and beheld the two condemned men on the scaffold. The lady, being in mourning dress, wore only a simple headcovering—a plain and humble costume, and one that should rightly have inspired pity. She there implored the people, tears in her eyes and her hair dishevelled, to have compassion on her two servants and render them to her.

A large number of the people wanted to accede to her supplication and spare their lives; others were opposed; and pikes were levelled at breasts, as if the two parties were going to do battle. Those who wanted the victims killed found themselves to be the stronger side, and they finally yelled to those on the scaffold to carry out the execution. To conclude, the two had their heads cut off, and the poor young lady returned in this sorry state to her dwelling, forlorn and griefstricken, for they were the men she trusted most.

After these people of Ghent had accomplished this feat, they removed from her side my lord of Ravenstein and the Dowager Duchess because they were likewise designated in the letter that the Chancellor and the lord de Humbercourt had delivered to the king. And then the people assumed all authority and rule over this poor young princess. She could thus well be called, not so much because of the loss of so many great towns, irrecoverable on account of the strong hand which now grasped them—for indeed by finding favour, friendship or a means of appointment [with the king] she could still have some hope regarding them—but because of being in the hands of her worst enemies, persecutors of her House. This was her real misfortune. Yet, in their conduct of affairs there is always more folly than malice. It is usually the crude artisans who enjoy credit and authority among them, men who have no knowledge of state affairs and the arts of governing. The cleverness of these people is confined to two issues: one is that in every way they seek to enfeeble and undermine their prince; the other is that when they have committed some offence or made a great miscalculation [i.e. in revolting], and see that they will get the worst of it, never do any people more humbly beg for terms than they do nor give greater gifts [in propitiation]. And they are better at finding just the right people to approach for securing terms than any other town I have ever known.

While the king was taking over the towns and places afore-mentioned on the borders of Picardy, his army was operating in the County and Duchy of Burgundy. Its nominal head was the Prince of Orange [Jean de Chalon], still living today, a native and subject of the County of Burgundy. However, he had recently become, for the second time, an enemy of Duke Charles. Thus the king made use of him, for he was a great lord both in the county and the duchy, had influential kin, and was much loved. My lord de Craon, the king's lieutenant, was the real commander of the army; and he was the one in whom the king had confidence. He was indeed a clever man, and completely loyal, but somewhat too greedy. This lord, on approach-ing the duchy, sent the Prince of Orange and others before Dijon to make the necessary declarations and demand its allegiance to the king. This embassy did its work so well, mainly because of the Prince of Orange, that the town of Dijon [the capital] and all the other towns in the duchy submitted to the king's authority, as did several places in the County of Burgundy, like Ausson and some other strongholds.

The prince had been promised, in addition to splendid estates from the king, possession of all the places in the County of Burgundy which had constituted the inheritance left by the Prince of Orange his grandfather. This inheritance he had disputed with his uncles, the lords de Châteauguion, who, he claimed, had been wrongfully favoured by Duke Charles—for the case had been pleaded before the duke, a splendidly formal occasion lasting several days, after which the duke, counselled by many learned jurists, pronounced judgement against the prince, unjustly, at least so the prince said. On this account he left the duke's service and came to the king.

Notwithstanding what he had been promised, when the lord de

Craon found himself in possession of so many places, including the best ones that the prince was to have and that belonged to the disputed inheritance, he refused to deliver them to the prince, despite all the prince's demands. The prince wrote to the king about it, and, without exaggeration, wrote many times. The king, for his part, knew well that the lord de Craon was treating the prince unjustly, but he feared to displease that lord, who was in complete charge of the Burgundies, and he did not believe that the prince had the desire or the means to bring about a revolt in the county and duchy—though in fact the prince did do, at least in a great part of that territory. However, I will now leave this subject for a later time. . . .

The enmity of the city of Ghent for the House of Burgundy leads Commynes to suggest that every nation has its 'thorn', its natural foe—as the English for the French, the Scots for the English, Portugal for Spain, the Italian Republics, such as Florence, for Italian princes like the King of Naples, the Swiss for the House of Austria, the Hanseatic cities for the King of Denmark. Commynes then discusses again a favourite subject, the evils committed by princes reared in ignorance and heedless of good counsel, whom God alone punishes. One of the chief evils is brutal and tyrannical taxation. A prince should secure the good will and consent of his people in levying taxes—and here Commynes instances the people whose institutions he most admires, the English, particularly for their Parliament. 'In my opinion, among all the lordships of the world of which I have some knowledge, it is in England where public business is best managed, where least violence is done to the common people, and where there are no buildings ruined and destroyed by war. And when war is waged there, its misfortunes fall upon those responsible for it' (i.e. upon the nobles rather than the commons). As an example of why Kings of France should be willing to consult the Three Estates, Commynes instances the Three Estates summoned in 1484 after the death of Louis XI, which proved themselves completely loyal to his son, the boy-king Charles VIII. Commynes then adverts to the kind of punishment God inflicts upon princes, particularly in raising up against them unexpected enemies. He cites Henry VI, overthrown by Edward IV and the Earl of Warwick, and Warwick's turning against King Edward, only to meet death in battle; he then recounts the career of Richard III, which story will be inserted, in this translation, where Commynes later reverts to it in its chronological order. He concludes with brief examples drawn from Spain, Scotland and Gelderland.

BOOK SIX

Harvest,
1477–83

... THOSE WHO WILL READ THESE MEMOIRS IN TIME TO COME, and who understand better than I do the affairs of this realm and of its neighbours, may be amazed that, from the time I reached the death of the Duke of Burgundy up to now, a span of almost a year, I have made no mention of the English nor explained how they could allow the king to take into his hands towns so near them [i.e. so near English Calais] like Arras, Boulogne, Hesdin, Ardres and numerous strongholds, and to have his army encamp before St Omer for several days. The reason is that the intelligence and statecraft of our king were much superior to Edward IV's, although King Edward was a very valiant prince and had won in England eight or nine battles, always fighting on foot [with his men], for which feats he well deserves renown. But these English wars were of short duration and King Edward's abilities were not tested by them. As soon as he had won a victory, he was master of his realm until the next trouble developed; and whatever strife breaks out in England, within ten days or less the issue is decided one way or the other. Our affairs on this side of the Channel are not like that: for when the struggle with the Duke of Burgundy was concluded, our king had to be intensely occupied with several matters in the realm and with foreign relations. Among all his other affairs, he was especially intent upon keeping the King of England satisfied, or humoured, by embassies, presents and fine words so that he would not meddle in our affairs.

Our king knew well that any time the English, nobles, commons and churchmen alike, are happy to make war upon this realm, under pretext of the rights in the realm that they pretend to and also in the hope of spoils. This attitude derives from the fact that God permitted their ancestors to win many great victories in this kingdom and to hold parts of it for a long time, such as Normandy and Guienne which they had possessed for 350 years at the moment that Charles VII reconquered Normandy [1449–50] and retook Guienne for the first time [in 1451, the final conquest occurring in 1453]. During their occupation they carried off great spoils and riches to England, partly taken from the poor and partly from lords of France whom they had held for ransom in great numbers and partly from the towns and places they had captured in the realm. And their constant hope is to do the same thing again. But such success could hardly have come to them in the time of the king our master, for never would he have hazarded his realm to the extent, as was done at Agincourt [25 October 1415], of having the whole nobility of the realm dismount and fight on foot against the English. That he would have proceeded more wisely had it come to such a battle, you will have seen by the way he got rid of them when Edward of England invaded the kingdom.

Now the king our master knew well that the King of England and his intimate advisers were very much in favour of keeping the peace and enjoying our king's subsidies. Our king was therefore careful to pay the pension of fifty thousand crowns that [in semi-annual instalments] he rendered to the King of England at London (the English calling it 'tribute'); and to Edward IV's intimates he paid some sixteen thousand crowns in pensions as well—namely, to the Chancellor [Thomas Rotherham]; to the Master of the Rolls [John Morton], now Chancellor [and Archbishop of Canterbury]; to the Great Chamberlain, [William] Lord Hastings, a man of intelligence and ability who enjoyed high authority; to Sir Thomas Mongomery; to [John] Lord Howard, afterwards created Duke of Norfolk by the evil King Richard [III]; to the Master of the Horse, [Sir John] Cheyney; to Sir Thomas St Leger; to the Marquess of Dorset [Thomas Grey], son of the Queen of England by her first marriage. Our king also gave very lavish gifts to all English envoys who came to him. Even when they arrived with rigorous demands, he sent them off with such winning words and handsome presents that they considered themselves satisfied. And whatever realization they had that the king our master was acting thus to gain time and attain his

Ansi comme deuant est dit alloient et venoient ces marchi; entre le roy et le roy dingleterre pour tousiours gaigner temps et se affoiblissoit ladicte Damoyselle de bourgongne/ Car de ce peu de gens de guerre qui luy estoient demourez apres la mort de son pere plussrs se tournerent. Sa partye du roy/ Et par especial apres ce que morissr des cordes sy fut mrs qui plusieurs en emmena auec luy. Les autres se tournoient par necessite/ pource quilz estoient situez ou demourans pres des villes ou dedans celles qui estoient ia en lobeissance dudit sr et aussi pour auoir de ses biens/ Car nul autre prince

The marriage of Marie of Burgundy and Maximilian

ends in this war that he had begun [with Burgundy], they put it out of their minds because of the great benefits they were deriving.

To all these men he had made gifts in addition to their pensions. I am certain that in less than two years he gave Lord Howard, in addition to his pension, money and plate worth at least twenty-four thousand crowns, and to the Great Chamberlain, Lord Hastings, he gave, as a single present, a thousand marcs of silver in plate. The receipts of all these persons [for their pension payments] will be found in the Exchequer at Paris, except for that of Lord Hastings, Great Chamberlain of England (there is only one such Chamberlain and therefore it is a high office).

Lord Hastings saw to it that he was ardently solicited to accept a pension. I was responsible for his accepting one, for I made him a friend of Duke Charles of Burgundy at the time I was with the duke, who gave him a thousand crowns a year. Afterwards, I reported this to the king, whose pleasure it likewise was that I should arrange to make Lord Hastings his friend and servant—in time past he had always been a great enemy of France, while Duke Charles was alive; even later, he favoured Marie of Burgundy, and it was not his fault that at one time or another England did not aid her against the king. Thus I began this friendship through letters; and the king gave Lord Hastings a pension of two thousand crowns, double the amount the duke had accorded him. The king our master sent the pensions to him and the others by Pierre Clairet, one of the royal masters of the household, straitly charging Clairet to secure quittances for them, in order that, in time to come, it would be seen and known that the Great Chamberlain, the Chancellor, the Admiral, the Master of the Horse, of England, and the rest, had been pensioners of the King of France.

Pierre Clairet, a most prudent man, had a private meeting with Lord Hastings in his chamber in London, just the two of them. After Clairet had recited the necessary preliminaries and said that he was presenting him, from the king, these two thousand gold crowns (for the king never gave any money except gold coin to great foreign lords), and after the Chamberlain had received the money, Pierre Clairet begged him, for Clairet's acquittance, to sign a receipt. Lord Hastings made some difficulty about it. Then Clairet asked him for a letter of but three lines, addressed to the king, acknowledging that he had received the money. This, Clairet explained, was for his acquittance in regard to the king his master so that he would not

s

think Clairet had appropriated the money, the king being a little on the suspicious side. The Chamberlain, realizing that Clairet was asking no more than what was appropriate, said, 'Sir, what you say is perfectly reasonable; but this gift is made at the good pleasure of the king your master and not at my request. If you want me to take it, then put it here in my sleeve. But you will have neither letter nor quittance, for I am entirely unwilling, for my part, that it should be said, *The Great Chamberlain of England has been a pensioner of the King of France*, and that my quittance should be found in his Exchequer.'

Clairet, saying no more, left him the money. On his returning to the king and making his report, the king was very much chagrined that he had not brought the quittance, but he praised Clairet for what he had done and thenceforth thought more highly of the Chamberlain than of any of the other intimates and advisers of the King of England. And after that the Chamberlain was always paid without being asked for a quittance.

In this manner did our king live with these English. Nevertheless, the King of England was often pressed, by those about the young princess, to provide aid. He therefore sent the king an embassy to make remonstrances concerning this matter and to urge him to make peace or at least a truce. There were some members of King Edward's council, and especially some members of his Parliament (which is similar to the Three Estates) who were sagacious people, and far-sighted, and did not receive pensions like the others. These people ardently desired (as did the commons of England) that King Edward give positive aid to the young lady of Burgundy and said that the French were deceiving them and that the marriage [of Edward's eldest daughter Elizabeth and the dauphin] was not being accomplished—this being obvious since, in the Treaty of Picquigny, it had been sworn and promised that within a year the daughter of the King of England, already called Madame la Dauphine, would be fetched to France and that year had long ago passed. [In fact, no such clause occurs in the treaty.]

No matter what remonstrances King Edward's subjects made, he was unwilling to listen to them; and there were several reasons for this. He was a fleshy and lazy man who dearly loved his pleasures, and it would have been impossible for him to endure the toils of making war in France. He saw himself delivered from the great adversities he had suffered, and he had no desire to encounter more. On the other hand, his greed for the fifty thousand crowns delivered to him yearly in his Tower of London turned his heart to jelly. Furthermore, when his ambassadors arrived in France, they were so well treated and given such handsome presents that they returned home satisfied. Never was there made to their demands a response that represented a real answer or decision, this evasion always gaining time. Instead, they were told that in a few days the king would send to the king their master a worthy embassy, which would give him such assurances concerning matters of which he was in doubt that he would be well satisfied.

Thus, three weeks or a month after these English ambassadors had departed—sometimes more, sometimes less—which was no brief interval for such a case, the king sent the embassy, which was always composed of persons who had not been members of his previous embassy, so that if the latter had made some offer that had not been fulfilled, this next embassy could disavow any knowledge of it. Furthermore, these embassies were at great pains to give such sureties in France to the King of England that he continued to have patience and do nothing; for he so ardently desired this marriage of his daughter, as did his queen, that that, with the other motives I have explained, caused him to close his eyes to the situation which some members of his council declared to be highly prejudicial to his realm; he also feared the rupture of the marriage agreement because of the ridicule of it that was already circulating in England, especially by those who wanted strife and war.

To clarify this subject a little, the king our master never had any intention of accomplishing this marriage, for the ages of the two were not compatible, King Edward's daughter, the present Queen of England [to Henry VII], being much too old [twelve, in February 1477] for the dauphin, our present king [six]. Thus, by these evasions —a month or two at a time gained in the going and coming of each embassy—the king's enemy lost a campaigning season in which to do him harm. For, without doubt, had it not been for the English king's looking forward to the marriage, he would not have permitted, over such a period, places so near Calais to be captured without making an effort to defend them; and if, at the beginning, he had declared for Marie of Burgundy, our king, who feared putting matters in hazard, would not have enfeebled this House of Burgundy to the extent that he has.

I say these things mainly only to illuminate how the affairs of this world are managed—either in seizing an advantage or avoiding a danger—as a possible service to those with such grand designs in hand who will read these Memoirs: however intelligent princes are, a little counsel is sometimes useful. It is true that if the young lady of Burgundy had been willing to marry [Anthony Woodville] Earl Rivers, brother of the English queen, he would have aided her with a goodly number of troops; but it was not a suitable match for he was but an earl and she was the greatest heiress of her time.

Several propositions were advanced between our king and the King of England. Among others, our king made the offer that if King Edward would join with him against Marie of Burgundy in invading her domains, he would agree to King Edward's having the county of Flanders, without doing homage to him for it [i.e. in full sovereignty], and also Brabant. Our king further offered to conquer at his own expense the four largest towns of Brabant [of which Brussels was the capital] and put the King of England in possession of them, and, in addition, to pay the expenses of ten thousand English troops for four months, so that King Edward could more easily bear the costs of his invasion. He likewise would lend him a powerful artillery train, with men and wagons to service it, and, while the King of England conquered Flanders, he would keep the Burgundians busy elsewhere.

The King of England replied that these towns of Flanders were great and strongly fortified, that it was a region difficult to keep after it was won, the same being true of Brabant, and that the English would be entirely opposed to such a war because of their trade with the Low Countries. However, since the King of France was willing to share the French conquest with him, let the king then deliver to him some of the places he had already conquered in Picardy, like Boulogne and others, and he would then declare for him and send troops, at French expense, to aid him—which was a very clever answer.

Thus, as I said above, these propositions went back and forth between our king and the King of England, our king's purpose being always to gain time while Marie of Burgundy grew weaker. For, of the few troops that remained to her after the death of her father, many turned to the king's side, especially after my lord des Cordes did so, who brought over many with him. Others went over to the king by necessity, because their property or residences were located near or within towns already in the king's possession; and some changed allegiance in order to enjoy the king's rewards, for no other prince ever treated his servants as generously as he did. And then there were the daily increasing troubles in these large cities, especially in Ghent, the prime mover of them, as you have heard.

Those about Marie of Burgundy had discussed several marriages for her, saying that she must take a husband to defend the remainder of what she possessed or else espouse the dauphin so that she could keep all. Some ardently desired this marriage, especially she herself before the affair of the letter. Others pointed to the dauphin's tender years, he being then only about nine [actually, he would turn seven on 30 June 1477], and to the marriage already arranged for him with Princess Elizabeth, and they worked on behalf of the son of the Duke of Clèves. Still others favoured Maximilian, the son of the Emperor [Frederick III], who is at present King of the Romans [i.e. emperor-elect].

The young lady had conceived a hatred of the king because of the letter, which, it seemed to her, had caused the death of those two distinguished persons above named and the ignominy she suffered when it was publicly delivered to her as you have heard. This occurrence had inspired the people of Ghent with the audacity to drive so many of her servants away from her and to separate her from her step-mother and the lord of Ravenstein; and as a result her waiting ladies were in such a panic that they did not dare open a letter without showing it to their mistress, nor speak to her in a low voice [for fear of being accused of plotting against the city]. . . .

At a council meeting summoned to discuss the marriage question, Madame de Hallwin [a cousin of Commynes], first lady in waiting to the princess, said—as it was reported to me—that they needed a man and not an infant; her mistress was of child-bearing age and an heir was what the country needed. The council adopted this view. Some blamed the lady for having spoken so frankly; others praised her for it, saying that she was merely discussing the marriage, and what was necessary for the country, in practical terms. Thus finding the husband became their complete preoccupation. I truly believe that if the king had wished her to marry the present Count of Angoulême [Charles, father of the future Francis I], she would have agreed, so much did she desire to remain within the House of France. [The count was of the younger branch of the House of Orléans, which was next in line to the throne after the male heirs of the king.]

However, God willed a different marriage—and perchance we still do not know why God so willed. We see from what has happened that great wars have sprung from that marriage, both here and in the Burgundian domain, which would not have occurred had she married my lord of Angoulême. And these wars and other calamities have been borne mainly by Flanders and Brabant. . . .

Thus negotiations were begun for the young lady's union with the son of the emperor, concerning which there had been communication between the emperor and Duke Charles and the marriage agreed upon [autumn, 1476]. By command of her father, a letter was written in the young lady's name and a ring with a diamond dispatched. The letter said that, following the will of her lord and father, she promised the emperor's son to accomplish the marriage that had been negotiated, in the manner prescribed by and according by the will of her lord and father.

The emperor sent certain ambassadors to the young lady at Ghent. . . . It was decided by her council that, after these envoys had recited their credence, the young lady would tell them that they were very welcome and that she would submit to her council the mission they had announced and then would have a reply made to them; and she would say nothing more. To this she agreed.

The ambassadors presented their letters, when asked to do so, and spoke their credence—namely, a marriage agreement had been concluded between the emperor and the Duke of Burgundy her father, with her knowledge and assent, as was evidenced by a letter written in her hand—which they produced—and by her giving of the diamond, which, they said, was sent as a marriage token; they therefore emphatically demanded, in their master's name, that the young lady fulfill the marriage contract in accordance with her father's and her own promise, and declare before those present whether or not she had written the letter and whether she was willing to keep her word.

Without taking counsel, the young lady answered immediately that she had indeed written the letter, at her father's order, that she avowed its contents and that she had sent the diamond. The ambassadors thanked her effusively and returned joyful to their lodgings.

The Duke of Clèves was very deeply displeased by this response, which was the opposite of what had been agreed upon in council, and remonstrated strongly with the young lady for having spoken as she should not have. She replied that she could not have done otherwise, for the promise of marriage had been made and she could not go against it. . . .

Thus was achieved this marriage; for Duke Maximilian came to Cologne, where he was met by some servants of the young lady. I have reason to believe that they found him short of funds and supplied him with some, for his father has been the absolutely stingy man, more so than any other prince of our times.

The son of the emperor was escorted to Ghent, accompanied by seven or eight hundred horse, and there the wedding was celebrated [19 August 1477]. This marriage, at the beginning, was not very useful to the young lady's subjects; for instead of Maximilian's providing money, they had to supply him with it. The people he brought with him were far from sufficient in number to make any headway against such a power as the king's; and their way of life was incompatible with that of the subjects of this House of Burgundy, who had lived under rich princes, princes who distributed high offices and maintained a splendid court, in furnishings, table service, and in their dress and that of their courtiers.

The Germans are very much the opposite; for they are crude and they live crudely. I have no doubt that it was sage counsel and the grace of God which produced the law in France [the Salic law] that daughters cannot inherit the realm, in order to prevent its falling into the hands of a foreign prince and foreigners; for the French could hardly have endured that.

Nor can other nations. In the long run, there are no lordships, especially among the great ones, in which, in the end, the rule does not remain in the possession of those who are of those countries. You can see this illustrated by France, in which the English held great power for four hundred years, and at this hour they have only Calais and two little castles to guard it, which cost them a great deal to keep. The remainder of their French holdings they lost much more quickly than they conquered them, for they lost more in a day than they had won in a year. The same thing can be seen in the Kingdom of Naples and the Island of Sicily and other provinces the French [of the House of Anjou] possessed for long years; and, by all signs, there remains no memory of them except in the sepulchres of their ancestors.

Even if one can put up with a foreign prince accompanied by only a few followers, they well disciplined and he prudent, the situation becomes far more difficult if the prince brings large numbers of men. In time of war it is almost impossible to prevent discord and strife in the army, partly because of the differences in custom and temperament between his subjects and his own people and partly because of the outrages his people commit on account of lacking that love of the country possessed by those born there. The worst occurs when these foreigners seek to have offices and benefices and the positions of greatest authority in the country. Thus a prince, when he goes to a foreign land, must act very wisely in order to maintain harmony; and if a prince lacks this ability, which, above all other talents, comes only from the grace of God, no matter what other virtues he has in him, he will hardly be able to succeed. And if he lives a normal span, he will have great troubles and difficulties, as will all those living under him, especially when he reaches advanced years and his men and officers can no longer hope for his amending.

After the marriage of Maximilian and Marie, their affairs scarcely went any better, for they were both young. Duke Maximilian had no knowledge of anything, partly because of his being in a strange country, and partly because of an inferior upbringing, at least as regards his learning anything about statecraft. Also he was utterly lacking the troops necessary for a great military effort. On this account that land has been in great trouble up to now, and looks to be in it still. . . .

A few days after this marriage the County of Artois was lost, or at least it was lost while the marriage was being negotiated—I am satisfied if the substance is correct, and should I make a mistake in dates, by a month or so, I hope the readers will forgive me. The affairs of the king went better and better, for he had no opposition. He continued to take places, unless there was a truce or an overture regarding terms, which, however, could never come to anything because their terms were not reasonable. Hence the war against Duke Maximilian and Marie went on.

They had a son the first year, Archduke Philip [the Handsome] as he is now. The second year they had a daughter, Margaret, who is at present our queen. The third year they had a son [who died within a few months], named Francis for Duke Francis of Brittany. The fourth year Marie of Burgundy died of a fall from a horse [27 March 1482], or from a fever—but she did suffer the fall. Some say that she was pregnant. Her death was a great misfortune for her people, for she was a very good lady and generous and well liked by her subjects, who gave her more respect and obedience than they did her husband. Also she was the lady of the land [and her feudal sovereignty passed to her son Philip, not to Maximilian]. She was completely devoted to her husband, and a lady of high repute.

In Hainault the king held the towns of Quesnoy-le-Conte and Bouchain. These he gave back, an action that amazed some people, considering that he demanded no terms and had appeared to be set upon winning the whole Burgundian domain and leaving nothing to the House of Burgundy. And I well believe that had he been able to parcel out that domain as he pleased and completely to destroy the rule of that House, he would have done so. But there were two causes that moved him to yield these places in Hainault [in accordance with truces of June–July 1478]. In the first place, he believed that a king has greater power and right in his own realm, where he has been anointed and crowned, than he has outside of it, and these places were outside the realm. In the second place, between kings of France and emperors there are great oaths and treaties prohibiting the one from attacking the other, and the towns were situated in imperial territory. For like cause, the king rendered Cambrai, or put it in neutral hands, content to lose it; and also the inhabitants had admitted the king only on his giving sureties.

In the County and Duchy of Burgundy the war went on and on, and the king could not reach an end to it, because the Swiss gave some little aid to the Prince of Orange, [now] lieutenant for Duke Maximilian and Marie. This aid, however, resulted from the money the Prince of Orange gave the Swiss, not at all from any desire they had to help Maximilian. For never was a man to be found who supported him, at least at the time of which I am speaking. These Swiss were mercenary companies who hired themselves out to any-body, for the Swiss are neither friends nor well-wishers of this House of Austria. . . .

However, the forces of the king proved to be too strong. The Burgundians ran out of money. Through secret understandings, place after place went over to the king.

On one occasion, the lord de Craon, the king's lieutenant, besieged Dôle, capital of the County of Burgundy. The garrison was small and he underestimated it; and he paid for his mistake. A sudden sally by the garrison took him by surprise and he lost some of his artillery and a few men, a reverse which brought personal humiliation, and blame from the king.

The latter, angered by this occurrence, began to think of appointing another governor in the Burgundies, and also because of the great pillaging of the lord de Craon, which in truth, was too excessive. Nevertheless, before being dismissed from his office, that lord won a small victory over a force of Swiss and Burgundians, in which the lord de Châteauguion, the greatest noble of the region, was captured. For the rest, the battle was nothing much—I speak of it only by hearsay—but the lord de Craon won repute for his conduct that day.

As I began to say, the king decided, for the aforementioned reasons, to appoint a new governor for the Burgundies, without, however, cancelling any of the winnings and benefits of the lord de Craon, save for relieving him of his command of troops of the standing army, except for six men of arms and a dozen archers for his personal service. The lord de Craon, very fat and quite satisfied, went off into private life, well supported by the offices he held.

The king appointed in his place Charles d'Amboise, lord de Chaumont, a very valiant, sagacious and diligent man. The king then began negotiations aimed at securing the withdrawal of all the Swiss who were warring in the Burgundies, not so much to make use of those mercenary bands himself as to facilitate the conquest of the Burgundies and to negotiate a permanent arrangement for taking Swiss troops into his pay. He therefore sent envoys to the Swiss, whom he called 'my lords of the Leagues', and made them very handsome offers: first, twenty thousand francs a year to the four chief cities, Berne, Lucerne, Zurich and, I believe, Fribourg too —and the three cantons, which are federations of villages in their mountains, namely Schwytz from which the Swiss take their name, Uri and Unterwalden also shared in this distribution; second, twenty thousand francs a year to individuals who were useful to him in these negotiations. He had himself made an honorary citizen and wanted the honour signified in writing, and also had himself named their primary ally, against which point they raised some resistance because the Duke of Savoy had always been their primary ally. Nevertheless they accepted his offers and also agreed to provide him with a fixed contingent of six thousand mercenaries, he paying them four and a half German florins a month; and this number of Swiss remained in his army until his death.

An impoverished king could not have brought off such a feat. The whole arrangement proved very profitable to him, though I believe that in the end it will turn out harmful for the Swiss; they are now so used to making money, of which hitherto they had little knowledge, especially of gold coin, that they have come very near to fighting among themselves. Otherwise, they are quite safe from harm: their lands being poor and barren and they are excellent soldiers, few people will essay to attack them.

[Following the negotiation of this treaty and vigorous operations by the new governor, Charles d'Amboise, including the capture of Dôle and Auxonne] the Burgundies were entirely conquered. The governor had acted with great diligence, and he had also been urged on by the king, who feared lest he should always arrange for one place or another to resist so that he would be continually needed there and the king would not recall him to make use of him elsewhere. For the Burgundies are fertile country and the lord de Chaumont governed as if they were his own. The lords de Craon and de Chaumont both feathered their nests there very well.

For a while the territory remained in peace under de Chaumont's governorship. Nevertheless some places then rose in revolt (I was in the region at the time, for the king had sent me there as commander of the gentlemen-pensioners of his household; and it was the first time that he had appointed a captain for his pensioners, a practice which has since remained in force up to this hour). [After several operations, the siege and capture of Beaune ended the revolt.] All was recovered, and henceforth the enemies in the region had no power.

I was there at that time with the royal pensioners, as I have said. The king had sent me off because of a letter accusing me of sparing some burghers of Dijon from quartering troops. That, with a further slight suspicion of his, was the cause of his sending me very suddenly to Florence. I obeyed his order, as was my duty; and I left there as soon as I received his letter. [Commynes omits, out of modesty, to add that the mission required a man of his calibre, as was undoubtedly evident to Louis XI, who to the Florentines recommended his counsellor as 'one of the men in whom we have the greatest trust'.]

I was sent by the king to Florence because of strife that erupted between two celebrated families there, the Medici and the Pazzi. The latter, with the support of the pope [Sixtus IV] and of King Ferrante of Naples, plotted the death of Lorenzo de' Medici [Lorenzo the Magnificent] and all his chief adherents. Nevertheless, as to Lorenzo, the Pazzi failed; but they assassinated his brother, Giuliano de' Medici, in the *duomo* of Florence, and also one Francesco Nori, a servant of the Medici, who attempted to shield Giuliano. Lorenzo, seriously wounded, managed to withdraw to the sacristy of the cathedral, the doors of which, given by his father [Piero], are of bronze.

A servant whom he had ordered released from prison two days before served him well in his need, and received several wounds for him. The attack occurred as High Mass was being sung. The signal to kill was set for the moment that the priest who was singing the Mass would recite the *Sanctus* [i.e. at the elevation of the Host].

The event turned out otherwise than the plotters had intended, for, believing to have won all, some of them ascended the palace stairs with the aim of killing the members of the *Signoria* who were there—there are some nine of these members, their offices renewed every three months, who have the entire administration of the city. But these plotters were followed by few supporters; and, as soon as they had mounted the steps, a door was shut behind them and they found themselves to be only four or five in number, suddenly terrified and not knowing what to say. Perceiving this, the members of the *Signoria*, who had already heard Mass, and the attendants with them looked out the windows and saw the rioting in the town. Giacomo de' Pazzi and others in the square before the palace were shouting *Libertà! Libertà!* and *Popolo! Popolo!*—words that they thought would sway the populace to their side. The people, however, made no move; and Giacomo de' Pazzi and his companions, not knowing what to do, fled from the square. Seeing these things from the windows, the governors of the town of whom I have spoken immediately seized the five or six plotters trapped on the top floor, and, without more ado, had them strangled and hanged from the casement windows. Among those hanged was the Archbishop of Pisa.

These governors, seeing that the whole town had declared for them and for the Medici party, sent orders at once to river-crossings and frontier posts that every fugitive should be captured and brought to them. Giacomo de' Pazzi was taken within the hour along with another conspirator, an agent of the pope in command of some troops of Count Girolamo [Riario, Sixtus IV's nephew], who was in this enterprise. Giacomo was immediately hanged at the windows with the others. The agent of the pope had his head cut off. Several plotters, including Francesco de' Pazzi, who were captured within Florence, were hanged in the heat of the moment. I believe that, in all, fourteen important persons were hanged and a number of menials were killed throughout the town.

Not many days after this event I arrived in Florence [about the beginning of July] as an emissary of the king. Since leaving Burgundy I had not dallied on the road, for I sojourned but two or three days with the Duchess of Savoy (our king's sister), who gave me a very good welcome. From there I went to Milan, where I likewise sojourned two or three days in order to ask that troops be sent to aid the Florentines, whose ally Milan then was: and the Milanese government [the queen's sister, Bona of Savoy, Duchess of Milan then being regent for her little son Giangaleazzo Sforza] freely granted my request, both as coming from the king and as representing their treaty obligation. They immediately furnished three hundred men of arms and afterwards sent still others.

To conclude this matter, the pope—as soon as the Pazzi conspiracy had failed—launched an excommunication [1 June 1478] against the Florentines and also dispatched an army, composed of his troops and those of the King of Naples, which was large and well equipped and numbered many men of rank. They set siege to La Castellina, near Siena, and took it and several other places; and it was only by great good fortune that the Florentines were not completely destroyed, for they had not been in war for a long time and did not realize their peril. Lorenzo de' Medici, the chief man of the city, was young and was governed by young people. Everybody had his own view and clung to it. There were few captains and the army was very small.

For the pope and the King of Naples, [Federigo] the Duke of Urbino was commander, a very sagacious man and an excellent captain. With him were Roberto Malatesta, lord of Rimini, who since has been a powerful man, and Costanzio Sforza, Prince of Pesaro, and several others including the two sons of King Ferrante of Naples, Alfonso, Duke of Calabria, and Federigo, Prince of Taranto, who are both still living. Thus they captured all the places they besieged, not so promptly as it would be done here for they do not know as well as we do how to establish and develop a siege; but when it comes to supplies and military equipment, they know better than we do.

The king's support gave some aid to the Florentines, not as much as I would have wished for I had no army to help them, but only my military escort [twenty-five horse, according to a Milanese ambassador at the court of Savoy]. I remained with the Florentines, or in their territory, for a month [leaving towards the end of August]—very well treated by them, they defraying my expenses, and better treated the last day than the first. I was then sent for by the king. In passing through Milan, I accepted on the king's behalf the homage of Giangaleazzo, present Duke of Milan, for the Duchy of Genoa—or rather, Madame his mother performed the ceremony of homage for him. I then returned to the king our master [about mid-October, at Tours], who gave me a warm welcome and discussed his affairs with me more intimately than he had ever done, I sleeping in his chamber, although I was unworthy of the honour and there were many others more suitable. But he was so wise that one could not go wrong with him, providing that one did precisely as he commanded, without adding anything of one's own.

I found the king our master somewhat aged, and he was beginning to suffer illnesses. Nevertheless this decline did not show itself immediately, and he managed all his affairs with his usual sagacity. The war in Picardy still continued, which the king took very much to heart. His adversaries felt the same way, but lacked his power.

[Maximilian] the Duke of Austria, having the Flemings at his command that year, laid siege to Thérouanne [on 29 July 1479); whereupon my lord des Cordes, the king's lieutenant in Picardy, gathered together all the garrisons and frontier guards that the king had in the region, along with eight thousand franc archers, and marched to succour the town. As soon as the Duke of Austria learned of des Cordes' approach, he raised the siege and moved to oppose the French. They encountered each other at a place called Guinegate. With the duke were a great number of Flemings, up to twenty thousand or more, and some few Germans and three hundred English commanded by Sir Thomas Aurigan, an English knight who had served Duke Charles. The king's cavalry, which far outnumbered Maximilian's, broke the cavalry [wings] of the duke and pursued them and their commander, Philippe, lord of Ravenstein, all the way to Aire. The duke then took up his position with his [Flemish] pikemen. The royal forces included at least eleven or twelve hundred men of arms of the standing army. All the French did not join in the pursuit, but my lord des Cordes, who was commander-in-chief, did so, and my lord de Torcy with him. Although it was a valiant feat, the commanders of the advance guard should not take part in a pursuit. Some of the Burgundians withdrew under pretext of going off to guard their places; others simply fled. However, the duke's pikemen [the centre of his army] stood fast, although harassed by attacks; they were commanded by some two hundred stout-hearted gentlemen who fought with them on foot—among them, [Jacques of Savoy] the Count de Romont and the Count of Nassau and several others who are still living. As a result of the steadfastness of these leaders the pikemen held their ground, which was a marvellous thing considering that they had seen their cavalry take to flight. The king's franc archers applied themselves to pillaging the duke's wagon train and that of his sutlers. Some of the duke's foot-soldiers attacked them and killed a considerable number.

The duke's army suffered heavier losses than ours in men killed or captured, but the field remained to him. Indeed I believe that if he had been advised to return to Thérouanne he would have found not a soul within, nor at Arras. He did not dare attempt this, and paid for his failure; but in such cases commanders are not always aware of the essential course to follow, and also he had matters to worry about on his side. I speak of this battle only by hearsay for I was not there, but to pursue the thread of my story I had to say something about it.

I was with the king when the news reached him. He complained bitterly about it, for he was not accustomed to being beaten. On the contrary he was so successful in all his affairs that it seemed everything went according to his desire; but his intelligence was in large part responsible for these fortunate results, for he put nothing in hazard and was entirely opposed to battles—and this one had not come about by his order. He made his armies so large that few people were willing to engage them in combat, and they were supported by an artillery superior to that of any preceding King of France. It was the king's tactic to make surprise attacks upon places, especially those that he knew to be weakly defended. And when he had them, he stuffed them with so many troops and cannon that it was impossible to win them back from him. If in such a place there was some captain or other person who had the power to yield the town and wanted to make a deal with the king, that captain could be sure that he was on to a good thing; and however large the sum that such a one dared ask for, the king freely granted it.

The king was at first very much upset by this battle, thinking that he had not been told the truth and that it was a crushing defeat; for he well knew that if it was such a reverse he had lost all that he had conquered from the House of Burgundy in that region and that the remainder of his conquests were in great hazard. Nevertheless, when he learned the truth, he accepted the situation coolly and decided to arrange matters so that his commanders did not undertake such moves without his approval. And he was well satisfied with my lord des Cordes.

From that time he was determined to treat for peace with the Duke of Austria, provided that the articles of the peace were entirely to his advantage and that he could so thoroughly bridle the duke by means of the duke's own subjects (whom he knew to be disposed to grant what he was seeking) that he would never have the power to do him harm.

At this time the king cherished a very special desire, one to which he gave his whole heart, of being able to establish a uniform legal system in this realm, principally in the matter of long drawn out suits and trials, and in this respect to bridle the Parlement of Paris— not to diminish its numbers or its authority, but he had at heart several causes for hating it. He also ardently desired to establish in the realm one 'custom' [in place of a diversity of provincial and municipal regulations handed down from time immemorial] and a uniform system of weights and measures, and he wanted all customs codified in French [rather than Latin], the code to be inscribed in a handsome book, in order to prevent the tricks and plunderings of lawyers, which in this kingdom are so enormous that there is no other like it —and the nobles of the realm must know this well. Had God granted him the grace of living five or six years longer than he did, without being too much oppressed by illness, he would have done a great deal of good for his realm. He had heavily burdened his people with taxes—more than ever did another king. Authority, grasp of affairs, means of making remonstrances by which to secure relief they lacked: the relief had to come from him, as it would have done had it been God's will to preserve him from illness. Hence it is well to do good while a man has the time and God gives health.

The settlement that the king desired to make with the Duke of

Austria and the Burgundian domain was, by means of the people of Ghent, to negotiate the marriage of the dauphin with the daughter [Margaret] of Maximilian and Marie, whereby they would leave to him the counties of Burgundy, Auxerre, Macon and Charolais, while he would render to them the County of Artois, but retaining the citadel of Arras as he had fortified it—for the town of Arras no longer meant anything because of the citadel's now being enclosed against it, with stout walls and a defensive ditch between the two. . . .

Of the Duchy of Burgundy, the County of Boulogne, and likewise the Somme towns and the districts of Péronne, Roye and Montdidier, the king made no mention. This proposition he put forward, and the people of Ghent lent ear to it, and were extremely rude and overbearing to Duke Maximilian and his wife. Some other towns of Flanders and Brabant were very much of the same mind, especially Brussels—which was a great marvel considering that Dukes Philip and Charles of Burgundy had customarily resided there and that the Duke and Duchess of Austria were then in residence there. But the easy life that these people had known under the aforementioned lords had caused them to forsake God and their rulers and seek for some miserable future, which has since come to them, as you have seen.

During this time, in March of 1479 [actually, 1481], there was truce, and the king wanted a peace treaty, especially for this region of which I have spoken, provided, however, that it was entirely to his advantage, as I have said. He had already begun to grow old and ill; and while having his dinner at Les Forges near Chinon, he suffered a seizure and lost the power of speech. He was carried from the table and held near the fire, the windows being closed. Although he struggled to get to the windows, he was restrained by some who thought they were doing the right thing. This seizure occurred in March 1480. [Commynes contradicts the date he has just given; and there is convincing evidence that neither 1479 nor 1480, but 1481, is the correct year.] He lost his speech entirely and all awareness and memory.

Within the hour you happened to arrive, my lord of Vienne, you being then his physician. He was immediately given an enema and the windows were opened so that he could have air. At once he was able to say a few words and regained some possession of his senses; he then mounted horse and returned to Les Forges, for this illness

T

had come upon him in a little parish a quarter of a league from there, where he had gone to hear Mass.

He was well cared for. He made signs to indicate his meaning. Among other things, he asked for an ecclesiastic of Tours in order to confess himself and made signs that I should be sent for—for I had gone to [my estates at] Argenton, some ten leagues from there. When I arrived, I found the king at table, and with him Master Adam Fumée, formerly physician to Charles VII and at this time a Master of Requests of the royal household. There was also another physician named Master Claude. The king understood very little of what was said to him, but he was suffering no pain. He signed to me that I should sleep in his chamber; he was scarcely able to form words. I served him for fifteen days at table and attended upon his person, like a *valet de chambre*, which I considered a great honour; and indeed I was under obligation so to serve him.

At the end of two or three days, his speech began to return, and his understanding. It seemed to him that no one comprehended him as well as I. He therefore wanted me always with him; and when he confessed himself to the priest from Tours, I was present, for otherwise they would not have understood each other. He did not have much to say for he had confessed himself a few days before. Whenever the kings of France are going to touch people suffering from scrofula [hence called in England 'the king's evil'], they made confession, and our king never failed to do so once a week.

When he had made some recovery, he began to ask for the names of those who had restrained him by force and prevented him from going to the windows. He was told. Immediately he drove them all from his household. Some he deprived of their offices and never afterwards saw them; others, like my lord of Segré and Gilbert de Grassay, lord de Champéroux, lost no offices, but he sent them elsewhere.

A great many people were amazed at this notion of his and criticized him for it, saying that those men had acted for the best; and they spoke true. However, the obsessions of princes are various and complex and not to be understood by all those who busy themselves talking about them. There was nothing the king so much feared as to lose his authority—and very powerful it was—and to be disobeyed in any matter whatsoever.

On the other hand, his father King Charles, when he became fatally ill, conceived the notion that someone was seeking to poison him at the request of his son, and he became so obsessed with it that he refused to eat. It was then decided, by the advice of his physicians and his greatest and most intimate officers, that he should be made to eat by force. Thus was it done: he was forcibly fed broth. Shortly after, King Charles died, [but other evidence indicates that a jaw infection, not fear of poisoning, prevented the king from swallowing]. King Louis, who had always sharply criticized this action, took it amazingly to heart that he had been held down by force, though he sought to dissemble this feeling, for the main basis of his attitude was his fear that someone would seek to deprive him of his authority over affairs on the pretext that he was not of sound mind.

When he had given this fright to all those of whom I have spoken [i.e. had dismissed those who had forcibly restrained him], he inquired about what business the council had done and what orders had been dispatched in the past ten or twelve days. The chief councillors were [Louis d'Amboise] the Bishop of Albi, his brother [Charles d'Amboise] the governor of the Burgundies, Marshal Gié, and the lord du Lude, for they were the ones with him when he fell ill, and they were all lodged under his chamber in two little rooms that were there. The king wanted to see the letters that had arrived and were arriving every hour. He was shown the main ones, and I read them to him. He pretended to understand them, taking them in his hand and feigning to read them, though he had no comprehension of them; and he said some word or made signs to indicate the replies he wanted made.

We did very little business while awaiting the end of this illness, for he was a master for whom one had to plough a straight furrow. This illness lasted about fifteen days, after which his speech and understanding were restored to normal. But he remained weak and he was fearful of suffering a relapse—for he was by nature inclined not to believe the advice of physicians.

As soon as he was recovered, he freed Cardinal Balue, whom he had held prisoner for fourteen years; many times the cardinal's release had been requested by the pope and by others, and in the end the king secured absolution by a bull sent by the pope at his request.

At the time of his seizure, those who were then with him thought he was bound to die and dispatched several orders to cancel a very cruel and excessive tax which he had recently levied by the advice of my lord des Cordes, his lieutenant in Picardy, to pay for the upkeep of

20,000 foot-soldiers and 2,500 military engineers (and these troops were called 'the camp corps'); and he had established a body of 1,500 men of arms of the standing army to fight on foot with them at need. He had had constructed tents and pavilions and a huge number of wagons with which to enclose the camp and thus make a laager, a device which he borrowed from the Duke of Burgundy's army; and this 'camp corps' cost 1,500,000 francs a year. When this military establishment was ready, he went to see it encamped near Pont de l'Arche in Normandy on a beautiful plain, and the 6,000 Swiss were there, of whom I have spoken. Never but once did he see this 'camp corps'. On his return to Tours he suffered another seizure. Again he lost his speech and for a good two hours he was believed dead. He was in a gallery, lying on a straw mattress, several people about him.

My lord du Bouchage and I vowed him to St Claude, and all the others there present joined in the vow. Immediately his speech returned and within the hour he was walking about the dwelling, very feeble. This second attack occurred [at his palace of Plessis-les-Tours outside Tours] in [September of] 1481. He rode about the country as before. He was with me at Argenton, where he sojourned for a month, and was very ill; from there he went to Thouars, where he was likewise ill; and he undertook the journey to [the shrine of St Claude at] St Claude [in the County of Burgundy] to which saint he had been vowed as you have heard.

He had sent me to Savoy, on his leaving Thouars, against the lords de la Chambre and de Miolans and [Prince Philip of] Bresse [one of the numerous brothers-in-law of Yolande, Duchess of Savoy, now deceased]—although he was aiding them secretly—because they had seized lord d'Illins, of Dauphiné, whom he had placed in control of the government of Duke Philibert, his nephew. The king sent after me a force of troops whom I conducted to Macon against Prince Philip of Bresse. However, he and I came to a secret understanding: he captured the lord de la Chambre while that lord was sleeping in Duke Philibert's chamber at Turin in the Savoyard province of Piedmont, and then sent word to me. I immediately withdrew my force of troops, for Prince Philip brought the Duke of Savoy to Grenoble [capital of Dauphiné], where the Marshal of Burgundy, the Marquis de Rothelin and I had gone to receive him. The king then sent for me to join him at Beaujeu in the Beaujolais. I was amazed at the sight of him, so thin and wasted he was; and I was astonished that he could ride about the country; but his great heart sustained him.

At Beaujeu the king received letters informing him that the Duchess of Austria [Marie of Burgundy] had died of a fall from a horse—she was riding a very spirited little 'hobby'. The animal caused her to fall, and she landed upon a big piece of wood. Some say that it was not the fall but a fever that killed her. Whatever it was, she died a few days after the fall [27 March 1482]; and her death was a great misfortune for her subjects and allies, because never since have they been at peace—the people of Ghent and other towns held her in greater respect than they did her husband, she being the Lady of the land.

The king recounted to me this news, which overjoyed him. The two children of the duke and duchess had remained in the keeping of the people of Ghent, whom the king knew to be disposed to revolts and uprisings against this House of Burgundy; and it now seemed to him that his opportunity had come, the more so because the Duke of Austria was young and a foreigner and at war on all sides, and his father the emperor was extremely tight-fisted.

From that hour the king began to intrigue with the leaders of Ghent, through my lord des Cordes, concerning the marriage of his son the dauphin and the duke's daughter Margaret. The two men especially worked upon were the chief official of the town, Guillaume Rym, a very clever and adroit man, and Jean Coppenolle, secretary to the municipal council, who was a shoemaker and enjoyed great credit with the people—for it is folk of such stature that they choose when they are thus in a state of revolt.

The king returned to Tours [from his pilgrimage to St Claude on 2 June 1482]. He so shut himself away [at Plessis-lès-Tours] that few people saw him. He became marvellously suspicious of everyone, fearing an attempt to diminish or deprive him of his authority; he sent away all his people customarily in attendance upon him, and the most intimate advisers he had ever had, without, however, depriving them of anything, and they went off to their offices and duties or to their homes. This situation, however, was not of much duration, for he did not long survive. He also did many strange things, which caused those who did not know him to think that he was losing his mind—but they indeed did not know him.

As to his being suspicious, all great princes are so, especially the sagacious ones and those who have had many enemies and people bearing grudges against them, as was the case with the king. In addition, he knew that he was not loved by the great lords of his realm nor by many lesser folk, and he had more heavily burdened the people than any other king ever did—though he genuinely wanted to lighten that burden, as I have said, but he should have begun sooner.

King Charles VII was the first (by means of several good and wise knights who had served in his conquest of Normandy and Guienne, then held by the English) to win the point of imposing taxes at his pleasure without the consent of the Three Estates [and the provincial Estates] of his realm. And at that time there were pressing affairs, such as provision for the defence of the newly reconquered provinces and the necessity of getting rid of the companies of free-booters [called *Écorcheurs*, Flayers] who were pillaging the realm. The lords of France consented to this measure regarding taxes, in return for certain pensions promised them in lieu of the taxes levied in their lands.

If Louis XI were still living, and those who were then with him in his council, he would have done a great deal indeed to relieve his people of taxes. But for what has happened, and will continue to happen, he sorely charged his soul and the souls of his successors, and inflicted a cruel wound upon his realm, which long will bleed, and likewise fastened upon it the terrible bridle of an army of mercenaries which he instituted in imitation of Italian princes.

King Charles VII raised, at the hour of his death, a total of 1,800,000 francs in taxes and had about 1,700 men of arms comprising the standing army, who, well disciplined, were established as the guards of the provinces of the realm and who for a long time before that king's death had ceased to ride all over the country, which state of affairs gave great repose to the people. At the hour of the king our master's death, he raised 4,700,000 francs a year; and he had some 4,000 or 5,000 men of arms and, in the 'camp corps' and auxiliary forces, more than 25,000 foot-soldiers.

Thus there is no need to be amazed if the king had many long thoughts and notions and if he believed himself unpopular—though of those whom he had cherished in his household and who had received benefits from him, he would have found a great number loyal to him to the death.

Hardly any people entered Plessis-lès-Tours, which was where the king remained, except for domestic servants and the archers, a body of four hundred men, a goodly number of whom stood watch daily, patrolling the grounds and guarding the gate. No lord or important person lodged within and great lords in groups rarely entered. Of such nobles only my lord de Beaujeu, present Duke of Bourbon, who was his son-in-law [being married to his daughter Anne], came there. All round the palace of Plessis the king had had erected a fence of stout iron bars and had had imbedded in the wall iron prongs with many points at places such as the opening through which one could enter the defensive ditch. He likewise had erected four towers [at the corners of the palace], all of iron and quite spacious, which gave his archers excellent firing positions—they were really wonderful things, and cost more than twenty thousand francs. Finally, he stationed forty crossbowmen, day and night, in the defensive ditch, with orders to fire upon anyone who approached at night, until the hour when the gate was opened in the morning. It seemed to him, furthermore, that his subjects were somewhat eager to take power, if they should find the opportunity.

In truth there was some talk by people of entering Plessis and dispatching business as they saw fit, because affairs were not being taken care of; but they did not dare attempt this, and they were wise in refraining, for effective provision had been made against such an attempt. The king often changed *valets de chambre* and all other household people, saying that fear of him and respect for him would be maintained by these tactics.

To deal with affairs, he kept a few men about him, insignificant people of ill repute, who might well have realized, had they been prudent, that as soon as he was dead they would lose all their offices as the least that could happen to them. Thus it came about. Of the letters and dispatches they received regarding whatever kind of business, they reported nothing to the king unless it concerned the safeguarding of the state and defence of the realm, for he cared about nothing else.

At this time he was at peace or had made a truce with everyone. To his physician [Jacques Coitier] he gave ten thousand crowns every month, the physician receiving in a space of five months fifty-four thousand crowns.

To God and to the saints he remitted his hope of life, knowing that he could hardly last without a miracle; and, since there are instances of Our Lord's lengthening the life of a king because of his humility and repentance and the prayers of some holy prophet, our king, who in humility surpassed all other princes in the world, sought for a man of religion or of good life who lived austerely so that he might mediate between God and the king for the lengthening of the king's days. From all parts of the world the king received names of such people. To a number of them he sent messages. When some came to speak with him, he talked to them only of this lengthening of life. Most replied wisely, saying that they possessed no such power. Rich offerings he made [to churches, saints' shrines and the like]—excessive offerings in the view of the Archbishop of Tours, a man of good and holy life, a Franciscan and a cardinal, who wrote to the king, among other things, that he would prefer him to take the money away from the canons of churches where he was making his great gifts, and distribute it among poor labourers and others who bear the burden of these high taxes, than to levy taxes on the poor in order to give the money to rich churches and rich canons, as he was doing. His vows, offerings, reliquaries and adornments of shrines, including the silver trellis for St Martin of Tours, which weighed almost eighteen thousand marcs, and the reliquary for St Eutropius of Saintes and other gifts he made to the shrine of the Three Kings at Cologne, to Our Lady of Aachen in Germany, to St Servais of Utrecht, to St Bernadine of Aquila, to shrines in the Kingdom of Naples, golden chalices sent to St John Lateran at Rome and many other gifts, gold and silver, to churches in his realm—all these amounted in the course of one year to at least 700,000 francs.

He gave a great quantity of lands to churches, but this gift of lands has since been rescinded—and indeed it was excessive.

Among men renowned for devout life, the king sought out a man in the province of Calabria [in the Kingdom of Naples] who went by the name of Brother Francis [of Paola, 1416–1507, later the founder of the Order of the Friars Minims, canonized by Leo X in 1519]. The king called him 'the Holy Man' because of his saintly life. In his honour our present King [Charles VIII] erected for him a monastery at Plessis-lès-Tours at the end of the bridge, in place of the chapel near Plessis [which he had been occupying]. This hermit, at the age of twelve years, had put himself under a rock, where he remained until the age of forty-three years or thereabouts [actually, sixty-six], that is, until the time that the king had him sought out by one of the masters of his household in company with [Federigo] Prince of Taranto, son of the King of Naples, for the hermit refused to leave without the permission of the pope and his king—which showed how knowing this simple person was, and indeed he had built two churches in his region.

He had not eaten—nor, once he adopted this austere life, did he ever eat—flesh or fish, eggs, dairy products or fat. I do not believe I ever saw a living man of such holy life, nor one in whom it seemed so clear that the Holy Spirit spoke from his mouth, for he was learned and yet had never been to school. True it is that his Italian language helped him [in understanding Latin and other languages]. The hermit, in passing through Naples, was as honoured and sought after as if he had been a high apostolic legate, among others by the king and the king's children, and he spoke as if he had been reared at court. He then went to Rome, where he was called upon by all the cardinals. Three times he had audience with the pope, the two of them alone, he seated close to His Holiness in a splendid chair, each audience lasting three or four hours—a great honour for so humble a man—and in all his replies he spoke so wisely that everybody was amazed. Our Holy Father accorded him the privilege of founding an Order called the Hermits of St Francis.

Proceeding on his journey, he then came to our king. He was honoured as if he had been the pope, the king going down on his knees before him and begging him to pray God for him so that his life might be prolonged. He replied as a wise man should reply. I have many times heard him speak before our present king, all the magnates of the realm being present—the last time, two months ago. He seemed to have been inspired by God because of the things he said and declared. Otherwise he would not have known how to speak of the things of which he spoke. He is still living and therefore there could be a change, either for better or for worse, and hence I will say no more. Several people ridiculed the coming of this hermit called the Holy Man, but they knew nothing of the thoughts of our wise king nor did they know the reasons which prompted him to act thus.

Such was the life our king led at Plessis, with few people about him save archers and he a prey to the suspicions of which I have spoken. . . . To see him, he looked like a man more dead than alive, so unbelievably wasted was he. He dressed richly, which had never been his custom, and wore only robes of crimson satin furred with marten, and he gave many garments away, without being asked for them, for nobody would have dared ask.

He dealt out severe punishments in order to be feared and for fear of losing his authority, for so he himself told me. He removed office-holders and cashiered soldiers, pared some pensions and cancelled others. He told me, a few days before his death, that he passed his time in making and unmaking people. He caused himself more to be talked about in the realm than he had ever been, and he did so from fear that otherwise people might think him dead. . . .

He sent people in all directions outside the realm: to England to maintain good relations with Edward IV and give assurances of the marriage [of the dauphin and Princess Elizabeth], and he was careful to pay King Edward's pension and the other pensions; to Spain, where his envoys spoke only of friendship and distributed presents everywhere. In many places he sent to have a good horse or a mule purchased, whatever the cost—this always in countries where he wanted to be thought in good health.

He sent everywhere for dogs: into Spain, for a kind of dog called *alano*; into Brittany for small greyhound bitches, greyhounds and spaniels, and he bought them at high prices; to Valencia for little shaggy dogs for which he paid more than the sellers asked. Into Sicily he sent to seek some mule or other, especially sending to an official of the country and paying double for the animal; to Naples he sent for horses; he sent for strange beasts from everywhere, as to Barbary [the North African coast] for a species of small wolves, no larger than little foxes, which are called *adive*. In Denmark he sought out two kinds of animals: firstly elks, which resemble deer and are big as buffaloes, with horns short and broad; secondly reindeer, which have the build and colour of deer, except that their horns are much larger—I have seen a reindeer with horns of fifty-four prongs. To buy six of each kind of these animals he gave merchants 4,500 German florins.

When all these animals were brought to him, however, he paid no attention to them, nor, most times, did he even speak with those who brought them. Indeed, he did so many such things that he was more feared by his subjects and his neighbours than he had ever been, and this was his purpose.

To return to our main subject and to approach the end of these Memoirs, we must come to the conclusion of the treaty of marriage of our present king, then dauphin, and the daughter of the Duke and Duchess of Austria. This was accomplished, through the people of Ghent, to the intense displeasure of King Edward of England, who considered himself betrayed in his hope for the marriage of his daughter with the dauphin, which marriage he and his queen had more ardently desired than anything else in the world. Never would they believe any man who warned them that it would not take place, whether a subject of theirs or a foreigner; for the English council had several times remonstrated to King Edward, at the moment when our king was conquering Picardy, near Calais, that once King Louis had won Picardy, he could as well try to win Calais and Guines [one of the strongholds guarding Calais]. King Edward was told the same thing by the envoys whom the Duke and Duchess of Austria were continually sending to England and by Breton envoys and others, but he believed not a word. It is my opinion that he did not act thus out of ignorance as much as out of greed, in order not to lose the fifty thousand crowns that the king gave him annually, and likewise not to relinquish the life of pleasure to which he was addicted.

Concerning the marriage [of the dauphin and Maximilian's daughter Margaret] an assembly was held at Alost in Flanders, at which were present the Duke of Austria and deputies from the Three Estates of Flanders, of Brabant, and of other provinces belonging to the duke and his children. There the deputies of Ghent did several things against the will of the duke, like banishing people and removing attendants of his son; then they expressed their will that this marriage take place in order to have peace, and they forced him to agree to it, whether he would or no. He was very young and ill provided with able advisers, for almost all the officers of the House of Burgundy were dead or had come over to our side—I mean the great persons and the best counsellors. For his part, he had come inadequately accompanied. And then, because he had lost his wife, who was the princess of the land, he did not dare speak so boldly as he had formerly done.

To put it briefly, the king was informed of this action on the part of the deputies of Ghent by the lord des Cordes, and was overjoyed by the news. A day was agreed upon for the Princess Margaret to be brought to Hesdin. A few days before [28 July 1482], the lord de Cohen, of the County of Artois, holding Aire for the Duke of Austria and the lord de Bièvres his captain, had delivered up that powerful stronghold in Artois, for a sum of money, to the lord des Cordes. This loss aided the Flemings in pushing their campaign for the marriage and for a peace, since Aire is on the border of Flanders.

And although they want their prince weakened, they do not want him weak on their frontiers, nor do they want the king to be so very near them.

Once the marriage had been agreed upon, as I have said, ambassadors of Flanders and Brabant came before the king [in January 1483]. But everything depended on those of Ghent, because of the power they possessed—they having the [duke's] children in their hands and being always ready to make trouble. There also came some knights on behalf of Duke Maximilian, young like him and poorly advised, for the purpose of securing peace. Messire Jean de Berghes, lord de Cohen, was one of them and Messire Baudouin de Lannoy the other, and there was a secretary.

The king was already very low and was very reluctant to let himself be seen, and he made great difficulty about swearing to uphold the treaty [of Arras, which had been signed on 23 December 1482, the mission of the ambassadors being to witness this ceremony of oath-taking]. The king acted thus because he did not want to be seen; nevertheless, he took the oath. The treaty was very advantageous for him: he had several times been willing to agree to the marriage, asking only the County of Artois or that of Burgundy, just one of the two; and my lords of Ghent (that is what he called them) had both the counties delivered to him, along with the Counties of Charolais, Macon and Auxerre. And if they had been able to deliver to him the Counties of Hainault and Namur and all other French-speaking Burgundian subjects, they would have readily done so in order to weaken their ruler.

The king our master was very wise and well understood the situation in Flanders: that a Count of Flanders needs to possess also the County of Artois, seated between the King of France and the Flemings, which is like a bridle upon them, for he can raise good troops there to help him chastise the Flemings when they make fools of themselves. Therefore the king, in depriving the Count of Flanders [i.e. Maximilian, though, in fact, his son Philip] of the County of Artois, left him the poorest lord in the world and one without power unless the people of Ghent were willing to concede it. The heads of this embassy of which I have spoken were Guillaume Rym and [Jean] Coppenolle, the Governor of Ghent, whom I have mentioned above.

After the embassy had gone home, Princess Margaret was brought to Hesdin and put into the hands of my lord des Cordes. She was brought by Madame de Ravenstein, bastard daughter of the late Duke Philip of Burgundy; and she was received by the present Duke and Duchess of Bourbon [Pierre de Beaujeu and Anne, Louis XI's elder daughter], the lord d'Albret and others on the king's behalf; and they escorted her to Amboise, where the dauphin dwelt.

Had the Duke of Austria been able to wrest his daughter from those who accompanied her to Hesdin, he would have attempted it before she left Burgundian territory; but the people of Ghent had provided a strong escort. Also the duke had begun to lose his authority, and many people joined with those of Ghent because the latter held the duke's son [Philip] in their hands and removed and appointed his attendants at their pleasure. Among others [of the little prince's entourage] was the lord of Ravenstein, brother to the Duke of Clèves, principal governor of the child, named Duke Philip, who is living still, in expectation of a great heritage if God gives him long life. [Already in possession of his mother's Burgundian inheritances, Duke Philip the Handsome could look forward to inheriting his father's Austrian lands and the Hapsburg succession to the imperial crown, now well nigh hereditary; but it was not until 1496 that he married Juana, daughter and soon to be heiress of Ferdinand and Isabella of Spain, adding the Spanish succession to his other expectations; it was their son Charles who gathered in this immense inheritance and became Emperor Charles V.]

Whoever else had joy of this marriage, it bitterly displeased the King of England, for he considered himself mocked and humiliated by it and feared that he had lost his pension from our king—or tribute, as the English called it. He also feared lest the people of England turn against him on this account and rise in rebellion, especially because he had refused to listen to his councillors. Also he now could see our king established in great strength on the borders of Calais. As soon as he had word of the Treaty of Arras, he was so overcome that he fell ill and soon after died, some say of apoplexy. Whatever the illness, it was the shock of the Treaty of Arras that brought about his death in a few days. [Edward IV must have learned of the Treaty of Arras by the first days of January 1483; it was at the beginning of April that he collapsed, probably from an attack of apoplexy or acute indigestion, and he died on 9 April; it seems likely that Commynes is right in supposing that his intense chagrin over the treaty sapped his will to live.] . . .

Very soon after the death of Edward IV, our king was informed of it. He took no pleasure in the news. Not many days later, he received letters from the Duke of Gloucester, who had made himself King of England and signed himself Richard [III], having put to death his brother Edward's two sons [Edward, Prince of Wales and, upon his father's death, Edward V, aged twelve, and Richard, Duke of York, aged ten].

King Richard asked for our king's friendship, and I believe he would have been happy to receive the pension; but our king refused to reply to his letters or hear his messenger [in fact, Louis XI did reply, noncommittally], and considered him very cruel and wicked; for, after Edward IV's death, the Duke of Gloucester had done homage to his nephew as his king and sovereign lord, and as soon as he had killed the two princes and seized the throne, he had the daughters of King Edward deprived of their rank and proclaimed bastards in open Parliament, under a pretext for proof of which he offered the testimony of a Bishop of Bath [Robert Stillington]. This bishop, who had formerly been King Edward's Chancellor, was then deprived of his office and held in prison, from which he was released upon compounding with the king for a sum of money. This bishop affirmed that King Edward, being enamoured of an English lady (whom the bishop named) had promised her marriage in order to have his will with her and she had consented. The bishop said that he had then married them, only he and they being present. The bishop was a man of court and said nothing about this matter and helped to keep the lady quiet. [Lady Eleanor Butler, a daughter of the Earl of Shrewsbury, according to the record of Richard III's Parliament.] Afterwards, King Edward married, also for love, the daughter of an English knight named Lord Rivers, a widow with two sons. The bishop, after concealing in his heart for perhaps twenty years a longing for vengeance [because of his having been imprisoned], revealed this secret marriage to the Duke of Gloucester, which greatly aided the duke in carrying out his evil purpose. But the bishop fared ill because of what he had done. He had a son he dearly loved, on whom King Richard wished to bestow great benefits; he also wished him to marry the eldest of the daughters of Edward IV—Elizabeth, at present Queen of England and the mother of handsome sons—who had been stripped of their rank and dignities. This son, while captaining a warship under the command of King Richard his master, was captured off the coast of Normandy and, by the decision of those who captured him, was brought before the court of Parlement and imprisoned in the Petit Châtellet in Paris, where he eventually died of hunger and deprivation.

King Richard did not lord it long, however. He had executed the Duke of Buckingham, who had had the two princes put to death, [Buckingham, at first his greatest supporter, having attempted an abortive rising, in favour of Henry Tudor, in the autumn of 1483]. Yet, though he had a great army ready, God suddenly raised up against him an enemy who had no power and, I believe, little or no claim to the crown of England [being illegitimately descended, on his father's side, from Henry V's widow, Katherine of France, and quasi-illegitimately descended, on his mother's side, from John of Gaunt, Duke of Lancaster, and as such both a half-nephew and distant cousin of Henry VI]. This was [Henry Tudor] the Earl of Richmond, once a prisoner in Brittany and today the King [Henry VII] of England. He at one time told me, a little before he sailed from this realm, that from the age of five he had been a fugitive or a prisoner. The Earl of Richmond had been for about fifteen years a prisoner in Brittany of Duke Francis, recently dead, into whose hands he came, and his uncle [Jasper Tudor] the Earl of Pembroke with him, as a result of their being driven there by tempest as they were attempting to flee to France. I was at Duke Francis' court when they were taken. The duke treated his 'prisoners' very well indeed; and, at the death of Edward IV, Duke Francis provided the Earl of Richmond with a goodly number of troops and ships; and the earl, having a secret understanding with the Duke of Buckingham—who met his death as a result of this enterprise—sailed for England. After being tempest tossed and buffeted by contrary winds, he sailed back to Dieppe, and from there returned overland to Brittany.

He began to fear lest he annoy Duke Francis because of the expense to which he put the duke, having some five hundred English with him, and lest the duke come to an understanding, to the earl's harm, with King Richard—and such an understanding was being negotiated. Without taking leave of the duke, he and his band therefore passed into France. A little later, with some money and some three thousand men—taken from Norman jails, and worse could not be found—provided by our present king, the earl was transported to Wales by Norman warships. He was joined by Lord Stanley, his stepfather, with some twenty-five thousand men. At the end of three or four days, the earl's forces met in battle the army of this cruel King Richard, who was killed in the field, and the earl was then and there crowned king with Richard's crown. . . .

Our king had now achieved the Flanders marriage he had so ardently desired; he had the Flemings at his beck and call; he was at peace with the Bretons, whom he hated, keeping them in great fear of him because of the large numbers of troops he quartered on their frontier; with Spain he likewise had peace, and the King and Queen of Spain [Ferdinand and Isabella], who desired nothing but his friendship, he held at a disadvantage because of the County of Roussillon which had been delivered to him by King John of Aragon, father of King Ferdinand, as pledge [for the repayment of a loan] and on other conditions that have not yet been satisfied.

The powers of Italy wanted him for a friend, they had some alliances with him, and they sent him frequent embassies. In Germany he had the Swiss, who obeyed him as if they were his subjects. The Kings of Scotland and Portugal were his allies. A part of the Kingdom of Navarre [split by opposing factions] did as he wished. His subjects trembled before him. What he commanded was immediately accomplished, no difficulties or excuses made.

From all parts of the world remedies thought necessary for his health were sent to him. Pope Sixtus IV, recently deceased [in August 1484], on being informed that the king devoutly desired to have the Corporal [altar linen] used by St Peter in singing Mass, at once sent it to him, along with several other relics, which were duly returned to the pope.

The Holy Ampule at Rheims, which had never been removed from its place, was brought all the way to his chamber at Plessis and was there reposing on a buffet at the hour of his death. His intention was to anoint himself with the holy oil as he had been anointed at his coronation, though many people believed that he wanted to anoint his whole body—which is not likely, for the Holy Ampule is very small and there is little oil within it. I saw it at the hour which I have mentioned and also when the king was interred in the church of Our Lady of Cléry [near Orléans].

The Turk, who is reigning today [Bajazet II], sent him an ambassador who came as far as Nice in Provence. But the king refused to hear him or allow him to come further. The ambassador was bringing him a great roll of relics which were still at Constantinople in the hands of the Turk, and he offered them to the king along with a large sum of money, provided that the king would keep well guarded the brother of the Turk [Djem] who was in this realm in the hands of the Knights of Rhodes. At present he is in Rome in the hands of the pope.

From this recital can be perceived the intelligence and grandeur of our king, how he was esteemed and honoured throughout the world, and how both spiritual and material remedies were employed to prolong his life. Nevertheless, they were useless, and he had to pass to the place to which the others have passed. Some grace God had granted him, for He had created him wiser, more generous and more talented than the other princes of his time who were his enemies and neighbours, and as he surpassed them in the aforementioned qualities, so did he surpass them in length of life, but not by much. Charles, Duke of Burgundy, Charles' daughter the Duchess of Austria, King Edward and Duke Galeazzo-Maria of Milan and King John of Aragon, all had died a few years before; and the Duchess of Austria, King Edward and he died almost at the same time. In all of them were good and evil, for they were human beings. Still, eschewing flattery, I can say that he possessed the abilities required for the office of king and prince in greater measure than any of the others. I have seen nearly all of them and have known their capacities; and therefore my statement is not guesswork.

In [September] 1482 the king had gone [to Amboise] to visit his son the dauphin, whom he had not seen for several years. He kept the dauphin isolated, partly out of fear for the child's health, partly out of fear that he might be forcibly removed from Amboise and used as a figurehead for some uprising in the realm. For this is what had been done with him against his father Charles VII, when he was but thirteen [actually, sixteen] years old, by some lords of the kingdom. This rising was called the War of the Praguerie [1440], but it was of short duration and no more than a struggle between factions at court. Among other things, the king recommended to his son certain of his servants and expressly commanded him not to change any offices. He pointed out that when Charles VII his father went to God and the crown came to him, he had discharged all the loyal and notable knights who had served and aided his father in conquering Normandy and Guienne, in driving the English from the realm, and in restoring peace and good order—for thus he had found the kingdom [on succeeding to the crown] and very prosperous. He paid

U

dearly for dismissing these officers, for the result was the War of the Public Weal, of which I have formerly spoken, which was aimed at taking the crown from him.

Soon after the king had spoken with his son the dauphin and accomplished the marriage of which I have spoken, he was seized by the illness which sent him from this world. It happened on a Monday [25 August 1483] and the illness lasted until Saturday, 30 August. I was present at his end and therefore wish to say something about it. As soon as he suffered the [apoplectic] seizure, he lost the power of speech, as he had done the previous time; and when it returned to him, he felt himself weaker than he had ever been, although, even before, he was so feeble that he could scarcely lift his hand to his mouth and so thin and wasted that he aroused pity in all who saw him.

The king considered himself done for, and immediately summoned my lord de Beaujeu, husband of his daughter [Anne] and present Duke of Bourbon, and ordered him to go to 'the king his son' (thus he entitled the dauphin) who was at Amboise. He commended 'the king his son' and his faithful servants to the lord de Beaujeu, gave him the entire charge and control of 'the king', ordered him to prevent certain persons from approaching [young Charles], and made many remarkable observations to him. Had the lord de Beaujeu obeyed most of these commands (not quite all, for there were one or two extraordinary injunctions that clearly were not to be followed) I believe that both the realm and he himself would have profited by them, considering the things that have since happened.

Then the king sent the Chancellor and all the Chancellor's officers to bear the seals of the realm to 'the king his son'. He also sent to him part of the archers of the guard and their captain and all his huntsmen and his falconers and everything else. All those who came to see him he likewise sent to Amboise to 'the king' (thus he entitled him), praying them to serve him well. And by everyone of these people he sent something to his son, especially by Etienne de Vesc, who had reared the new king and served as his premier *valet de chambre*; and already the king our master had made him Bailli of Meaux.

His speech never failed after it came back to him nor his mind; in fact, never had his mind been so clear, for he continually voided, which removed all fumes from his brain. Never throughout his

illness did he complain, as do all sorts of people when they feel ill—
at least, I am of this nature, and I have seen many others like me, and
then, it is said that to complain relieves suffering. He was continually
making sagacious observations; and his final illness lasted, as I
have said, from Monday to Saturday evening.

At this point, I wish to make a comparison between the ills and
sufferings he inflicted on a number of people and those that he himself endured before dying; because I hope that those sufferings of his
will have brought him into Paradise and will have been part of his
purgatory. If these pangs were not so great nor lasted so long as those
he caused some to suffer, he, on the other hand, held a far higher
office in this world than they did. Also he had never experienced
pain inflicted on him by anyone, but was so completely obeyed that
it seemed all Europe had been made only to bow before him; hence,
the little that he did suffer, being contrary to his nature and customary experience, was the harder for him to bear. [Commynes
overlooks the severe haemorrhoidal attacks that Louis XI had from
time to time suffered since 1467.]

Always he maintained his hope in the Holy Man at Plessis, whom
he had brought from Calabria, and incessantly sent to him, saying
that if the Holy Man so willed, he could indeed prolong his life—
for notwithstanding all the final commands he had given to those
whom he had sent to the dauphin, his spirits revived and he had hopes
of escaping death. Had it so come about, he would have quickly
dispersed the company of people he had sent to Amboise to the new
king. Because of the hope he had in the hermit, a certain man of
religion and others decided that he should be told that he was
deluding himself, since in his case there was no more hope except in
God's mercy; and they also decided that when these words were
spoken, his physician would be present, Master Jacques Coitier, to
whom he gave each month ten thousand crowns, hoping that he
would prolong his life. This decision was taken by Master Olivier
[le Daim, the king's barber] and this Master Jacques, the physician,
in order that the king think of nothing but his conscience and
abandon all other thoughts, including his hope in the Holy Man.

Just as the king had raised these men—too suddenly and without
due deliberation—to positions greater than were suitable for them,
so did they take charge without fearing to say things to such a
prince that it was not their place to say, nor did they maintain due

respect and humbleness as they should have, and as would have done those who had long been his intimates and whom, a little before, he had sent away from him because of his imaginings. Thus, just in the way two great persons had been executed by his order—concerning one of whom he felt remorse at his death but not concerning the other (they were the Duke of Nemours and the Count of St Pol)—to whom the death sentence was signified by commissioners, who in terse words pronounced their condemnations and provided a confessor for them to settle their consciences in the little time allowed them, just so did the three above mentioned individuals signify to the king his death in terse, rude words. 'Sire', they told him, 'we must do our duty. Put no more hope in the Holy Man nor in anything else, for you are without question done for; and therefore think of your conscience, since there is no remedy.' And each one added an abrupt word or two. He replied, 'I hope that God will aid me, for perhaps I am not so ill as you think'.

What dolour was it for him to hear this news and this sentence! For never man so much feared death nor made so many attempts to avoid it. All his life he had requested his servants, including me, that if he was seen to be mortally ill, he should not be so informed but only urged to make confession, without the cruel word 'death' being pronounced; for he felt that he lacked the courage to hear so cruel a sentence. Nevertheless he accepted his fate and all his sufferings until death more patiently and courageously than any other man I have ever seen die.

To his son, whom he called king, he sent several things; and he confessed himself very well and said several prayers in accordance with the sacraments he took, which he himself asked for. And, as I have said, he spoke as alertly as if he had never been ill. He talked about matters that could be useful to his son. He said, among other things, that he did not want my lord des Cordes to leave the king his son's side for six months and that that lord should be asked not to undertake anything against Calais or any other place. It had been decided, he said, that my lord des Cordes would undertake such enterprises—to the good of the king and the kingdom—but they were risky, especially an attempt upon Calais, because of the danger of stirring up the English. Above all things, he wanted the realm, after his death, to be kept at peace for five or six years—which in his lifetime he would never have been able to endure. In truth, the realm needed peace: great of resources and of extent though it was, it was

The death of Louis XI

also wasted and poor, especially because of its being trampled by troops [of the standing army], who moved from one province to another, as they have since done, and with even worse results.

He ordered that there be no strife with Brittany and that Duke Francis be left to live in peace, without being troubled, and likewise all the neighbours of the realm so that the king his son and the kingdom could remain at peace until the king had reached his majority and was of an age to dispose of matters as he pleased.

In a foregoing paragraph I began to show the parallel between the sufferings he had inflicted upon certain people and the sufferings he endured before dying. . . . For a period of five or six months preceding his death he suspected everybody, especially those whose status fitted them for authority. He had fears regarding his son and had him closely guarded; and no man saw him or spoke with him, unless by the king's express command. He had fear, in the end, of his daughter [Anne] and his son-in-law [Pierre de Beaujeu], the present Duke of Bourbon, and wanted to know what people entered Plessis with them; and at the end he broke off a council that Pierre de Beaujeu was holding there by his order.

At the time that his son-in-law and the Count de Dunois [Jean, son of the Bastard of Orléans] came back to Plessis after heading the deputation [on the king's behalf] that attended the wedding of the dauphin and Princess Margaret at Amboise, and brought with them many people, the king, who had had the gates strongly guarded, was in the gallery which looks out upon the courtyard of Plessis. He summoned one of the captains of his guards and commanded him to touch the people with the two lords in order to discover whether they were wearing cuirasses under their gowns, and he ordered the captain to carry out this command while pretending to chat casually with these people so that what he was doing would not be obvious.

Consider then whether, if he had made many people live in doubt and fear under him, he was not paid back in his own coin; and consider also what people he could be sure of, when he was suspicious of his son, his daughter and his son-in-law! I do not say this only in regard to the king but also for the benefit of all other lords who desire to be feared. Never do they feel what revenge is until they reach old age, when, for their penance, they fear every man.

What dolour was it for this king to experience such fears and emotions. He had his physician named Master Jacques Coitier, to whom in five months he gave fifty thousand crowns in coin, Master Jacques' salary being at the rate of ten thousand crowns a month; to Jacques' nephew he gave the Bishopric of Amiens and he also gave other offices and lands to Master Jacques and his friends. This physician was so rude to him that one would not say to a menial the coarse and outrageous words that he used to the king; and the king so much feared him that he did not dare send him away. He complained about him, but would not have dared dismiss him as he did all other servants. The reason was that the physician had brashly said these words to him: 'I know very well that one morning you will send me away as you have done others, but, by the . . . (a great oath that he swore), you will not be alive eight days later!' This statement so much frightened the king that ever after he did nothing but flatter him and load him with gifts. To be so fearful was for the king a great purgatory in this world, considering the obedience that he had had from all people, even princes.

It is true that the king our master had constructed rigorous prisons, such as cages of iron and others of wood that were covered with iron plates outside and inside, terrible enclosures eight feet wide and a foot higher than a man's height. The first who conceived them was the Bishop of Verdun, who was himself imprisoned in the first one made and slept there fourteen years [see, above, p. 97]. Many people since have cursed him for it, and I also, who, under the present king, experienced one of these cages for eight months.

He had also had metal rings made by Germans, very heavy and terrible, to be fastened on feet—one ring only on one foot, like an iron collar, with a heavy chain attached and an iron ball at the end of it, much heavier than it should have been. These were called 'the king's little girls'. However, I have seen a great many people of rank thus imprisoned with iron collar on foot, who afterwards emerged in great honour and great joy and received high rewards from the king. Among others was a son of the lord de la Gruthuse, of Flanders, captured in battle, whom the king provided with a wife, made him chamberlain and Seneschal of Anjou and gave command of a hundred lances [of the standing army]. There were also the lord de Piennes, a prisoner of war, and the lord de Vergy, both of whom received army commands and chamberlainships, either from him or his son, and other great offices; and as much was given to [Jacques] the lord de Richebourg, brother of the [late] Constable, and to a man named Rocaberti, of Catalonia, likewise a prisoner of war; and there were many others from various regions, whom it would take too much time to name.

Now this is not our main subject, but I had to come back to it to point out that, just as in his time there were bad prisons of various kinds, so, before dying, he found himself in a comparable one, and worse, and in as great a state of fear as those he had kept in that state. This situation I consider to be the greater grace for him and as part of his purgatory. I speak thus to demonstrate that there is no man, of whatever rank he may be, who does not suffer, either in secret or publicly, especially those who make others suffer.

The king, towards the end of his days, had his palace of Plessis-lès-Tours entirely enclosed. . . . He well knew that this fortification would not suffice against an army or a large number of people, but of such possibilities he had no fear. He feared only that some lord, or several lords, might attempt to take the place by night, half by persuasion and half by force, having had something of a secret understanding with people within, and that they would deprive him of his authority and treat him like a man of unsound mind who was unfitted to govern. The gate of Plessis was not opened until eight in the morning, nor the drawbridge lowered; at that hour the officers entered, and the captains of the guards placed the customary gatekeepers and then established their watch of archers at the gate and around the courtyard, as if in a frontier post closely guarded. No one entered except through the wicket of the gate and with the king's knowledge, save for some master of the household and people of that sort who did not come into the king's presence.

Is it then possible to detain a king, keeping him under honourable guard, in a narrower prison than he kept himself? The cages in which he had imprisoned others were eight feet square; and he, so great a king, had a small castle courtyard to walk in. Even then, he rarely went there, but stayed in the gallery, and he went to Mass without crossing the courtyard. . . . It is true that this place was larger than a common prison, but he was also greater than common prisoners.

It could be said that others have been more suspicious than he. There has not been, perhaps, in my time either a man so wise nor a king who had such loyal subjects. And it could be that other suspicious rulers were cruel and tyrannical, but this king did evil to no one who had not committed some offence against him. . . . It is true that he oppressed his subjects, but he allowed no one else to do so, whether [a great lord] of his realm or a foreigner.

After such fears, suspicions and pains, Our Lord passed a miracle upon him and cured him both in soul and in body, as He always does in making His miracle, for He took him from the miserable world in full possession of his intellect, understanding and memory, he having received all the sacraments without suffering any pain that could be perceived, but speaking continually till within a paternoster's time span of his death. He gave orders regarding his sepulchre [in the Church of Our Lady of Cléry], regarding those who would accompany him there and the route of the funeral journey, and he said he hoped to die on no other day except the Saturday and that Our Lady, in whom he had always had his trust and to whom he had addressed great devotions and prayers, would procure him this grace and that he was to be interred the Saturday following. And thus it all came about; for he died Saturday, 30 August 1483, at eight o'clock in the evening, at Plessis, where he had had his seizure the preceding Monday. May Our Lord receive him into his realm of Paradise! Amen!

Little hope should the poor and humble have in the things of this world since so great a king suffered and toiled so much and then left all without being able by so much as an hour to postpone death, despite all his diligence in seeking to do so. I knew him and was his servant in the flower of his years and in his great prosperity, but I never once saw him without cares and troubles. Above all pleasures he loved hunting and falconing in season; but he did not take nearly so much pleasure in birds as in dogs. With the ladies he did not meddle from the time that I was with him, for soon after my arrival he lost a son [François, in July 1473], and, grief-stricken, then vowed to God, in my presence, never to touch another woman except the queen his wife. Though thus he should do according to the marriage commandments, it was a great thing, with so many ladies at his disposal, for him to persevere in this promise, considering also that the queen was not physically attractive, but a very good lady.

Again, hunting gave him almost as much annoyance as pleasure, for he worked very hard and zealously at it. Rising very early in the morning, he vigorously coursed stags; on occasion he pursued game long distances and would not abandon the hunt, no matter what the hour. Hence he sometimes returned very weary and almost always angry with someone—for hunting is a vocation that does not always go according to the pleasure of those who follow it. Nevertheless, he was recognized to be better at it than any other man of his time, in everybody's opinion.

He hunted incessantly, lodging in villages, until there came news of war—for almost every summer there was trouble between Duke Charles of Burgundy and him, and they made a truce every winter.

He also had strife, over this county of Roussillon, with King John of Aragon, father of the King [Ferdinand] of Spain now reigning . . . which cost him and his realm dear, for many men of rank died and he had to spend large sums there.

The pleasure he enjoyed, and that was itself laborious as I have said, did not occupy much of a year. The times when he did take repose, his mind was working; for he had affairs in so many directions that it was amazing; and he was as actively involved in the affairs of his neighbours as in his own and placed people in their households and thus created factions which weakened their power. When he was waging war, he desired peace or truce; when he had peace or truce, he could hardly endure it. He busied himself about innumerable small things in his realm, many of which he could well have passed by; but such was his nature and so he lived. Also he had such a magnificent memory that he retained everything, and he knew everybody in all the countries about him. In truth he seemed made to rule a world rather than a kingdom.

I do not say anything about his youth, for I was not then with him. However, at the age of eleven [actually, sixteen] he was involved, by some lords and others of the realm, in a rising against his father, Charles VII; but the war, called the Praguerie, was of short duration. He was married to a princess of Scotland [Margaret, daughter of James I] against his will; and while she lived he regretted the marriage. [She died in August 1445.] Afterwards because of the factions and strife in the household of his father, he withdrew to his province of Dauphiné, to which many men of standing followed him, and more than he could support. While there, he married [Charlotte] a daughter of the Duke of Savoy. Immediately after the marriage, he quarrelled with his father-in-law and they waged bitter war against each other.

King Charles, seeing that his son enjoyed the services of many men of standing and of a goodly force of troops, decided to go to Dauphiné in person with a large army and eject his son from the province. He took pains to order a number of people, as being his subjects and under the customary penalties for disobedience, to abandon his son and return to him. Some of them obeyed, to the great displeasure of our King [Louis], who, perceiving his father's angry state of mind, decided, notwithstanding that he had a strong position, to depart from Dauphiné and leave it to the king. With but few followers, he went off, via the County of Burgundy, to the court of Duke Philip, who received him with great honour and provided generous support in the form of annual pensions for him and his principal officers, like [Jean, Bastard of Armagnac, and later] the Count of Comminges, [Jean] the lord de Montauban and others; and, throughout the time Louis Dauphin was there, the duke continued to make gifts to his servants. Nevertheless, because of his expenses and the number of men in his entourage, the dauphin was often out of money, a situation which caused him great trouble and anxiety and required him to look everywhere for funds and to borrow, for otherwise his people would have left him—great anguish for a prince unaccustomed to such an occurrence. Furthermore, it was not smooth sailing for him in this House of Burgundy; for he had to make himself agreeable to the duke and the duke's chief officers, lest they become weary of his being there so long, for he was there six years [September 1456–August 1461: five years]. And incessantly his father sent embassies to the duke to demand either that he be forced to leave the Burgundian domain or be sent back to the king. Thus you can see that he was far from idle and not without long thoughts and cares.

Now then, given all these things, how often did he experience joy or pleasure? I believe that, from his childhood, he did nothing but labour until his death; and I am certain that, if all the days in his life on which he experienced more happiness than travail were counted, they would be few in number—I think there would be twenty of toils and anxieties to every one of pleasure and ease. He lived to be about sixty-one. However, he had always thought that he would not reach sixty, and he said that for a long time—some say, since Charlemagne—no King of France had lived to be more than sixty. Nevertheless, the king our master, at sixty-one, had gone well beyond that. [Actually, he died a little less than two months after his sixtieth birthday on 3 July 1483.]

Commynes then reviews the careers of Duke Charles of Burgundy, Edward IV, and 'two wise and valiant princes', Mathias Corvinus, King of Hungary, and Sultan Mahomet II, conqueror of Constantinople in 1453, in order to demonstrate the trials and labours they all endured. He regards the King of Hungary and Mahomet II, along with Louis XI, as 'the three greatest men who have reigned for a century; but in his way of life our king proved himself much superior to the other two'.

Thus you have seen so many great men dying within a few years of one another, men who laboured so hard to increase their power and attain glory, but who experienced such sufferings and toils, and thus shortened their lives—and perchance their souls could be the worse for it. I do not include the Turk; for I consider that this point is irrelevant in his regard and that he is lodged with his predecessors. Concerning our king, I have hope, as I have said, that Our Lord has had mercy upon him and will have mercy, if it be His will, upon all others.

But to speak plainly, as a man who has no learning, save for some little experience he has gained, would it not be better for them and all other princes, and for men of medium station who have lived under these great ones and will continue to live under those now reigning, to choose the middle way in these matters? That is, to burden themselves with fewer cares, to work themselves less hard, to undertake fewer enterprises—and to have greater fear of offending God and persecuting their people and their neighbours by cruel means, as I have demonstrated at length previously—and, instead, enjoy ease and honourable pleasures? Their lives would be the longer for it, illnesses would come later, and their deaths would be the more regretted by a greater number of people, and looked forward to by fewer, and they would have less reason to fear death.

The most splendid examples of humanity give us to realize what an insignificant thing is a man and how miserable and brief this life is. Neither the great nor the small, as soon as they are dead, are anything; and everyone holds the corpse in horror and loathing, while the soul, on the instant, must go to be judged. And already sentence has been passed upon it, according to the works and merits of the body.

1. *The House of France*

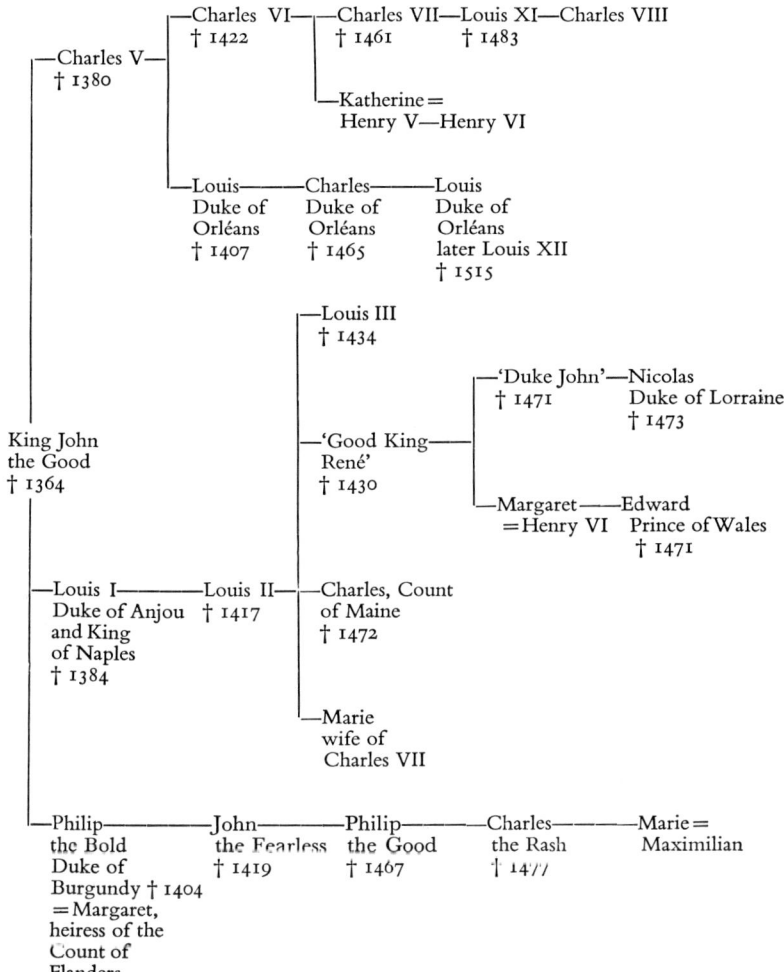

```
                    ┌─Charles VI──┌─Charles VII─Louis XI─Charles VIII
                    │   † 1422    │   † 1461      † 1483
    ┌─Charles V─────┤             │
    │   † 1380      │             └─Katherine =
    │               │               Henry V─Henry VI
    │               │
    │               └─Louis───────Charles───────Louis
    │                 Duke of     Duke of       Duke of
    │                 Orléans     Orléans       Orléans
    │                 † 1407      † 1465         later Louis XII
    │                                            † 1515
    │
    │                           ┌─Louis III
    │                           │   † 1434
    │                           │                    ┌─'Duke John'─Nicolas
    │                           │                    │   † 1471    Duke of Lorraine
    │                           │                    │                † 1473
    │                           ├─'Good King─────────┤
King John                      │  René'
the Good                       │   † 1430
† 1364                         │                    └─Margaret──────Edward
    │                          │                      = Henry VI   Prince of Wales
    │                          │                                     † 1471
    │
    ├─Louis I───────Louis II──┼─Charles, Count
    │  Duke of Anjou  † 1417  │  of Maine
    │  and King               │  † 1472
    │  of Naples              │
    │  † 1384                 │
    │                         │
    │                         └─Marie
    │                           wife of
    │                           Charles VII
    │
    └─Philip────────John──────────Philip─────────Charles───────Marie =
      the Bold      the Fearless  the Good       the Rash      Maximilian
      Duke of        † 1419        † 1467         † 1477
      Burgundy † 1404
      = Margaret,
      heiress of the
      Count of
      Flanders
```

† = died

2. Rulers and Principal Lords

Rulers

HOUSE OF VALOIS

Louis Dauphin; later Louis XI (1423–83)

His father: Charles VII, Joan of Arc's 'gentil Dauphin' (reigned 1422–61)

His mother: Marie of Anjou, sister of 'Good King René'

His first wife: Margaret (died 1445), daughter of the poet-King, James I of Scotland

His second wife: Charlotte, daughter of Louis, Duke of Savoy

His son and heir: Charles; later Charles VIII (1470–98)

His daughters: Anne, married to Pierre de Beaujeu of the House of Bourbon; Jeanne, married to Louis, Duke of Orléans (later Louis XII)

His bastard daughters: Jeanne, married to Louis, Bastard of Bourbon, Admiral; Marie, married to Aymar, Lord of St Vallier

His brother: Charles, Duke of Berry; later Duke of Normandy, and then Duke of Guienne (1446–72)

His sisters: Jeanne, married to Jean, Duke of Bourbon; Yolande, married to Amedée, Prince, later Duke, of Savoy; Madeleine, married to Jean, heir of the Count of Foix; also other sisters

HOUSE OF LANCASTER

Henry VI (1421–71); reigned 1422–61; 1470–71

His father: Henry V, victor of Agincourt and conqueror of northern France (died 1422)

His mother: Katherine of France, daughter of the mad Charles VI and sister of Charles VII

His wife: Margaret of Anjou, daughter of 'Good King René'

His son: Edward, Prince of Wales (killed at the battle of Tewkesbury, 1471)

His half-brother: Jasper Tudor, Earl of Pembroke, son of widowed Katherine of France and Owen Tudor

HOUSE OF YORK

Edward, Earl of March; later Edward IV (1442–83); reigned 1461–70; 1471–83

His father: Richard, Duke of York, killed at the battle of Wakefield, 1460

His mother: Cicely Neville, aunt of Richard Neville, Earl of Warwick ('The Kingmaker')

His wife: Elizabeth Woodville, daughter of Richard, Lord, later Earl, Rivers, and of Jacquetta, formerly Dowager Duchess of Bedford, sister to Louis of Luxembourg, Count of St. Pol

His sons: Edward (Edward V) and Richard, Duke of York, murdered (?, 1483?) following the seizure of the throne by their uncle Richard, Duke of Gloucester (Richard III) in June of 1483

His daughter: Elizabeth, betrothed to Charles, Dauphin of France (also other daughters)

His brothers: Edmund, Earl of Rutland, killed at Wakefield, 1460; George, Duke of Clarence, executed 1478; Richard, Duke of Gloucester, later Richard III (1452–85)

His sister: Margaret, married in 1468 to Charles the Rash, Duke of Burgundy

HOUSE OF ARAGON

Alfonso V, King of Aragon and of Naples (1385?–1458)

His bastard son: Ferrante, King of Naples (1423?–1494); Ferrante's sons Alfonso, Duke of Calabria, married to Ypollita Sforza; Federigo, Prince of Taranto, married to Louis XI's sister-in-law, Anne of Savoy

His brother: John, King of Navarre; later John II, King of Aragon (reigned 1458–79); John's sons Don Carlos (died 1461); Ferdinand, married to Isabella of Castile and, with her, joint ruler of Spain; John's third daughter Eleanor, heiress of Navarre, married to Gaston, Count of Foix

HOUSE OF HAPSBURG

Frederick III, Emperor of Germany (1415–93)

His son: Maximilian (later the Emperor Maximilian), married to Marie, heiress of Charles the Rash, Duke of Burgundy; their children: Philip, married to Juana the Mad, heiress of Spain; Margaret, married to Louis XI's heir, the Dauphin Charles (the marriage later dissolved)

His cousin: Sigismund, Duke of Austria, ruler of the Tyrol and portions of Alsace

THE POPES
Nicholas V (1447–55)
Calixtus III (1455–58)
Pius II—Aeneas Sylvius Piccolomini (1458–74)
Paul II (1464–71)
Sixtus IV (1471–84)

Lords

HOUSE OF BURGUNDY
Philip the Good, Duke of Burgundy
His third wife: Isabella of Portugal (descendant of John of Gaunt, Duke of Lancaster)
His son and heir: Charles, Count of Charolais; later, Charles, Duke of Burgundy (duke, 1467–77); Charles's heiress, Marie, married to Maximilian of Hapsburg; Charles's second wife, Margaret of York, sister of Edward IV
His most famous illegitimate son: Antoine, the Grand Bastard of Burgundy

HOUSE OF ANJOU
'Good King René' (died 1480), Duke of Anjou, of Bar, and of Lorraine, Count of Provence, titular King of Naples
His first wife: Isabella of Lorraine
His son: John, Duke of Calabria (Duke John); John's son Nicolas, Marquess of Pont-à-Mousson and later Duke of Lorraine (died 1473, Nicolas's cousin René becoming René II, Duke of Lorraine)
His daughter: Margaret of Anjou, wife of Henry VI of England
His brother: Charles, Count of Maine
His sister: Marie, wife of Charles VII

HOUSE OF ORLÉANS
Charles, Duke of Orléans, poet (captured at the battle of Agincourt and twenty-five years a prisoner in England)
His son: Louis; later Duke of Orléans and then King Louis XII
His half-brother: Jean, Bastard, Count of Dunois (companion-in-arms of Joan of Arc)

x

HOUSE OF BOURBON

Jean, Duke of Bourbon

His father: Charles, Duke of Bourbon (leader of the 'Praguerie', 1440)

His mother: Agnes, sister of Philip the Good, Duke of Burgundy

His wife: Jeanne, sister of Louis XI

His brothers: Charles, Archbishop of Lyons; Pierre de Beaujeu, married to Louis XI's daughter Anne and later Duke of Bourbon; Louis, Prince-Bishop of Liége

His half-brother: Louis, Bastard of Bourbon, Admiral, married to Louis XI's illegitimate daughter Jeanne

HOUSE OF ARMAGNAC

Jean, Count of Armagnac (killed, 1473)

His sister and 'wife': Isabel

His uncle: Bernard, Count of Pardiac, governor of the Dauphin

His cousin: Bernard's son Jacques d'Armagnac, Count of La Marche, and later Duke of Nemours, executed 1477

HOUSE OF BRITTANY

Francis II, Duke of Brittany

His daughter and heiress: Anne, married first to Louis XI's son Charles VIII, and then to Louis XII

HOUSE OF SAVOY

Amedée, Duke of Savoy

His father: Louis, Duke of Savoy

His mother: Anne of Cyprus

His wife: Yolande, sister of Louis XI, Duchess and then Regent of Savoy

His son and successor: Philibert, Duke of Savoy

His brother: Philip, Count of Bresse; numerous other brothers

HOUSE OF SFORZA

Francesco Sforza, Count of Pavia, Duke of Milan (1450–66)

His wife: Bianca, illegitimate daughter of the last Visconti Duke of Milan, Filippo-Maria (died 1447), whose sister Valentina was the mother of Charles, Duke of Orléans

His son and heir: Galeazzo-Maria, Duke of Milan (assassinated 1476);
Galeazzo's wife Bona of Savoy, sister-in-law of Louis XI, later
Regent of Milan for her son Giangaleazzo

His daughter: Ypollita, married to Alfonso, Duke of Calabria, son
of King Ferrante of Naples

His brother: Lodovico ('The Moor'), usurper of the Duchy from his
nephew Giangaleazzo; numerous other brothers

HOUSE OF NEVILLE

Richard Neville, Earl of Warwick ('The Kingmaker'), killed at the
battle of Barnet, 1471

His father: Richard, Earl of Salisbury, brother of Cicely, Duchess of
York

His wife: Isabel, heiress of Richard Beauchamp, Earl of Warwick

His daughters: Isabel, married to George, Duke of Clarence; Anne,
married first to Edward, Lancastrian Prince of Wales, and then to
Richard, Duke of Gloucester, later Richard III

His brothers: John, Lord Montagu; later Earl of Northumberland
and then Marquess Montagu, killed at Barnet, 1471; George,
Bishop of Exeter, then Chancellor of England and Archbishop of
York (deprived of his chancellorship, 1467)

Index

Set in 12 point Bembo type, leaded 1 point, with Castellar for display.
Text printed by Richard Clay (The Chaucer Press), Limited,
Bungay, Suffolk
on Fineblade coated cartridge paper.
Illustrations printed by Alabaster Passmore & Sons Limited, Maidstone,
by four-colour lithography.
Bound by W & J Mackay Limited, Chatham,
in calf-finish skiver leather and cloth.

FIFTEENTH CENTURY
FRANCE

English Channel

Dieppe

Rouen

Normandy

Brittany

Maine

Anjou   Tours   Touraine

Nantes

Poitou

Poitiers

La
March

Bay

of

Biscay

Saintonge

Bordeaux

Guienne

R. Garonne

Armagnac

Toulouse

Béarn

Pamplona

Navarre

Comming

0   50   100   *Miles*   200